Social Entrepreneurship in the Greater China Region

T0303927

This book offers the first exploration into the development of social enterprises in the Greater China region, consisting of Hong Kong, Macau, Taiwan and Mainland China. By drawing on the research and experience of over a dozen scholars and practitioners from across the area, it offers a picture of how a strong State can play an important role as a catalyst in developing the social entrepreneurship sector, particularly by legitimizing it. It delves into the role and impact of institutions and policy on the development of social enterprises, and explains how micro and macro factors might interact in influencing social entrepreneurship. Structured in two parts – policy and cases – it reveals the historical development of the Social enterprises sector in the Chinese context and then illustrates this using cases studies. Providing an alternative view of social entrepreneurship by highlighting the importance of context in this new sector, the book questions whether or not social entrepreneurship is preferable to more conventional models of development.

Sparking new interest and offering fresh insight into social entrepreneurship in the Greater China region, this book will be useful to students and scholars of Chinese Studies, Business Studies and Sociology.

Yanto Chandra is Assistant Professor at the Department of Public Policy, with joint appointment with the Department of Management, at the City University of Hong Kong. His research interests are social, sustainable, developmental entrepreneurship, social investment, and entrepreneurship in general.

Linda Wong is a former professor in the Department of Public Policy at the City University of Hong Kong. She was the founder and director of Project Flame, the City University of Hong Kong's platform to promote social innovation and social entrepreneurship for students.

Routledge Contemporary China Series

Social Entrepreneurship in the Greater China Region

Policy and cases

**Edited by Yanto Chandra
and Linda Wong**

Routledge
Taylor & Francis Group

LONDON AND NEW YORK

First published 2016
by Routledge

2 Park Square, Milton Park, Abingdon, Oxfordshire OX14 4RN
711 Third Avenue, New York, NY 10017

Routledge is an imprint of the Taylor & Francis Group, an informa business

First issued in paperback 2017

British Library Cataloguing in Publication Data
A catalogue record for this book is available from the British Library

Library of Congress Cataloging-in-Publication Data
Names: Chandra, Yanto, editor.
Title: Social entrepreneurship in the greater China : policy and cases /
    edited by Yanto Chandra.
Description: Abingdon, Oxon ; New York, NY : Routledge, 2016. |
    Series: Routledge contemporary China series ; 147 | Includes
    bibliographical references and index.
Identifiers: LCCN 2015042347 | ISBN 9781138947498 (hardback) |
    ISBN 9781315670065 (ebook)
Subjects: LCSH: Social entrepreneurship—China.
Classification: LCC HD60.5.C5 S63 2016 | DDC 658.4/080951—dc23
LC record available at http://lccn.loc.gov/2015042347

ISBN: 978-1-138-94749-8 (hbk)
ISBN: 978-0-8153-6880-9 (pbk)

Typeset in Times New Roman
by Apex CoVantage, LLC

Contents

Figures

Tables

Contributors and Bios

Kevin Au co-founded the CUHK Center for Entrepreneurship and serves as the current Director. He is also Director of the Centre for Family Business. His research interests are international management, entrepreneurship, family business, and social network. He has published dozens of academic articles, teaching cases, and book chapters, and served on the editorial boards of several academic journals. He has provided consulting and training for the government and business corporations. His clients include the Central Policy Unit, Hong Kong Cyberport, and a number of business startups and family businesses in Hong Kong.

Besides research and consulting, he serves as a director for the Hong Kong Business Angel Network Ltd.(HKBAN), Family Firm Institute (USA), and International Study of Entrepreneurship Education Outcomes (ISSEO). He is an active angel investor on a few startups. In the capacity as Chairman of the Successful Trans-generational Entrepreneurship Practices (STEP) Project of the Asia Pacific Consortium, he worked with dozens of schools in Asia and Babson College to promote family business research in the region. In the public domain, he is currently member of the Social Enterprise Advisory Committee and the Social Innovation and Enterprise Task Force, a sub-committee of the Commission for Poverty.

Yanto Chandra, PhD, is Assistant Professor at the Department of Public Policy and the Department of Management, City University of Hong Kong. Chandra's research focuses on social entrepreneurship/innovation, entrepreneurship, social investment and research methods. Chandra won the Outstanding Paper Award Winner at the Literati Network Awards for Excellence 2010. He serves on the Editorial Board of the *Journal of International Marketing* and the *Journal of Data Mining & Digital Humanities*. His work has been published in, among others, *Asia Pacific Journal of Management, Journal of International Marketing, and Journal of World Business*. Prior to these, he was a faculty member at the University of Leeds and University of Amsterdam, and had around seven years of work experience in multinational companies.

Jennifer H. Chen, PhD, is an associate professor in the Graduate Program of NPO Management in Nanhua University, Taiwan. Actively involved with civic groups, she has founded a chapter for the Society of Wilderness and an association dedicated to the promotion of cultural events in rural areas. Her recent research topics cover social innovation and entrepreneurship, as well as the collaborative governance in creating collective impact. Her research proposal receives scholarly distinguished recognition by the National Science Council in Taiwan, and her papers have been published in various English and Chinese journals. She obtained her PhD in Strategy from National Taiwan University, and prior to joining an academic career, she was a certified public accountant in California, US.

Kee Chi-Hing is Adjunct Associate Professor of the Business School in Hong Kong Baptist University, a member of the Social Innovation and Entrepreneurship Development Fund Task Force of the Commission on Poverty, a member of the Social Enterprise Advisory Committee of Home Affairs Bureau and a member of the Community Investment and Inclusion Fund of the Labour and Welfare Bureau. He is the chair of Fullness Social Enterprises Society. Before retirement, he was the former Corporate Vice President and Hong Kong Managing Director of Hewlett-Packard.

Hang Chow was a senior research associate in Project Flame: Social Innovation and Entrepreneurship at City University of Hong Kong. He obtained his BSocSc in Policy Studies and Administration from CityU and his MA in China Development Studies from the University of Hong Kong. He was responsible for the promotion of social innovation and entrepreneurship education both inside and outside campus. He also organized student activities to raise their social awareness and to enhance their capacity of service leadership. Hang is now working at Hong Kong University of Science and Technology.

Cora Chu is the Chief Executive Officer of Dialogue in the Dark Hong Kong. Cora has extensive sales and marketing management experience in the telecommunication industry for local and global markets. She was inspired to pursue her second career in DiD HK Limited in 2013 with key focus on transforming team culture and crystalizing key learning impacts of experiential learning workshop and entertaining events. She took up the CEO role in 2015 with the vision to empower more People of Differences (PoD) to live out their lives with respect and dignity. Cora holds a masters degree in Family Education and Family Counselling from the Chinese University Hong Kong.

Yu-Yuan Kuan, PhD, is Professor of Social Welfare and Social Policy at National Chung Cheng University, Chiayi, Taiwan. His current research focuses on governance of non-profit organizations, civil society, political economy of the welfare state and social entrepreneurship and social economy. Recent publications include *Social Enterprise: A Comparison of Taiwan and Hong Kong* (co-editor). Kaohsiung: Chu-Liu Book Company, 2012; *The Non-profit Sector: Organization and Operation* (co-editor). Taipei: Chu-Liu Book Company, 2011; *A Historical Review of the Family Helper Project in Taiwan.* Taichung: Taiwan Fund for Children and Families, 2010; *Non-profit Organizations and*

Evaluation: Theories and Practices (co-editor). Taipei: Hung Yeh Book Company, 2008.

Jane C. Y. Lee, PhD, is Director of the Hong Kong Sheng Kung Hui (Anglican) Welfare Council. She has been the Chair of the Organizing Committee of the Social Enterprise Summit since 2008. Currently, she serves on a number of government committees, in particular Social Enterprise Advisory Committee (2009–2015) and the Vice Chair of Hong Kong Social Entrepreneurship Forum. She also sits on a number of NGO's Boards and Executive Committees in Hong Kong, including St. James Settlement and Sheng Kung Hui St. Christopher's Home Limited. She is also Council Chair, Vice-chair and School Manager of a number of Secondary Schools in Hong Kong and Macau.

Ji-Ren Lee, PhD, is a professor of Strategy and Management at the College of Management, and Director of Creativity of Entrepreneurship Program, National Taiwan University. He received his doctoral degree with concentration in strategy from the University of Illinois at Urbana-Champaign. His research interests focus on competence-based growth strategy, entry strategies into emerging markets and corporate transformation, among others.

Zhao Meng, PhD, is an associate professor at the School of Business at Renmin University of China. He was an assistant professor at the Moscow School of Management Skolkovo. He received his PhD from the Said Business School, Oxford University. Previously, he was a visiting scholar at the Harvard Kennedy School of Government and Stanford University's Philanthropy and Civil Society Research Center. He was the cofounder of Youth Business Development International, an Oxford-based nonprofit organization to support youth social entrepreneurs worldwide. His research focuses on social innovation in the business context, stakeholder management strategy, corporate social responsibility and social entrepreneurship.

Julian Zhu Min is the Head of Learning & Development of Dialogue in the Dark Hong Kong. Julian was a proofreader at the China Braille Press and later a vocational trainer for blind people with the China's Association of Disabled People. He joined the Dialogue Social Enterprise (Germany) under its Dialogue in the Dark business since 2007 and has been in charge of recruiting, initial training and continuous talent development of blind employees, as well as maintaining and sharing knowledge of employment diversity among DiD teams. He also supported DiD in mainland China and Taiwan in building up their teams for delivering dark experiences.

Antony Pang is the Founder of The Dots Company which is a consultancy company offering co-transformation strategies for "venturers of social heart and business mind". He was the CEO of Dialogue in the Dark Hong Kong, from July 2010 to June 2015. He received training in the areas of Social Work, Marketing and Criminology, and is a Registered Social Worker (Hong Kong), Certified Gambling Counselor (Canada) and Narrative Therapy Practitioner

(Australia). He worked in NGOs for more than fifteen years focusing on children and youth work. He pioneered the first Asset Based Approach project in Hong Kong and in 2008 he started "BiciLine – Bicycle Eco-tourism" in Hong Kong under the Tung Wah Group of Hospitals, which creates employment opportunities for disadvantaged youths in Tin Shui Wai district.

Jessica Tam is Head of HKCSS-HSBC Social Enterprise Business Centre (SEBC), the first tripartite platform in HK in driving social entrepreneurship and advocating social innovation. Since the launch of SEBC in 2008, Ms. Tam has been initiating a wide range of cross-sectoral initiatives, including the setup of the 'Good Goods' Sales Platform, DBS Social Enterprise Advancement Grant, Impact Incubator and the Good Point Social Enterprise Lifestyle Hub. Ms. Tam obtained her M.Phil in Sociology at the Chinese University of Hong Kong and received executive training on social entrepreneurship at INSEAD. Prior to her current position, Jessica served as a Policy & Research Officer in HKCSS and tertiary institutes with a focus on poverty and employment.

Shu-Twu Wang, PhD, is Professor and Director of Department of Social Work at National Pingtung University of Science and Technology, Pingtung, Taiwan. His research focuses on the issues of non-profit organizations (NPOs), social enterprise, and program evaluation. He has done several projects with respect to the institutions analysis of NPOs, the development and characteristics of social enterprise in Taiwan, social performance evaluation of NPO and community-based social enterprise research in Taiwan. Recent publication includes *Social Enterprise: A Comparison of Taiwan and Hong Kong* (co-editor, Kaohsiung: Chu-Liu Book Company, 2012).

Fiona Wat is the Founder of Dialogue Experience Silence and Silence le Cabaret at the Dialogue in the Dark Hong Kong. Dialogue Experience Silence received the respected 2013 Social Enterprise Champion Award. Silence le cabaret is the world's first silent theatrical dining experience, which offers a unique "Impactainment – Impact + Entertainment" experience and exposes a different vision of the art world to the general public. She has over fifteen years of marketing and brand management experience in collaboration with well-known brands and international corporations.

Linda Wong, PhD, is a former professor in the Department of Public Policy at the City University of Hong Kong. She was the founder and director of Project Flame, the City University of Hong Kong's platform to promote social innovation and social entrepreneurship for faculty and students. She was a social worker and social planner before joining the academia. Her teaching and research interests include social welfare, the third sector, social entrepreneurship, comparative social policy and China studies. She has published widely in monographs, book chapters and top journals.

Hsiang-Hsun Wu, PhD, is the New Business Development Director at Wiskey Capital. Prior to being on leave to the industry, he served as an assistant professor at Yuan Ze University from 2010 to 2015. He received his doctorate in Strategy from National Taiwan University. His research interests include the social interactions in large-scale networks and negative emotions at workplace; currently he is conducting a social network study of top web forums in Taiwan. He has dedicated several years as a pro bono consultant for two social enterprises.

Terence Yuen, PhD, is a research associate at the Centre for Social Innovation Studies at the Chinese University of Hong Kong. Apart from picking up the university appointment, Dr Yuen is also the founder and chief executive of the Hong Kong Institute of Social Impact Analysts, a professional body offering social impact assessment services to a wide range of organizations, including social enterprises. A qualified accountant and a seasoned evaluation researcher, Dr Yuen has been undertaking research and consultancy projects on program evaluation, nonprofit management and social entrepreneurship in various capacities for over fifteen years. Dr Yuen obtained an MPA and a PhD in Politics and Public Administration at the University of Hong Kong.

Foreword

Benefiting from close cross-sector partnerships, social enterprises (SEs) in Hong Kong have become an increasingly important component of our economy, injecting much energy and innovation for the city to overcome mounting social challenges through commercially viable solutions and collaborations.

I have a long association with SE development in Hong Kong which has lasted for some 15 years. I started championing SE in 2000 in my then capacity as the Director of Social Welfare. Inspired by a non-governmental organization (NGO) in the rehabilitation sector, the Department launched the Enhancing Employment for People with Disabilities through Small Enterprise Project. In 2007, in my then capacity as the Permanent Secretary for Home Affairs, we supported SEs in poverty alleviation work especially at the district level. In 2008, as the Secretary for Development, I took a further step in introducing the SE model to the adaptive re-use of Hong Kong's historic buildings. In 2013, the Commission on Poverty, which I chair, decided to move from SE to SI (social innovation) with the creation of the Social Innovation and Entrepreneurship Development Fund. Over these years, the number of SEs in our city has more than doubled, surpassing 570 and representing the highest density in East Asia in terms of population size. The sector has shown a greater diversity both in terms of the scope of business and the target beneficiaries. What is more encouraging is their sustainability, with over 60 percent of SEs achieving break-even or making a profit according to a recent survey.

The headway made in promoting SEs in Hong Kong would not have been possible without the enthusiasm of many NGOs, business groups and dedicated individuals. It is the Hong Kong Special Administrative Region Government's policy objective to focus on jointly building the SE ecosystem with various sectors to enable Hong Kong's SEs to thrive and grow organically. Examples of our key initiatives include providing seed funding to SEs, adjusting our procurement policy, supporting capacity building programs to nurture social entrepreneurs, enhancing public awareness of SEs, and promoting cross-sector dialogue and collaboration through the annual SE Summit and ethical consumption campaigns, as well as award and mentorship schemes.

New technology, rapid urbanisation, expanding education and consumption-driven damage to the environment are creating unprecedented pressures as well as opportunities for community leaders and social practitioners, calling for visionary responses through innovation and partnership. Nowhere is the pressure higher or the need for innovation greater than in Asia, where patterns of population and business methods that have helped drive rapid growth need to adapt rapidly to an ageing population and to the imperative of efficient use and maintenance of resources. I see a path for Hong Kong, thanks to its openness, its social conscience and its entrepreneurial flair, to lead the way through social innovation to new patterns of business and society that sustain hope and prospects in the region for generations to come. There is surely much to be done.

I must therefore congratulate the editors of this book, Dr Yanto Chandra and Professor Linda Wong, and all contributors, for their collaboration in producing this most timely collection of articles on the state of social entrepreneurship in Greater China. By taking stock of what we collectively have achieved in the social entrepreneurship sector, everyone can be better informed and better equipped to build the SE ecosystem stronger and better.

I look forward to walking hand in hand on the SE journey with you.

Carrie Lam
Chief Secretary for Administration
The Government of the Hong Kong Special Administrative Region

"Social enterprise", the next engine for social progress

The idea of social enterprise is growing rapidly and attracting increased attention from many people. I believe that "social enterprise" will be the next driving engine for human civilization and an essential mechanism of value innovation for the society.

Over the years, I have been concerned about society's sustainability and competence; therefore, for the past five years, I have actively devoted myself to promoting the ideas and mindset of "Wangdao". The three core values of Wangdao are value creation, balance of interests, and sustainable development. Ultimately, permanent sustainability is achieved by constant creation of innovated value for the society while balancing the interests of all stakeholders.

The value refers to the total value taking into consideration all six aspects of value (Wangdao), which include tangible, intangible, direct, indirect, and present and future value. In other words, one needs to deliberate on both the visible (tangible, direct, and present) and the invisible (intangible, indirect, and future) perspectives to create balanced value.

Even though social entrepreneurship will emphasize more of the invisible perspective of social value, it still needs to create the visible value and establish its revenue model so that it can prosper and become a comprehensive system that generates value for society.

After my retirement, I have set my mission to become a social entrepreneur. The Stans Foundation, which that I founded, has been operating in compliance with the spirit of social entrepreneurship, promoting all kinds of projects to cultivate talents. I believe the mechanism of value innovation of social enterprise is the only way to utilize limited resources most effectively and hence will gain sustainable development.

With the arising development of social enterprises, the exchange of experience is important. This book presents many social enterprise cases as reference, which can help whoever has his/her vision on social entrepreneurship and withstands challenges to make a difference in society. I congratulate the editors, Dr Yanto Chandra and Prof Linda Wong, and the authors for their hard work in putting together these state-of-the-art articles on social entrepreneurship in Greater China.

Stan Shih
Co-founder and Honorary Chairman of the Acer Group/Chairman of
Stans Foundation

Book Comments

This book represents an important new contribution both to regional perspectives on social entrepreneurship and, specifically, to scholarly analyses of the Asian contexts of this growing field. As the first collection to take stock of the development of social entrepreneurship in the Greater China region, the book sets out a compelling agenda to consider social entrepreneurship as a solution to many of the complex and pressing social problems in the region. Social entrepreneurship is still a nascent and ill-defined sector in the region, and this fascinating and timely collection argues that a strong state can play an important role as a catalyst in developing the social entrepreneurship sector, particularly by legitimizing it. However, at the same time, the local innovative traditions around private enterprise – notably in Hong Kong – can act as the driver of social innovation locally and across the Greater China region. Elsewhere, this book suggests that much can also be learned from adapting existing practices and models found in the West to the Chinese context. The book contains a compelling blend of academic and practitioner perspectives from mainland China, Hong Kong and Taiwan that are particularly powerful and should generate considerable interest across the public, commercial, and not-for-profit sectors in the region. I welcome this wonderful work of scholarship as a vital new addition to our understanding of social entrepreneurship around the globe.

Professor Alex Nicholls
Professor of Social Entrepreneurship
Said Business School
University of Oxford
Editor, *The Journal of Social Entrepreneurship*

Overview and Introduction

The rise of social entrepreneurship (SE) – defined as organizations that seek to create societal value by combining social welfare and commercial logic (Battilana & Dorado, 2010) or practices and processes of using business principles to solve social-environmental problems (Short, Moss, & Lumpkin, 2009) – highlights the increasing importance of new types of actors and organizations as solutions to various "inefficiencies", or what economists call "failures", left by the three pillars of society: the state, the non-profit sector and the for-profit sector (Defourny, Hulgard, & Pestoff, 2014). If the state cannot efficiently solve a social problem, the for-profit sector avoids taking part in solving it, as it generates no (large) profits, and the non-profit sector lacks the efficiency and innovation to perform the social function, who else can or is/are willing to fix those inefficiencies if not the society itself?

Despite its relative newness, social entrepreneurship has roots that can be traced back to the broader practices of social innovation. Social innovation involves the invention of new ideas, artefacts, organizations or systems that seek to benefit the society and is not necessarily motivated by profit. The invention of money (which enables market exchange efficiently and precisely), management (a modern practice in organizing work), mass movements (as strategies to collectively organize people to achieve certain goals), and benefit corporations (innovations in a legal entities that protect their directors in "doing good" and against shareholder lawsuits) are some of the major examples of social innovation in the history of mankind (Drucker, 1987). In fact, social entrepreneurship is about *internalizing* social innovation into an organization and wrapping it with an identity, a system that transforms input to output to outcomes and impact and with unique value proposition.

The emergence of social entrepreneurship in the past decade may reflect disenchantment or even anger by individuals or groups with pressing societal issues, including poverty, social exclusion, human rights, ageing, sanitation, water, and pollution. Social entrepreneurs recognize these problems as opportunities. But instead of pointing fingers as to who causes and must be held responsible for such problems, they take initiatives, gather personal as well as external resources and advocate people to support a good cause through "trade", "innovation" and "compassion", not "aid" (e.g., donation or charity) or costly "political action" or "indifference." Some label them as "unreasonable people" (Elkington & Hartigan, 2008) with big ambitions but no clear plan of how they would change the world. Obviously social entrepreneurs are highly reasonable individuals, as they employ the entrepreneurial method by making the best use of what they have and know and of their identity (Sarasvathy, 2001) and reconnect previously unconnected ideas, resources, people and institutions to create something new that solves problems (Baker & Nelson, 2005) and develop opportunities based on what they already know, i.e., their prior knowledge (Chandra, Styles, & Wilkinson, 2012, 2015; Shane, 2000). They are also reasonable because they seek financial and operational "sustainability" in their activities such that every single cent invested in the social enterprise will make a return. Thus unlike a non-trading form based on "doing good", such as a charity, the lifespan of the social enterprise (or broadly, social investment) can be endless and can attract more investment to create larger social impact.

The bulk of scholarly work in social entrepreneurship has focused on the macro level (i.e., institutions and organizations) and to a smaller extent on the micro level (i.e., the social entrepreneur). However, extant research has almost completely ignored the role of *context* in the study of social entrepreneurship. Context matters. It is our purpose in this book to bring to the world the first book that examines – systematically and using rich evidence – how social entrepreneurship is adopted in the *non-Western, non–Anglo Saxon context*. Perhaps there are alternative viewpoints, meanings or models of social entrepreneurship that one might find in the *Greater China context*.

While social entrepreneurship is in its infancy in most parts of the world and has yet to become "legitimate" (Dacin, Dacin, & Tracey, 2011; Nicholls, 2010), it is even a newer and often not well understood phenomenon in the Greater China context (i.e., mainland China, Taiwan, Hong Kong and Macau). Greater China has distinct and unique institutional heritage, history, law, culture, social and family values, propensity to create voluntary organizations, social welfare system, innovation system and the concept of "giving and helping others". However, most of our understanding of what works and what does not and why in social entrepreneurship has so far come from the West and the rest of the world. *But what can the world learn about social entrepreneurship from Greater China?* Specifically, *how are the unique local environments or institutions shaped by the nature of social enterprises in this region? How do policies affect social enterprise in this region? What social problems have social entrepreneurs from Greater China tackled? How did they do it?* Although a small army of social entrepreneurs have pioneered social enterprises successfully in Hong Kong, mainland China and Taiwan, to date we know very little of them. These were the overarching questions or challenges that we pose to our contributors.

Therefore, we hope to provide an alternative view of social entrepreneurship by acknowledging that context matters in this new sector. Specifically, this book delves into the role and impact of institutions and policy on the development of social enterprises, and uses rich cases to explain how the micro and macro factors might interact in influencing social entrepreneurship in Greater China.

The book is structured as follows. Part I is entitled *Policy*. This part provides a macro-level perspective of the development of social enterprises in Greater China. As most of the chapter demonstrates, the government and its policies play a *pioneering or catalyst role* in starting up the social enterprise sector in Greater China and *resource provision role* in the subsequent growth of the sector. The *legal and legislation role* of the government in the social enterprise sector has yet to emerge. Importantly, Greater China demonstrates a gradual shift from a *pure social welfare model* to the *social economy model*, where social enterprise is an element, as stakeholders at the government, business and civil society levels attempt to make and give sense to the social enterprise as a new model of development. An important part of this development is the role of *language and discourse about social enterprises*, where the concept of "social enterprises" may need a clever reinvention or reinterpretation so that its meaning is not lost in translation to the Chinese language. These are among the key characteristics of the social enterprise sector in Greater China as compared with the West. Among the theoretical lenses used in the chapters in Part I are institutional theory and logic, structuration, politics and impact assessment.

Professor Meng Zhao, in Chapter 1, examines social enterprise as a "foreign concept" to mainland China and highlights how the social enterprise concept could be translated and mean various things in Chinese, including "social startup", "private enterprise" and "startup for public good", which deviate from their original meanings in the West. He shows the social-cognitive tensions that complicate the meaning of social enterprise and how the government and grassroots supporters strategically explore local meanings and political opportunities to facilitate social enterprise development. Zhao downplays the heroic focus in social entrepreneurship and invites future research to further examine how contextual forces shape local form(s) of social enterprises. In short, Zhao characterizes social enterprise development in mainland China as a *process of institutional reinvention*.

In Chapter 2, Professor Kevin Au, Terence Yeung and Jessica Tam examine the birth and rise of social enterprises in the Hong Kong Special Administrative Region (SAR). Drawing on institutional theory, and particularly the structuration view and reflexive isomorphism concepts, they document how the Hong Kong government shifted its policy from "social welfare" to "welfare-to-work" as it sought to tackle unemployment after the Asian financial crisis, or what they call *"from sociality to market orientation"* and argue how the acts of pioneer social enterprises and their success stories help legitimize the *social enterprise as a new institutional logic* that is based on quality and efficiency, financial sustainability and business models. They argue for building a more *pluralistic* SE sector, beyond the dominant work-integrated social enterprise (WISE) sector, as the solution to strengthen Hong Kong's social entrepreneurship space.

In Chapter 3, Dr Jane Lee argues how social enterprises have become *politically embedded* in the Hong Kong government's policy and the critical role that political support plays to advance SE as a new approach to tackle Hong Kong's social problems. Extending and broadening Au et al's argument, Dr Jane Lee argues for relevant policy issues, such as *definitions and legal framework, governance and audit, public education and publicity, as well as training and talent development* as key drivers to the legitimacy of SE in Hong Kong's free market system.

Kee Chi-Hing, in Chapter 4, offers one of the first attempts to evaluate the effectiveness of the social enterprise policies of the Hong Kong government. By analyzing the data on 3E (Enhancing Employment of People with Disabilities through Small Enterprise) Project and ESR (Enhancing Self-Reliance through District Partnership) Program and comparing them with commercial and social enterprises in the US and UK, Kee finds that the *median life span, financial performance and social impact of social enterprises in Hong Kong are more favorable* than those in the US and UK. Kee proposes future research that adopts a more holistic way of evaluating the impact of social enterprises, including those that include the affective, cognitive, behavioral, narrative and financial dimensions.

Professor Yu-Yuan Kuan and Shu-Twu Wang, in Chapter 5, analyze the role of the government and public policy measures (e.g., the Law for Protecting Disabled People, Multi-Employment Service Program) on the development of social enterprises in the Taiwanese context. Using data from three surveys on the social enterprises in Taiwan in 2006, 2010 and 2013, they portray that the most effective support measures provided by the Taiwanese government since the mid-2000s have been *financial measures*, followed by *capacity building of business operation through consulting services or trainings* and *marketability*. They also find that the Taiwanese government has given less attention to the "legal framework" for social enterprises and "cross-organizational and cross-sectoral cooperation", which could offer avenues for future research.

In Chapter 6, Professor Jennifer Chen and Ji-Ren Lee offers a historical overview of the concept of social enterprise in Taiwan by deconstructing its ecosystem. Drawing insights from the development of the Fairtrade movement in the US (i.e., plantation/scaling up vs. small producers/empowerment focus), they argued for a bipolar model of SE in Taiwan, one that is based on mission focused with income-generating activities and the other business focused with social issues in mind. Next, they offer five key challenges that hamper the development of social enterprises in Taiwan: innovation, human resources, business development, governance and funding, as well as the ongoing debate on whether to create a legislation and certification system to define social enterprises.

Part II is entitled *Cases*. This part provides a micro-level perspective of the development of social enterprises in Greater China and how macro-level variables might influence the micro-level variables. As the chapters demonstrate, the key success factors of social enterprises in Hong Kong, Taiwan and mainland China do not seem to differ from social enterprises in other parts of the world or the West. In general, the key success drivers in the cases shown include a *deep personal motivation* to start enterprises for social purposes (be it driven by family- or work-related problems), *entrepreneurial techniques and strategies* in dealing with resource constraints and lack of legitimacy in the early stage of the ventures such as *bricolage* (Nelson & Baker, 2005), the role of *social and professional networks* as sources of ideas and capabilities, *relational competence* including building relations and persuading the government, *social innovative capacity* in creating innovative social intervention solutions that add value to stakeholders and some element of "luck", as any entrepreneurs would claim to have it. In addition, it reveals the role of higher education systems in promoting and instilling the social entrepreneurial culture among young people.

In Chapter 7, Dr Yanto Chandra argues that little is known about *how and why certain social enterprises are successful in the Chinese context*. Drawing on one of the most successful social enterprises in Hong Kong, Diamond Cab, which has successfully created a specialty taxi market from the ground up and turned it into a legitimate market in less than five years, Chandra conducted in-depth interviews and compiled secondary data and finds several key mechanisms behind Diamond Cab's high performance as a social enterprise: *a focused strategy, social design orientation, social bricolage and informal and formal advice networks*, as well as *biographical variables including personal values, traits and distress*. Chandra argues for future research that focuses on the *micro-foundations* of SE, particularly the role of people behind social enterprises, their emotions, cognition and behavior, as well as the entrepreneurial method, such as effectuation as a means to address uncertainty in better understanding the performance drivers of social enterprises.

In Chapter 8, Ding Li offers a historical account of the rise of the Non-Profit Incubator (NPI), which has cultivated over 1,000 social entrepreneurs annually in China, showing a perplexing relationship between government and social entrepreneurship development in China. Li traces the development of NPI through the journey of its enterprising founder, Zhao Lu; how he gained the trust and support from local government agencies, secured funding from international foundations, used the English-based "Non-Profit Incubator" name for his organization and finally was included by the Civil Affairs Ministry as a nationwide model. It highlights Zhao's ability to satisfy the heterogeneous requirements of multiple stakeholders in China as a critical success factor of NPI's rise into one of China's largest SE support organizations.

In Chapter 9, Professor Linda Wong narrates her experience as a social intrapreneur at the City University of Hong Kong and the bottom-up and multiple-stakeholder construction of Project Flame (previously SE Group) and how she and colleagues co-crafted its identity, created high-profile events and turned it into one of the most successful campus-wide initiatives at the university level. Wong further describes the motivation behind the creation of Project Flame and argues how universities in Hong Kong could learn from among the best universities in the West by balancing research, teaching and making contributions to society and how social innovation and entrepreneurship education could be a viable option to liberate and prepare young people as future leaders. Wong concludes with a summary of Project Flame's experience, which could be adopted and replicated by other educational institutions with a "flame" in their hearts.

In Chapter 10, Antony Pang, Hang Chow, Cora Chu, Fiona Wat and Julian Zhu adopt an *empowerment perspective in social entrepreneurship* and offer a critical reflection of why and how Dialogue in the Dark (DID) Hong Kong, a social franchise from Germany's DID enables the innovative processes of empowerment at various levels. They find the explicit role of psychological empowerment; narrative therapy for visually and hearing impaired individuals; *transformational experiential learning process via role reversal and change in power relations for "customers"*, organizational empowerment via the social mission and values that provide plenty of room for innovative projects; and community empowerment as being critical processes that strengthen multiple stakeholders (beneficiaries, customers, funders, society). They argue for DID Hong Kong as a unique and all-round model in empowering various stakeholders in the community with innovative ideas.

The last chapter, Chapter 11, written by Professor Hsiang-Hsun Wu and Jennifer Chen, offers an in-depth analysis of the development of one of Taiwan's most well-known social enterprises, Duofu, which offers barrier-free transport services. Wu and Chen analyzed its founder Jeff Hsu's personal experiences with his injured grandmother and low service quality problems of public-managed private rehabus services which led to an opportunity to establish Duofu. The two authors concluded that the *multi-sided platform strategy* (which enables direct interactions between people with disabilities with accessible travel service providers, and other related service providers), *cross subsidy model of products and services* and *service innovation* as key mechanisms led to the success of the social enterprise in the Taiwanese context.

This book offers the first exploration into the world of social enterprises in the Greater China context. Our objective is to show the progression of social entrepreneurship in this region and its historical color, shed light onto some of its success stories to spark an interest in the area and open up new debates so as to facilitate a better understanding of whether, why and how social entrepreneurship may or may not be preferable to more conventional models of development. This book remains exploratory in nature and is far from providing conclusive evidence on the state of social entrepreneurship in Greater China. Therefore, we believe that more research is needed to understand the strategies, patterns and models that may explain the boundary conditions of social entrepreneurship in and beyond Greater China and how it can be fruitfully used to create a better, sustainable world. We do hope that this book will spark a greater interest in social entrepreneurship in this region.

The Editors
Yanto Chandra and Linda Wong

References

Baker, T., & Nelson, R. (2005). "Creating Something from Nothing: Resource Construction through Entrepreneurial Bricolage", *Administrative Science Quarterly,* 50(3): 329–366.

Battilana, J., & Dorado, S. (2010). "Building Sustainable Hybrid Organizations: The Case of Commercial Microfinance Organizations", *Academy of Management Journal,* 53(6): 1419–1440.

Chandra, Y., Styles, C., & Wilkinson, I. (2012). "An Opportunity Based View (OBV) of Rapid Internationalization", *Journal of International Marketing,* 20(1): 74–102.

Chandra, Y., Styles, C., & Wilkinson, I. (2015). "Opportunity Portfolio: Moving Beyond Single-Opportunity Explanations in International Entrepreneurship Research", *Asia Pacific Journal of Management*, 32(1): 199–228.

Dacin, M. T., Dacin, P. A., and Tracey, P. (2011). "Social Entrepreneurship: A Critique and Future Directions", *Organization Science*, 22(5): 1203–1213.

Defourny, J., Hulgard, L., & Pestoff, V. (2014). *Social Enterprise and the Third Sector: Changing European Landscapes in a Comparative Perspective*. Abingdon, Oxon: Routledge.

Drucker, P. F. (1987). "Social Innovation – Management's New Dimension", *Long Range Planning*, 20(6): 29–34.

Elkington, J., & Hartigan, P. (2008). *The Power of Unreasonable People: How Social Entrepreneurs Create Markets that Change the World*. Boston: Harvard Business Press.

Nicholls, A. (2010). "The Legitimacy of Social Entrepreneurship: Reflexive Isomorphism in a Pre-paradigmatic Field", *Entrepreneurship Theory and Practice*, 34(4): 611–633.

Sarasvathy, S. D. (2001). "Causation and Effectuation: Toward a Theoretical Shift from Economic Inevitability to Entrepreneurial Contingency", *Academy of Management Review*, 26(2): 243–288.

Shane, S. (2000). "Prior Knowledge and the Discovery of Entrepreneurial Opportunities", *Organization Science*, 11: 448–469.

Short, J. C., Moss, T. W., & Lumpkin, G. T. (2009). "Research in Social Entrepreneurship: Past Contributions and Future Opportunities", *Strategic Entrepreneurship Journal*, 3: 161–194.

1 Reinventing social enterprise in China

Language, institution and strategy

Meng Zhao

Introduction

Social enterprise (SE) is a flourishing phenomenon that attracts remarkable attention from academics and practitioners around the world (Austin, Stevenson, & Wei-Skillern, 2006; Mair & Marti, 2006; Zahra, Rawhouser, Bhawe, Neubaum, & Hayton, 2008). A recent literature review (Short, Morris, & Lumpkin, 2009) reported that there were fifteen countries represented in a systematic search for academic publications on the topic of SE. On the practitioner side, the global presence of the SE movement is even more impressive if one counts the nationalities represented by the award receivers of prestigious championing organizations such as the Skoll Foundation, the Schwab Foundation and Asoka. For example, Asoka has selected over 2,000 social entrepreneurs as its Asoka Fellows from more than sixty countries on the world's five main continents.

Yet we know little about how SE, as an institutional idea that is still evolving, has made its way into so many countries that vary in their political, economic and cultural contexts. SE presents itself as a foreign idea, and thus requires skilful importation into local realities (Boxenbaum & Battilana, 2005). What is underspecified in the extant research on the antecedents of SE (Bacchiega & Borzaga, 2001; Johnson, 2000) is the emergence of SE as a process of institutional reinvention, where social cognition, economic and political system and organizational strategy play intertwined roles. I draw on the literature of institutional translation and bricolage and social movement theory (e.g., Campbell, 2002; Czarniawska & Joerges, 1996) to define institutional reinvention as the foreign concepts or practices being modified to fit local realities and being combined with local elements to shape a course of development different from that in its home context. Institutional reinvention takes place through the collective action of multiple local social actors such as governments, business firms and nonprofit organizations.

The idea and practice of SE is taking off in China. It is undergoing a reinvention process that is shaped by the social-cognitive reframing, the institutional pressure and the strategic revision of newly born SE supporters (Zhao, 2012). For this chapter, twelve interviews were conducted with pioneers among SE supporters in China, and an analysis was done on 932 major Chinese mass media reports on SE in 2009. I disclose from this dataset an updated scenario about how the SE concept is translated, what the social-cognitive tensions are that complicate the perception and acceptance of the concept, how incumbent government officials open up opportunities for SE development and how grassroots supporters utilize local translations and political opportunities to facilitate SE development.

China's legal, political and social support for grassroots nonprofit initiatives has been known to be weak, but the time has come for the government to search out innovation to address social problems at a transitional time. This poses an interesting and important question about the relationship between the existing institutional system in China and an emerging community of social innovation practitioners. Making clear the tension and innovation in SE development in China provides a realistic view to understand how an imported social innovation practice gains access to a politically and legally restrictive environment.

SE has established itself as a legitimate organizational form in the Western world as well as in some developing countries, but it was introduced into China as a novel institutional idea only a few years ago. China's unique, complex and dynamic institutional environment provides an informative context for scholars to develop a more complete understanding of how SE is imported, recreated and accepted.

I introduce a realistic view about how the historical and linguistic traditions in China have generated tensions that influence people's acceptance of SE by starting with a small language analysis of SE. The term "social enterprise" has taken on three forms when it is translated in China. They are "社会企业" (social enterprise), "社会创业" (social startup) and "公益创业" (startup for public good). "Social" in Chinese does not have a strong connotation of "nonprofit", "philanthropy" or "charity" as it has in English, considering the popularity of "social sector" or "social economy" in English. In Chinese, "public good" is used to refer to "philanthropy" or "charity". "Enterprise" in Chinese does not clearly imply innovation, risk taking, or venture as it has in English. It narrowly indicates "business" or "company". Instead, "startup" has a clearer reference to innovation and venture. This composes the fundamental connections of meaning underlying the Chinese translation of "social enterprise". See Figure 1.1 for the language structure of "social enterprise" before and after translation. See Figure 1.2 for the growth of Internet coverage on "社会企业" (social enterprise), "社会创业" (social startup), "公益创业" (startup for social benefit) and "非营利" (nonprofit) in 2000–2009.

The next part of the chapter will provide details on this, while the following part will move on to who SE supporters are and how they build on the existing institution to make a change.

Methodology

This chapter draws conclusions from interviews and a content analysis of media articles. Twelve semi-structured interviews were conducted with founders and key decision makers in organizations ranging from nonprofit organizations (NPOs) to business firms to research institutes. All interviewees are experienced practitioners

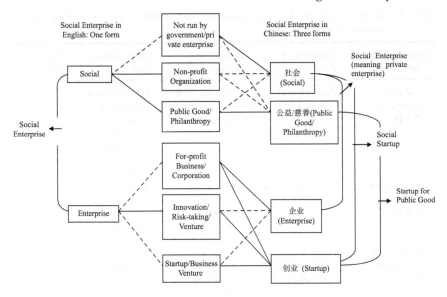

Figure 1.1 Language structure before and after SE reinvention.

Note: Solid lines refer to meaning connections in use. Dashed lines refer to weak or absent meaning connections.

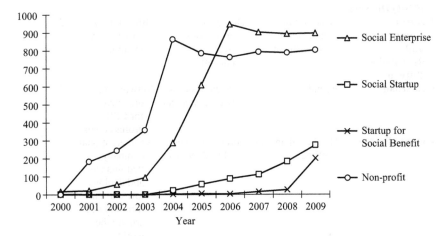

Figure 1.2 The growth of Internet coverage on "社会企业" (social enterprise), "社会创业" (social startup), "公益创业" (startup for social benefit) and "非营利" (nonprofit), 2000–2009.

Source: Google News Archives

or observers in the area of social innovation in China. The interviews lasted one or two hours and all of them were recorded and transcribed. See Table 1.1 for a description of interviewees.

In order to examine how the concept of SE is used in the Chinese context, I did a content analysis of 932 news articles (identified through Google News in 2009)

Table 1.1 Backgrounds of key organizations and interviewees promoting social entrepreneurship in China

Organization Name	Interviewee Position	Interviewee Background	Organization Type	No. of Interviews
Non-Profit Incubator (NPI)	Founder and director	Domestic bank and nonprofit; domestic education	NPO incubator, operating Lenovo's venture philanthropy program since 2007	2
Global Links Initiative (GLI)	Co-founder and director	Foreign and domestic nonprofit; overseas education	SE and NPO information service provider	2
China Social Entrepreneur Foundation	Head of Social Innovation Division	Domestic nonprofit; overseas education	Private foundation	2
Lenovo's Corporate Social Responsibility (CSR) Division	Head of CSR	Domestic business; domestic education	Corporation CSR division	1
Central Compilation and Translation Bureau	Head of Social Innovation Department	Domestic academics; overseas education	Official think tank/research institute	2
Crossroad	Founder	Foreign business; white American	Networking organization for CSR professionals	1
Climate Bridge	Head of Shanghai office	Foreign business; white American	An international company that finances and deploys low-carbon technologies around the world	1
Social Venture Group	Founder	Foreign business; American Chinese	Consulting agency for NPO, foundation and company CSR	1

that include any one of the three terms – "社会企业" (social enterprise), "社会创业" (social startup), "公益创业" (startup for public good). The purpose is to disclose how social meanings underlying the interpretation of SE are embodied by the language structure of news discourse. I focus on mass media accounts because they are the easiest and assumably the most widely used means for the general public to learn about SE in the Chinese language, considering the novelty of this concept and the high accessibility of the Internet in the country. This strategy is consistent with the academic convention in organization studies that treats news media as an important social institution where practices and fields are theorized and new logics emerge and are legitimated (Kennedy, 2008).

The coding strategy builds on an understanding that the structural analysis of the pentadic dimensions of "who gets to do what, where, when, how, and why" in texts can reveal how new concepts are framed in the local context (Green Jr., Carroll, Huang, & Goodnight, 2010). I started the coding process by reading through all news articles, following an open coding process (Miles & Huberman, 1994). In order to identify these relationships and hence the meanings of SE, I coded themes that include the Background of Term User (who writes the texts); the Context of the Term Usage (around what events, activities or ideas the term "social enterprise" is used); the Source of Term (where is the term from: foreign sources such as books and cases vs. local interpretation); the Outcome

Table 1.2 Coding themes and keywords indicating distinct ways of reinventing SE in China

Outcome of Term Use (local reinvention of SE)	Background of Term User (who is the author)	Sample Keywords for the Context of the Term Usage (what does SE refer to)	Source of Term (where is the term from)
SE as private enterprise	Government, mass media	Business enterprise, private enterprise, for-profit enterprise	Local interpretation
SE as nonprofit	Foundation, non-governmental organization practitioner, SE practitioner, scholar, mass media	Public goods, philanthropy, nonprofit, social organization	Mainly local interpretation, a few foreign book/article and foreign NPO/SE cases
SE is incumbent	Scholar, mass media	Social welfare enterprise, co-operative, community service organization	Local interpretation
SE as CSR	Business firm, mass media	Righteous view of wealth, safety, environment protection, climate change, employment	Local interpretation

of Term Use (what the term users get to do by using the term). Term users are important because the existing research reveals that an idea becomes popular not primarily because of its properties but because of who transports and supports it and how it is packaged and formulated (Czarniawska & Joerges, 1996; Tolbert & Zucker, 1983).

See Table 1.2 for detailed coding themes. I use these themes to identify distinct local meanings of "social enterprise". A nontrivial proportion of articles interpret SE in a similar way as that in the West. For example, they describe SE as a new business model or social innovation that adopts business means and market-based logics to serve social missions. I purposefully exclude these articles and only focus on those implying the Chinese variance of the SE concept. The content analysis reveals four types of local understandings of SE. They reflect social-cognitive tensions that reinvent the SE concept in China.

Social-cognitive tensions that reinvent social enterprise language

Social enterprise as private enterprise: a planned economy legacy

In order to examine how the different terms about SE are used in practice, I analyzed 932 news articles in 2009 that included any one of the three terms "社会企业" (social enterprise), "社会创业" (social startup) and "公益创业" (startup for the public good).

Enterprise (企业) as a for-profit entity is a hard-won concept in China. As China was based on a planned economy, basically all forms of organizations engaged in profit-making activities are run by or affiliated with the government. Before the economic reform in 1978, the private for-profit enterprise was seen as the symbol of capitalism and was officially forbidden and socially discriminated against. The economic reform has brought about a legal and cognitive transformation in Chinese society. It has taken a long time for people to accept that the for-profit business is a legal and officially legitimate choice. In 1982 and 1987, the government issued the *Provisions on Several Issues Concerning Urban Individually Owned Enterprises* and the *Tentative Regulations on the Administration of Urban and Rural Individually Owned Enterprises*, respectively. They represent the government's early efforts at formalizing the administration of private businesses.

"社会企业" (social enterprise) started appearing in the mass media and in official expressions. In the media release, "社会企业" (social enterprise) is used to refer to "enterprise in society" rather than "enterprise for society", meaning the private sector enterprise. The purpose is to make a contrast to public sector organizations such as party agencies, government agencies, universities or hospitals and state-owned enterprises. For example, an article published in *Guangming Daily* says that "the meteorological service charges government departments according to the principle of cost recovery, while it charges SEs or the economic sector based on the market rate". An article in *Guangzhou Daily* says: "the local Bureau of Sports provides policy support for both SEs and state-owned enterprises." It actually refers to the sales companies subordinated to these state-owned enterprises' (SOEs) local oil refineries. Therefore, before the translation of "social enterprise" as a new concept, the term "社会企业" (social enterprise) existed in China with a meaning different from the West.

Today "企业" is widely understood as a for-profit enterprise or a corporation. "企业" in the Xinhua (New Chinese) Dictionary is defined as the basic unit of economy that engages in manufacturing, distribution and service businesses and has an independent operation. It therefore loses the features of "enterprise" in English with respect to innovation, value creation, risk taking, the pursuit of opportunity and the possibility of going beyond the for-profit sector. Therefore, a closer translation of "社会企业" is "social business" rather than "social enterprise". "I think when people talk about '企业家' [entrepreneur] they see things that are different from entrepreneur in English. The first response of most people to this term in Chinese would be a business man. As to '企业家精神' [entrepreneurship], people tend to think more of profitability and making money than innovation or creativity. We are not very keen to use the term 'social enterprise' because it may lead to misunderstanding" (interview with the head of the social innovation unit in the China Social Entrepreneur Foundation, September 2009). Drawing on the hard-won understanding of the for-profit nature of business enterprises, Chinese people can easily lean towards an image that SEs actually make money in the name of social benefits. It therefore requires extra efforts to cultivate the public comprehension of and trust in the innovation and social essence of SE.

Social enterprise as nonprofit: a rising and suspicious concept

Chinese people and government are just becoming familiar with the idea of a nonprofit organization (非营利组织). Although not-for-profit and philanthropic practice enjoys a tradition as long as Chinese history, to our knowledge they were rarely framed in a way to contrast to "for-profit" practices. This is partly because in history the for-profit sector as a whole did not obtain the social status and political influence as it had in the West. Chinese today are more familiar with terms such as "公益" (public good) and "慈善" (philanthropy/charity). These concepts do not clearly refer to a sphere of activities that have grown to a degree that can parallel economic or for-profit activities, as strongly connoted in concepts such as "the third sector", "nonprofit" and "the social economy". This partly accounts for why the analysis of the 2009 media reports finds that it is more likely for the mass media to use "public good" than "not-for-profit" to discuss the social aspect of "social enterprise".

The very fact of the NPO sectors' newness partly leads to its lack of legitimacy. NPO is still a sector that is suspicious in the eyes of companies and government authorities. Policymakers have little interest in putting SE on the policy agenda, since they are not sure about how the business elements of an SE will impact its social mission or even raise public concerns. "The reality is that NPOs have low accountability and social trust. In the course of NPO development in China, a few bad cases raised great concerns among people and government agencies.

If the NPOs are commercialized, we can hardly tell them apart from for-profit businesses. We are hence doubtful about their commitments to social benefit. This will contradict the philanthropic nature of the NPOs that the government highlights. So officials have concerns about this. Some think that the commercialization of NPOs is a mistake" (interview with the head of the social innovation research division at the Central Compilation and Translation Bureau,[1] September 2009).

This understanding of a sharp distinction between charity and economic activities is a prevalent social cognition. "The public has an ideal and heroic view of people working in the charity sector. They expect that you devote every minute of your life to philanthropy and give up personal needs. It is difficult for them to accept that NPO practitioners talk about salary or other business stuff" (interview with the head of the social innovation unit in the China Social Entrepreneur Foundation, September 2009). The director of corporate social responsibility (CSR) at Lenovo has the same observation: "In China, doing philanthropy means being a good person and doing good for society. People will for sure doubt your motivation if you do philanthropy but talk about making money" (interview, September 2009).

In addition to the history of local NPO development and related social perception, the background of the concept promoter and the means of promotion also have an influence on how well a new concept will be received. NPO as an imported concept did not avoid an issue of global-local tension that is typical of practice translation across institutional contexts. The CSR director of Lenovo comments on this in detail: "SE as a foreign concept could be suspicious for many people. Every organization has its purpose. We know that some Western NPOs have met difficulties in China. I do not see this simply as government repression. The thing is that an organization will not be welcomed if it aggressively instills its own value into China" (interview, September 2009).

Social enterprise is incumbent: confusion with existing activities

The widely recognized issue of NPO registration in China has furthered the confusion in the understanding of SE. The restrictive legal system forces a great deal of grassroots NPOs to register as companies, which generates a group of NPOs with a legal appearance of SE but which actually do not have a sustainable business mechanism. "Because the legal structure is not available for people, so if you want to be legal in China your best option is to register as a business. But if you register as a business, you cannot do fundraising, so you cannot be traditional charity. . . . Many NPOs are illegal technically. The government accepts NPOs that do a good job. If you are formally registered, you will be limited as to what you can do. If you stay with your business status, you can do whatever you want. . . . We almost need to redefine what is an NPO and what is a social enterprise in China, because the regulation is so different" (interview with the founder of Crossroad, September 2009). This traditional treatment of "社会企业" can cause nontrivial confusion when it is used together with nonprofit organizations. For example, an article from *China Weekly* says that "the Sun Village [an NPO by nature] is a social enterprise that registers with the Bureau of Industry and Commerce." "Social enterprise" actually refers to the private business enterprise as opposed to the nonprofit organization. This is because it registered as a business enterprise rather than as a social organization (or an NPO) due to the restrictive registration system and operational reasons.

Meanwhile, some for-profit enterprises have received social welfare status from the government so that they actually possess the social and commercial features of an SE. One thing to argue concerns their administrative relationship with the supervisory government agency, which renders them hardly grassroots SEs. The Ministry of Civil Affairs issued a *Provisional Ordinance on the Administration of Social Welfare Enterprise* in 1990. The Social Welfare Enterprise (社会福利企业) needs to have more than 35 percent disabled people among their employees. They are business enterprises that register under the Ministry of Industry and Commerce, like other for-profit enterprises. But they need to receive supervision from the local bureaus of civil affairs. They are required to get a "Social Welfare Enterprise Certificate" in order to enjoy tax benefits, government loans and other government support.

Indeed, some scholars in the government-run research institutes view existing forms of social organizations such as "社会福利企业" (social welfare enterprise) and "合作社" (co-operatives) as quasi-social enterprises (准社会企业). The head of the social innovation research division in the CCTB said that "if we look at the fundamental spirit of social enterprise, there have been social enterprises in China for a long time. I name them as quasi-social enterprises. The welfare factory is an example. Another example is the professional cooperative and the community-based service organization or service center" (interview, September 2009). The existence of similar activities and organizational forms in China is likely to engender a "we already have this" syndrome. The understanding and adoption of social entrepreneurship could be limited when people tend to narrowly equate the existing forms with the new concept and are blind to important differences.

Social enterprise as corporate social responsibility: a convenient misreading

Quite a few media reports treat "social enterprise" as an equivalent of corporate social responsibility. When they mention "social enterprise" they actually highlight business enterprises that take on social responsibility. A large proportion of media reports described private business entrepreneurs as "social entrepreneurs" and their businesses as "social enterprises" when their activities are in effect CSR projects. These articles typically use "社会企业" without any further explanation and hence they seem to be doing more of a branding work. For example, an article by the Xinhua News Agency argues that "we need to have a righteous view of wealth, a corporation needs to become a social enterprise when it grows to a certain scale." An article on the Phoenix website said that "as a car manufacturer, [the company] puts safety as the priority. This presents it as a social enterprise." Several articles discussed "social enterprise" as a useful public policy solution to address the unemployment problem or promote community development. For example, an article in *Shenzhen Special District News* suggested that "[the government should] support social entrepreneurs to set up social enterprises so that the social sector can provide a great deal of employment." The majority of this understanding comes from government officials and domestic business people. The concept of CSR has obtained firm legitimacy in China and has taken a foothold in both official and grassroots discourses. In this background, SE has become a convenient tool for CSR promotion and business practitioners' self-labeling.

Political opportunities for social enterprise development

China is indeed a transitional society. What flows is not only the language and cognition about SE, but also the political and regulatory governance on the NPO sector. SE supporters have managed to exploit opportunities in the government system. The revision of the language indicates how the history, regulatory arrangement and social trend complicate the translation process. The existing political and regulatory institutions in China are also opening up opportunities for SE development. Some key government officials take on a proactive role in building a more favorable environment for grassroots NPO in general and fostering the work of SE supports in particular. Meanwhile, the regulation on NPO administration is undergoing a change, and experiments with new policies have appeared in Shenzhen and Beijing. Regarding the government's attitude on SEs and on NPOs in general, the head of the social innovation research division in CCTB said:

> There are debates among the supervisory government officials about SE. Some find it appealing, some find it a new label for old stuff . . . . The government may not explicitly promote SE, but you will note that the policy is gradually loosening up in practice. The government is trying to improve the environment for NPO development. For example, we are entrusted by the government to study the experience in other countries so that we can amend the dual administration system in China.
>
> (Interview, September 2009)

As a matter of fact, central government officials have been pushing an "opening up" policy for social organizations[2] for years. For example, Fan Baojun was the vice minister of the Ministry of Civil Affairs and is now the chairman of China Charity Federation. He has frequently picked on the restrictive dual administration system and appealed for speeding up the process of NPO legislation. Wang Zhenyao was the director of the Ministry of Civil Affairs' Disaster Alleviation office. He accomplished the implementation of the minimum living security system and health care system in urban and rural areas. He then led the establishment of the Social Welfare Office and the Philanthropy Promotion Office at the ministry, with an announced objective to build up an advanced social service system and facilitate grassroots philanthropy. Partly due to their constant efforts, now the draft of Philanthropy Law is under review by the State Council.

They are not the only cases. Xu Yongguang is the general secretary at the Narada Foundation, one of the major SE facilitators in China. He was the head of the Organization Department of the Youth League of the Central of the Communist Party of China, the general secretary of the China Youth Development Foundation, and the vice chairman of the China Charity Federation. So from the former central official in the Party system and the head of two of the largest government-run nonprofit organizations in China, Xu moved to a small but pioneering grassroots foundation set up by a private company in Shanghai. Another case is that of Shang Yusheng, who was the general secretary of the Research Institute of China Science Foundation. He then retired from the government and founded China NPO Network, which provides free training to grassroots NPOs all over China.

The recent reform of NPO registration gives a clue of the emerging social "opening up" policy. Shenzhen has started experimentation with "registration without supervisory agency" since 2008, which applies to NPOs of industrial and commercial types, social welfare types and charity types. In July 2009, the Shenzhen government signed an agreement with the Ministry of Civil Affairs to promote civil administration reform. The agreement allows public foundations to register directly with the city's civil affairs authorities without requiring permission from the ministry. This kind of work is far-reaching but is not as visible as economic feats in the newspaper. The NPO sector remains representative of a generally restrictive political environment in the eyes of both foreign observers and the general public in China. However, underlying a seemingly inertial system could be unexpected breakthroughs derived from constant but often overlooked endeavors from within the system, as shown by the recent case of the One Foundation.

The One Foundation is a charity set up by Chinese movie star Jet Li. It just transformed to a public foundation in Shenzhen this January, four months after Jet Li disclosed the possible termination of the agency in a television interview, and three years after its operation. The problem is common for grassroots NPOs in China. The One Foundation is not able to register as a public foundation, so it cannot receive money from society. The foundation tried to address this by working with the China Red Cross Society and raising money through the latter's account. This worked fine for a few years but was finally suspended by the Shanghai Bureau of Civil Affairs, where it registered. Liu Runhua, the head of the Shenzhen Bureau of Civil Affairs, initiated a call to invite Jet Li to come to Shenzhen before the suspension. Liu claimed that he expects that the One Foundation case will inspire more business entrepreneurs to come to Shenzhen to do philanthropy.

In February 2011, one month after the One Foundation case, the Beijing Bureau of Civil Affairs announced that four types of NPOs, including the three types in Shenzhen and another one specializing in social service, do not need to secure a professional supervisory agency any more when they register. They only need to register at the Ministry of Civil Affairs. Meanwhile, government and Party employees often work part time in the board of NPOs. The Beijing city government claimed to enhance the grassroots nature of NPOs by requesting them to gradually move out. The policy stipulates that, in principle, an NPO should not have government or Party employees in its staff at registration. For exiting NPOs, government or Party employees should drop out in the next board selection.

Cross-sectoral strategy that facilitates social enterprise practice

SE supporters in China strategically draw on local translations and leverage political opportunities to facilitate SE practices. Reinventing concepts to fit local realities and mobilize political resources is critical to making SEs actually happen and grow in a generally restrictive and suspicious social-political environment. Governments in the US and UK have stepped up to support SEs through legislation and various works of institution building. Given the Chinese government's inactive status, SE supporters in China face tasks that involve not only advocating the concept and theorizing how it could benefit various stakeholders, but also securing an official recognition so as to formalize SE development.

But how do you reach the government and lobby for change? This job is longitudinal and collective. In fact, since at least 2004, people from various professional backgrounds have started to build up a knowledge base and organizational support for SEs in China. This was done primarily from the bottom up. Starting with interviews with well-recognized pioneers in China, my colleagues and I followed a snowball process to collect important events concerning SE development. These activities fall into two sections: theorization through writings and trainings, and formalization through setting up organizations and formal mechanisms.

China has seen the publication of books, magazine articles and academic journal papers that specialize on the SE topic. Self-entitled SEs may have been there for a while, but the past decade has witnessed the first set of grassroots supporting agencies such as membership organizations, the incubators, training sessions and teaching curriculums. While most other initiatives were taken by grassroots agencies, the government-run Journal of Comparative Economic and Social Systems is a leading force in the theoretical discussion on SE. See Table 1.3 for a chronology of important early events about SE development in China. Most of these events are the first of their kind. Not clearly demonstrated in this chronology, however, is that the most influential SE supporting agencies in China have commonly adopted a cross-sectoral strategy through which they familiarize government officials with SE and mobilize their support to expand SE practices. The Non-Profit Incubator (NPI) and China Social Entrepreneur Foundation (CSEF) are influential cases.

NPI was founded in 2006 by Lu Zhao, a former journalist and a business entrepreneur, with the aim of cultivating grassroots NPOs and SEs in China. Xu Yongguang and Shang Yusheng were selected as NPI's board director and vice board director, respectively. NPI is proposing a concept of a "New Privatization Movement", where social entrepreneurs are primary players. This movement is compared to the privatization of business enterprises in China three decades ago. Interestingly, NPI views both movements as being fulfilled via top-down mobilization. This way, NPI is appealing for the government to stir up a wave of "liberation of mindset" about mutual assistance and grassroots philanthropy among Chinese people through the development of grassroots NPOs and SEs.

Table 1.3 Chronology of key early events that reinvented the SE concept in China

Reinvention Process	Strategy	Agency	When	What
Theorization of SE through building a knowledge base	Academic publication	*China Social Work Research* journal	2004 Jan	Published a translated article named "The Social Enterprise"
	Academic publication	*Comparative Economic and Social Systems* journal	2006 Mar	Published an article named "What Is Social Entrepreneurship?"
	Academic publication	*Comparative Economic and Social Systems* journal, the British Council China	2007 Oct	Published a special issue about "Social Enterprise Overview: A UK and China Perspective"
	Academic publication	*Comparative Economic and Social Systems* journal	2010 Aug	Published a special issue to introduce venture philanthropy in the US and in Europe
	Media report	*21 Century Business Review* magazine	2006 Jan	Published about 10 articles on social entrepreneurship
	Media report	*Chinese Society* newspaper	2006 Aug	Published "Social Enterprise and the Localization of Social Management"
	Book publication	A female Chinese business leader	2006 Apr	Published the Chinese version of "How to Change the World: Social Entrepreneurs and the Power of New Ideas" (by David Bernstein)
	Book publication	GLI	2006 Sep	Published the Chinese version of "The Rise of the Social Entrepreneur"
	International communication	GLI	2004 Nov	Organized a group of Chinese social entrepreneurs, journalists and government officials to visit UK social enterprises
	International communication	GLI	2007	Organized a group of Chinese social entrepreneurs, journalists and government officials to visit UK social enterprises
	Conference/forum	GLI	2004 Dec	Hosted the first social entrepreneurship forum in China
	Conference/forum	The Global Entrepreneurship Research Center of Zhejiang University, the Skoll Centre for Social Entrepreneurship of Oxford University and the Entrepreneurs School of Asia	2007 May	Organized the International Forum on Social Entrepreneurship

(Continued)

Table 1.3 Continued

Reinvention Process	Strategy	Agency	When	What
	Conference/forum	China Social Entrepreneur Foundation, British Council, Ashoka and other organizations	2010	Organized the Greater China Social Entrepreneur Forum
	University curriculum	China Social Entrepreneur Foundation, the Research Centre of Civic Society of Peking University	2009 Sep	Launched an elective course at Peking University titled "Social Entrepreneurship and the Practice of Social Innovation"
	SE training	China Social Entrepreneur Foundation, British Council	2008 June	Developed the Social Entrepreneur Skill Training Workshop
	SE contest (government-NPO partnership)	The Bureau of Civil Affairs of Shanghai, NPI	2009	Organized the first Shanghai Community Venture Philanthropy Contest
Formalization of SE through founding organizations	Social enterprise membership organization	GLI	2004 July	Global Links Initiative (GLI) was founded in the UK
	Grassroots foundation specializing in SE	China Social Entrepreneur Foundation	2007	China Social Entrepreneur Foundation founded in Beijing
	Nonprofit/SE incubator	NPI	2007	NPI was founded and started to promote the model of an "NPO Incubator" in Shanghai
	Company-sponsored venture philanthropy fund (business-NPO partnership)	Lenovo Venture Philanthropy Fund	2007 Nov	Lenovo entrusted NPI to plan and run the Lenovo Venture Philanthropy Fund. This is the first time the domestic company practiced venture philanthropy in China

A few months after the launch, NPI was entrusted by the Bureau of Finance of the Pudong New District of Shanghai to draft a *Guideline on Government's Purchasing Social Organization Services*. By the end of 2010, NPI had received visits by the minister and the vice minister of the Ministry of Civil Affairs and the vice mayor of Shanghai city. They applauded an incubation model for NPOs and SEs and encouraged a nationwide replication. So far, The Venture Philanthropy Funds managed by NPI have supported more than 300 NPOs and SEs.

CSEF was established in 2007 by a group of business entrepreneurs, with senior officials from the Poverty Relief Office of the State Council in the board. It proposed a concept of "New Philanthropy" with social entrepreneurship as a core part of the philosophy and SE as the major form of practice. The CSEF model is special. It incorporates the social entrepreneurial model into a conventional social problem area heavily invested by the government: poverty relief. Its programs on poverty relief have received extensive support from ministers and government agencies. In turn, CSEF appropriates government resources to further expand social entrepreneurship in various areas through training, incubation and advocacy. In fact, the Chinese name for CSEF is the You Cheng Poverty Relief Foundation. CSEF's claimed core strategy lies in exploring a sustainable solution of poverty relief in China by linking up government resources and grassroots initiatives.

Neither NPI nor CSEF starts exactly with SE. They integrate the idea of SE into an ideological system and a working area familiar to and legitimate for government officials. In contrast to SE, the terms "organization for public good", "philanthropy" and "social innovation" are more used by NPI and CSEF in their programs. Adopting these locally decent terms of social enterprise addresses aforementioned social-cognitive tensions and smoothens the cross-sectoral strategy.

Conclusion

SE has to a large degree been accommodated into the local discourse space despite the various social-cognitive tensions that complicate the translation. This concept has basically settled into a few versions of translation that avoid local negative implications and help retain the nature of SE that combines entrepreneurial attributes with a purpose of creating social value or addressing social problems. This is a nontrivial achievement for SE development in China, since a critical factor that often causes an imported concept to die young is the conflict of values.

Although the state is unlikely to dramatically revise the regulation on NPOs and other organized grassroots initiatives in the short run, it is probing into different possibilities. Several key government officials are moving to the grassroots NPO sector themselves. Incumbent senior officials have publicly applauded new social innovation models such as NPOs with income-generating mechanisms or a venture capital approach to support charities. Also, experiments with a new NPO administration system have taken off in Shengzhen and Beijing. The government's twelfth five-year plan stresses a need to innovate in the public administration system. More importantly, social welfare indicators like education, health care and environment protection have increased their weights in the formal evaluation system for local government officials. Meanwhile, grassroots supporting agencies have strategically utilized local translations and political opportunities to facilitate SE practices.

This chapter examines SE development in China as a process of institutional reinvention. Although the initial influence originated from the translation of foreign literatures, the actual opportunity of comprehending and practicing SE in China is to a large extent a collective and local enactment process. The arguments are in line with scholars who urge downplaying the heroic focus in studying the social entrepreneur. This chapter intends to bring SE development in China to academic audiences around the world and invite more researchers to join the efforts of studying common and distinct patterns of social enterprise diffusion across diversified institutional contexts.

Recommendation for practice and policy

Launching social innovation in China, as in other countries, is an institutional work. Namely, effective social innovation adapts not only to social needs but also to cultural-cognitive expectations and social-political conditions. Understanding the local meanings of SE allows practitioners to frame the concept in a way that avoids negative local implications and hence mobilizes support from multiple stakeholders such as governments, business firms and foundations. For example, "社会创业" (social startup) and "公益创业" (startup for social benefit) go beyond the social-financial dichotomy and highlight innovation natures and social impacts. This reinvention of the SE concept helps reduce the tension between the two sides perceived by governments and the general public. It also helps distinguish the SE concept from conventional NPO activities that have relatively low, albeit growing, social trust. In addition, the CSEF and NPI cases indicate the importance for practitioners of taking a framing strategy that clarifies the SE concept's alignment with current government and social agendas.

Thanks to the reinvention initiatives in the past decade ranging from SE theorization to SE formalization, SE is gaining a legitimate conceptual root in public, social and business sectors in China. Meanwhile, as introduced in this chapter, anecdotal government officials and local authorities have actively engaged in SE development. Nevertheless, it remains unclear whether policymakers could find it a priority among massive social-economic reform tasks to promote the SE concept and practice. It seems more likely that the government will keep tracking SE dynamics and focus on pushing existing agendas in the social sector. This chapter suggests that the government may capitalize on the rise of SE awareness and supporting mechanisms to facilitate the existing reform initiatives by cultivating a more favorable regulatory and administrative environment for SE development.

Foreign government initiatives and Chinese reform experiences show that at least two types of policy work are worth exploring in China. First, a legislation effort is key to handle the confusion of SE meanings so as to shape a consolidated understanding of related concepts and practices in the society. This effort needs to recognize SE as a separate legal category of organizational form (e.g., community interest company in the UK or low-profit limited liability company in the US) and clarify how SEs depart from general nonprofit, philanthropy and CSR activities. The government could develop broad guidelines by leveraging existing regulations on business corporations and social organizations and allow local authorities to specify operational details. Second, a viable business model is crucial for SE to meet its social objective. Government policies need to open opportunities and reduce uncertainty for practitioners to pursue different business models. Examples may include regional policy experiments on SE registration, public purchasing, funding access and legal and professional advisory services. Creating a policy environment that facilitates organization registration, revenue mechanism innovation and operation professionalization could generate chain effects in favor of the reform of social organization management and government system transformation.

Notes

1 The Central Compilation and Translation Bureau (CCTB) reports directly to the Central Committee of the Communist Party and is responsible for informing China's top authorities on international academic thought in social and economic areas.
2 The officially registered grassroots NPOs primarily include "Social Organization" (*shehui tuanti*) and "Civil Non-Business Unit" (*minban feiqiye danwei*). The 1998 Regulation on Social Organization Registration and Administration specifies a social organization as a not-for-profit organization founded on a voluntary basis by Chinese citizens and operating according to the common mission of its members. The 1998 Interim Regulation on Registration and Administration of Civil Non-Business Unit defines civil non-business unit as an agency founded by business enterprise, public service units, social organization, other social forces or individual citizens that uses non-state-owned assets to provide non-profit social services. Social organization is a major legal category of NPOs in China. For the sake of convenience, I will use NPO hereafter to indicate all related legal forms in China.

References

Austin, J., Stevenson, H., & Wei-Skillern, J. (2006). "Social and Commercial Entrepreneurship: Same, Different, or Both?" *Entrepreneurship: Theory & Practice*, 30(1): 1–22.
Bacchiega, A., & Borzaga, C. (2001). "Social Enterprises as Incentive Structures: An Economic Analysis", in C. Borzaga & J. Defourny (Eds.), *The Emergence of Social Enterprise*. London, New York: Routledge, pp. 273–294.
Boxenbaum, E., & Battilana, J. (2005). "Importation as Innovation: Transposing Managerial Practices Across Fields", *Strategic Organization*, 3(4): 355–383.
Campbell, L. J. (2002). Where Do We Stand? Common Mechanisms in Organizations and Social Movements Research. Prepared for a conference on "Social Movements and Organizations Theory," University of Michigan.
Czarniawska, B., & Joerges, B. (1996). "Travels of Ideas", in B. Czarniawska & G. Sevon (Eds.), *Translating Organizational Change*. Berlin: De Gruyter, pp. 13–38.
Green, S. Carroll, C., Huang, N., & Goodnight, T. (2010). "Institutional Logics and the Rhetorical Encoding of Legitimacy: A Dramatistic Pentadic Analysis of an Emergent Field". Working paper.

Mair, D. J., & Marti, I. (2006). "Social Entrepreneurship Research: A Source of Explanation, Prediction, and Delight", *Journal of World Business*, 41: 36–41.

Miles, M. B., & Huberman. A. M. (1994). *Qualitative Data Analysis: An Expanded Sourcebook*. Thousand Oaks, CA: Sage Publications.

Johnson, S. (2000). "Literature Review on Social Entrepreneurship", Canadian Centre for Social Entrepreneurship website, http://www.bus.ualberta.ca/ccse/Publications/Publications/Lit.%20Review%20SE%20November%202000.rtf, accessed August 31, 2006.

Kennedy, M. T. (2008). "Getting Counted: Markets, Media, and Reality", *American Sociological Review*, 73: 270–295.

Short, J. C., Morris, T. W., & Lumpkin, G. T. (2009). "Research in Social Entrepreneurship: Past Contributions and Future Opportunities", *Strategic Entrepreneurship Journal*, 3: 161–194.

Tolbert, P. S., & Zucker, L. G. (1983). "Institutional Sources of Change in the Formal Structure of Organizations: The Diffusion of Civil Service Reform, 1880–1935", *Administrative Science Quarterly*, 28: 22–39.

Zahra, S. A., Rawhouser, H. N., Bhawe, N., Neubaum, D. O., & Hayton, J. C. (2008). "Globalization of Social Entrepreneurship Opportunities", *Strategic Entrepreneurship Journal*, 2(2): 117/131.

Zhao, M. (2012). "The Social Enterprise Emerges in China", *Stanford Social Innovation Review*, Spring.

2 Social enterprise development in Hong Kong

Legitimacy and institutional logics

Kevin Au, Terence Yuen and Jessica Tam

Introduction

Social enterprise (SE) and social entrepreneurship have gained increasing attention from academic research. In this young area, scholars in recent reviews have characterized its research as multidisciplinary, embryonic, lacking a coherent paradigm. Besides, the majority of these reviews are theory treatises. Among the empirical studies, more of them are anecdotal analyses and case studies (Dacin, Dacin, & Tracey, 2011; Galaskiewicz & Barringer, 2012). Further, almost all of the empirical studies are on work-integrated social enterprises (WISEs), and this is true for both overseas (e.g., Pache & Santos, 2013; Shaw & Carter, 2007) and Hong Kong studies (Ho & Chan, 2010). This focus is likely a result of the development history of WISEs, their sheer number, and unemployment as the common triggers for many governments to promote SE. For instance, while Hong Kong faced economic restructuring and public financial reform in the late 1990s (Chan & Yuen, 2013; see also review below), France suffered from long-term unemployment due to its rigid labor policies (Pache & Santos, 2013). WISEs were established as a possible solution to deal with the prevalent unemployment in these two places.

Behind the dominant scene of WISEs are more than just non-governmental organizations (NGOs) and the government. As analyzed below, Hong Kong SEs have been developing with the active involvement of social entrepreneurs (who transformed themselves from working in other sectors) and many stakeholders, including businesses, professionals, academics, and various charity and family foundations. That is to say, SE development in Hong Kong has been a dynamic field. In an attempt to achieve social goals in the uncertain environment, multiple actors introduced their ideas, competed for resources and attention, and in the process have shaped the institutional environment and the ecology. Nicholls (2010) discussed the emergence of social entrepreneurship as a field and advocated *structuration* as the process through which it developed in UK. Accordingly, competent agents (social entrepreneurs and SEs) actively and reflexively reproduce the conditions that determine their behaviors, but they do so in a way that enables changes to happen (Giddens, 1984). Following this, he also proposed *reflexive isomorphism* as the legitimating strategy of SEs such that "dominant organizations can shape the legitimacy of an emergent field to reflect their own institutional logics and norms," and they "actively engage in processes that align field-level and internal logics to shape emergent institutional fields as closed systems of self-legitimisation" (p. 617).

Although the UK and Hong Kong are different in their environments and institutions, the two places share a common public management philosophy (Au, Wang, & Vertinsky, 2000) and involve similar groups of stakeholders and social entrepreneurs, as active agents, in the development of SEs. For instance, Au and Birtch (2010) analyzed how a youngster could acquire skills, acquired clients, hire jobless labor, and form a WISE doing gardening, as he nimbly sought resources by interacting actively with different stakeholders, including the church, government, and NGOs. His endeavor, likewise in other SEs, created social capital across different levels of the society and thus helped shape the norms supporting SEs（阮耀啟，2008）. This case example thus hints that drawing on the approach of Nicholls (2010; Nicholls & Cho, 2006), particularly the concept of reflexive isomorphism, is useful to make sense of SE development in Hong Kong.

The objectives of this chapter are the following. We first review and update the development of SE vis-à-vis the changes in the social and policy environment since the last batch of studies on Hong Kong SEs (Ho & Chan, 2010; Ng, Cheung, & Prakash, 2010). Then, we analyze and make sense of such development using Nicholls' (2010) framework. Lastly, based on the analysis, we discuss and highlight social innovation and citizen coproduction as the priorities for SEs and other stakeholders in Hong Kong to establish legitimacy for future development of the SE sector[1] and conclude with an analysis of how the SE sector may change based on institutional logic framework (Thornton, Ocasio, & Lounsbury, 2012).

Social enterprise development over the past decade

Policy shift – from poverty alleviation to social innovation

The practice of "social entrepreneurship" is hardly new in HK. For many years, quite a few non-profit organizations have been initiating various self-financed projects which were hybrids of social missions and business models. However, the phrase "social enterprise" had not come on stage until early 2000. The Social Welfare Department pioneered the first social enterprise scheme, called Enhancing Employment of People with Disabilities through Small Enterprise (the 3E scheme) in 2001 as the first attempt to tackle employment obstacles of people with disabilities (PWDs) by means of a "welfare-to-work" approach. This 3E scheme has successfully established a foundation for the subsequent social enterprise movement and has since incubated many successful social enterprises, a few of them now major players in the current social enterprise sector.

Social enterprises have gained government's attention as a means to alleviate poverty and unemployment problems since 2005. The first Commission on

Poverty (CoP) took up the agenda in that year; the Enhancing Self-Reliance Through District Partnership Program (ESR Program) was set up under the Home Affairs Department in 2006 to encourage NGOs setting up WISEs on a district-based level. From that time the target beneficiaries have been extended from PWDs (for 3Es scheme) to other able-bodied unemployed. In 2010, the Social Enterprise Advisory Committee (SEAC) was formed under the Home Affairs Bureau; this high-level committee has steered social enterprise–related policies and launched a number of new initiatives.

Government's blessing to SE has never been lacking, as well after the current chief executive, C. Y. Leung, took office. He set up the second Commission on Poverty and paid due recognition to SE's significance by allocating HK$500 million from the Lotteries Fund to set up the Social Innovation and Entrepreneurship Development Fund (SIEDF) under the second CoP.[2] The SIEDF aims to support innovative social solutions and presents a new perspective of the government and the society. By engaging intermediaries to manage the Fund and relaxing the application criteria to the business sector and individuals, the SIEDF is a new attempt at experimenting with cross-sector partnership and a risk-taking approach to tackle social problems.

Yet a concrete direction and coordinated efforts from different SE-related bureaus and departments are weak. This problem was raised by the Audit Commission in a recent report.[3] Despite the government's great efforts and significant resources allocated to the SE sector, stakeholders are still looking for a forward-looking, high-level policy direction.

Bottom up – unleashed power of civil society

The civil society sector, particularly the welfare organizations, is a key agent promoting social entrepreneurship in the beginning stage of Hong Kong SE development. Against the backdrop of the Asian financial crisis in the late 90s and the subsequent economic downturn as well as the new welfare policy reform, developing SEs has been regarded as not only a strategy to alleviate the unemployment problem, but also a strategy for NGOs to ignite internal innovation and organizational regeneration.

We have observed the emergence of a number of NGO-run social enterprises since the launch of the 3E scheme mentioned above, with a focus on the rehabilitation subsector. Social enterprise has been positioned as an extension of the Supported Employment service, such as Mental Care Connect. Meanwhile, some community-based, grassroots organizations initiated "community economic development" projects (CEDs) in relatively deprived districts. By trying different types of income-generating activities with social missions, such as discounted price markets, postnatal care service, and secondhand shops, these organizations were engaging grassroots with an objective to activate community assets. The gardener SE discussed above is one of the examples (Au & Birtch, 2010).

However, it was not until 2007 that there was a clear scoping of the social enterprise landscape, when the Hong Kong Council of Social Service (HKCSS) published the first Social Enterprise Directory. HKCSS adopted an inclusive approach by including all NGOs and non-NGO-operated SEs, co-operatives as well as individual community economic projects in the list; this exercise took stock of some 200 social enterprise projects at that time. In 2007, the Council continued its efforts by setting up the first social enterprise support platform, the Social Enterprise Resources Centre.

The years 2007–08 were a watershed of SE movement in HK. Since that time a number of notable SE support organizations and network platforms have entered in the field. The Chinese University of Hong Kong launched the first intercollegiate social business plan competition, the Hong Kong Social Enterprise Challenge, which has incubated many young social entrepreneurs. Social Ventures Hong Kong, the first social investment platform using a "venture capital" model, was established in the same period. In 2008, the Social Entrepreneurship Forum, the Social Enterprise Summit, and the Hong Kong General Chamber of Social Enterprises also came on stage. In subsequent years, the Fullness Social Enterprises Society, Good Lab, Education for Good, and Project Flame of the City University of Hong Kong have emerged and become important players in the SE ecosystem.

The active participation of these independent organizations and civil society organizations is a unique characteristic of the HK social enterprise movement. These organizations carrying different missions join hands to promote the SE movement. The annual flagship event, the Social Enterprise Summit, a joint effort of these SE support platform, attracts over 1,000 local practitioners and overseas visitors every year. These SE platforms emerged along with government's support of SE, yet they are independent in operation, with their own visions and agendas. These SE platforms leverage an untapped market and societal resources, talents, and a network to build a vibrant, diversified, and dynamic SE ecosystem.

Table 2.1 illustrates the development of the SE sector in past few years. The number of social enterprise projects substantially increased from 269 in 2008/09 to 457 in 2013/14, amounting to a 69.9 percent growth over past five years. The majority of the SE projects were operated by charitable organizations registered under section 88 of the Inland Revenue Ordinance, for tax-exempt organizations, yet there was a rising number of non-tax-exempt organizations engaging in the SE sector (estimated to be 16 percent in 2013; 34 percent in 2014). SE projects registered in different legal forms. According to the latest figures of the SE Directory 2013/14, 53.2 percent of the SE projects were operated as separate units under non-profit organizations, 46.2 percent registered as private companies, and 0.6 percent registered as co-operatives.

Table 2.2 compares the business nature of SE projects in 2009/10 and 2013/14. 'Food production and catering', 'lifestyle and retail', and 'medical care' were the most popular HK SEs. We observed a rapid surge in the industries of 'medical care' and 'education and training'. For instance, the former offers competitive medical and health services such as patient escort support, postnatal care, and community-based health care to meet social and market needs.

Table 2.1 Number of social enterprise projects in HK, 2008–2014

	2008/09	2009/10	2010/11	2011/12	2012/13	2013/14
No. of SE projects	269	320	329	368	406	457
Growth in no. of project over previous year	47 (+21%)	51 (+19%)	9 (+3%)	39 (+12%)	38 (+10%)	51 (+13%)
Total no. of operating organizations	103	99	116	124	150	190
No. of charitable organizations registered under section 88	87 (84%)	84 (85%)	100 (86%)	95 (77%)	105 (70%)	125 (66%)
No. of organizations not registered under section 88	16 (16%)	15 (15%)	14 (14%)	29 (23%)	45 (30%)	65 (34%)

Source: *Social Enterprise Directory* compiled and published by the Hong Kong Council of Social Service

Table 2.2 Comparison of business segments of SE projects in HK, 2009 /10 vs. 2013/14 (multiple answers)

	2009/10 (no. of projects)	2013/14 (no. of projects)	Growth by Business Segment
Food production and catering	114	144	+30
Lifestyle and retail	103	127	+24
Medical care	68	125	+57
Ecoproducts and recycling	48	87	+39
Business support	56	75	+19
Education and training	14	58	+44
Domestic cleaning and renovation	48	33	−15
Others	0	25	+25
Logistics and auto services	19	17	−2
Clothing	3	16	+13

Source: *Social Enterprise Directory* compiled and published by the Hong Kong Council of Social Service

New opportunities – beyond corporate social responsibility

Support from business and professional sectors to SE is ample, though never enough. Since the early stage of SE development, mainly around WISEs, the government encouraged active participation by corporations in the forms of matching funds, responsible consumption, and volunteer service. Apart from the government's efforts, initiatives by responsible procurement and ethical consumption campaigns have also been taken up by other SE platforms, such as the Fullness's Ethical Consumption Month and the HKCSS's Good Goods sales platform.

Donation is the most direct way for corporations to show their support. To name a few, the Henderson Land Group waived the rental fee and sponsored the setup of Good Lab; the Hongkong Bank Foundation supported the establishment of the HKCSS-HSBC Social Enterprise Business Centre; and the DBS Bank HK set up the first Social Enterprise Advancement Grant. Some companies and professional associations adopt more engaging approaches by mobilizing their staff members to provide free consultancy services to social enterprises.

Forming a social enterprise is not necessarily a corporate social responsibility (CSR) project – it could bring social value and business value to the corporation. Recently, we observed the emergence of 'corporate shared value' (CSV) in Hong Kong. Some corporations had started to invest in this new sector. For examples, the Hong Kong Heritage Conservation Foundation, founded in 2008 by the Ng Family, Sino Group's majority shareholder, used a social enterprise model to conserve and revitalize the old Tai O Police Station into the Tai O Heritage Hotel. In fact, the SME (small and medium-sized enterprise) sector could become an important player by venturing into the SE sector and setting up social enterprise subsidiaries. A local herbal tea company, Health Works, has partnered with a group of social economy groups and grassroots organizations to set up the first joint-venture social enterprise, which will come into birth in the near future. SEs in Hong Kong has reached a new stage of development (阮耀啟、陳健民, 2014; Chan & Yuen, 2013).

Legitimacy of SEs in Hong Kong

Defining Hong Kong SEs: sociality, market orientation, and innovation

Nicholls and Cho (2006) proposed three defining dimensions of social entrepreneurship which are central to SEs. These dimensions also have local relevance to Hong Kong. Regarding sociality, Hong Kong SEs had to deal with social welfare reform and funding model change. During the tough times, economic downturns caused massive unemployment and job renewal that led to the rise of WISEs in Hong Kong. Recently, change in economic conditions (e.g., no massive unemployment), the emergency of non-WISEs, and maturity of some WISEs, as the statistics showed, have prompted SEs to pursue social goals other than merely reducing welfare. The rising interest in CSV and impact investment will blur the boundaries between business and social contexts as well. In consequence, the meaning of "social" has been debated and become contested.

As to market orientation, SEs in Hong Kong, most of them WISEs, had to respond to the pressure of competing in the market and operating with business efficiency. The financial and political situation during the economic downturn prompted policy changes in funding NGOs and charity organizations. Social workers who managed welfare for disadvantaged groups and the unemployed had to embrace the business principles. Further, subsequent funding agencies formed to support SEs, such as 3E and ESR, were in fact focused to support WISEs. The reason is two-fold. On one hand, most applicants were NGOs or charity organizations making do to survive the new funding models or to continue their services for disadvantaged groups. They would not have the entrepreneurship mindset or motivation in the business sense to take risks to invent new products or explore uncharted markets (Morris, Webb, & Franklin, 2011). Many of them resorted to grabbing viable business concepts, such as eatery, retailing, etc., and running them with workers from the disadvantaged groups. Their challenge was how to achieve operational efficiency and financial sustainability.

On the other hand, the funding agents operated to evaluate applicants and allocated grants, from the public pocket, as short-term seed funding for SE ventures. They organized themselves to create funding criteria and guidelines that enacted market pressure on WISEs. Given their mandate to evaluate WISEs using market principles, these agents recruited members chiefly from the business sector, since they were supposed to know the principles well. In evaluating the applications, as most applicants were from NGOs and lacked business experience, the funding agents naturally saw risk in proposals that required prolonged R&D and new products/services. Supporting the seed stage, to them, meant only allowing a short period of support. This further drove the agents to prefer proposals stringent in finance and capable of breaking even quickly. As it turned out, the NGO applicants gradually learnt how to play the game and reflexively submitted proposals that suited the taste of the agents. In this way, the agents and NGO applicants "acted together" to reproduce conditions that favored SEs doing mundane business employing disadvantaged groups. As a result, WISEs turned out to be the dominant form of SEs. Yet, recent public inquiry concerning the agents, the success and maturity of some WISEs, and the emergence of new breeds of SEs has started challenging the status quo. Having said all this, we are not trying to undermine the contributions of WISEs. Indeed, they have made tremendous inroads to promote employment and contribute to the development of the SE sector in a creative way too.

Therefore, lastly, SEs in Hong Kong are innovative in trying to improve the society. They "seized opportunities others [missed] and improv[ed] systems, inventing new approaches and creating sustainable solutions to change society for the better" (Nicholls & Cho, 2006, p. 102). As a case in point, WISEs in Hong Kong have adapted sheltered workshops, retail franchises, and ordinary businesses to suit market niches employing disadvantaged groups. Doing this involved not taking risks or investing much in new technology. They astutely transformed resources to implement viable ideas. Their perseverance and creative efforts to achieve the double bottom lines are recognized even without the need to deal with the uncertainty in invention. Fundamentally it is not easy to sustain profit through hiring disadvantaged groups, who are usually not productive labor (Morris, Webb, & Franklin, 2011). The results are welfare reduction and empowerment of the disadvantaged groups (紀治興, 2014). Yet, as hinted in the review above, recent public inquiry, internal reflection of matured WISEs, and skepticism from the business sector challenge whether these efforts can continue to contribute and justify further attention and support.

Taking a different path, some SEs have spotted unmet community needs and market gaps, such as child care, fair trade, and environmental awareness. They innovatively develop new business models to address these needs and gain the attention of potential consumers while demonstrating how to disrupt the existing markets. Their efforts have empowered many forward-looking individuals, who expect to plow new, alternative ways to solve social problems. Yet, their initial success does not guarantee growth or big impact. Many of these SEs remain at an early stage or stuck in the middle, as further development (scaling up) requires resources that are not easy to come by in Hong Kong. The capacity to support disruptive social innovation is in the making. Most resources are still in the hands of large corporations and funding agents – conventional players in the society. These players are aware of and sympathetic to the SE movement but hesitant to engage in it wholeheartedly, either because they cannot bridge their views and practices (e.g., CSR) with new perspectives (e.g., shared value; see Porter & Kramer, 2011) or because they still do not clearly see the impact of social innovativeness advocated by many SEs.

Legitimacy in the past

Over the past decade, Hong Kong SEs, as active agencies, have overcome difficulty and reflexively reacted to the challenges. We observe that they have, as in the UK (Nicholls, 2010), resorted to the two prioritized narrative logics to establish legitimacy. The first logic is the hero entrepreneur model. Heroic stories of successful SEs, such as the Senior Elderly Citizen Association, Mental Care, Dialogue in the Dark, are publicized, and so are innovative social entrepreneurs, such as Kee Chi-Hing, K. K. Tse, and Francis Ngai, among others.[4] Another logic to establish legitimacy is the ideal business type. Many SEs and funding agencies for WISEs have promulgated and adopted business tools and principles such as quality and efficiency, financial sustainability, business models, and entrepreneurship.

These narrative logics bring legitimacy to SEs in Hong Kong. Accordingly, they have succeeded because the SEs and social entrepreneurs have shaped the discourses and institutional logics of various stakeholders in their attempt to reflect their own norms and internal logics (Nicholls, 2010). However, due to power and resource imbalances (Lounsbury & Strang, 2009), the "hero entrepreneur working within a business" has prevailed (Nicholls, 2010, p. 626), such that SE development in Hong Kong has taken an off-balance stance against the social and community side (阮耀啟、陳健民，2014). The consequence is dissatisfaction from various stakeholders. The public and government may misunderstand the purposes of SEs as merely to reduce unemployment of disadvantaged groups, while the enterprises may regard SEs as second-class (uncompetitive) members in the business sector. The social sector finds SEs twisting their core value of serving the needy in the emphasis of WISEs on market principles. This imbalance may not only marginalize social entrepreneurs and their peers, but also undermine the legitimacy of the SE sector in the long run.

Institutional logics for the future

Our analysis suggests that such negative consequences can happen and may actually be happening. Fortunately, several counterbalancing forces have emerged that may prompt a change in course for SE development towards a model of social innovation and community engagement. According to Thornton, Ocasio, and Lounsbury (2012), organizations and individuals (and their attention, values, and behaviors) are not completely constrained by institutions, as the view of neo-institutionalism implies (DiMaggio & Powell, 1991). Instead, individual agency and institutional logics both play a role in the reproduction and transformation of organizations and institutions. Changes can come from several paths (see their chapter 4).

First, diverse social actors are being exposed to alternative institutional logics. Discussed in review and analysis above, the players on the social enterprise scene have become diversified. They are not simply coming from NGOs and the social sector, but include, for instance, volunteer, retired, and converted business people and professionals. As they come from different sectors and have different networks and work histories, they bring in and expose each other to different contexts and institutional logics.

Second, following the introduction of diversity of institutional logics is a fertile ground to enable different forms of interaction and organizational practices in organizations and institutional fields. Different forms of interaction and practices can lead to institutional complexity. As a case in point, since some successful WISEs develop, they tap into new sectors and interact with organizations outside the social sectors. They experience new forms of doing things and develop new strategies, including the CVS examples. Their governance, organization, and management become more complex than before.

Third, exogenous changes provide opportunities for the reexamination of prevailing logics and their constitutive identities, goals, and schemas. Family foundations have started to show interest in social enterprise, and new funding sources (such as the SIE Fund and SVhk) have also appeared. They bring in new ideas or new attention to social innovation, social impact, and impact investment. Though not directly, the annual Social Enterprise Summit, arguably the largest in Asia, has introduced advanced and diverse ideas from all over world that challenge the local SE sector continually. Fourth, the introduction of market logic to form WISEs, on one hand, put pressure on NGOs to adopt market principles (which are against the need principles). On the other hand, however, market logic imbues the positive side of the market in that the market is generative of endogenous change. The market is dynamic and changes all the time. WISEs and other SEs, since they are in the market, inevitably compete with each other and other enterprises, and thus sense the sentiment of change and directions for improvement. Market competition as a result prompts the emergency of a new breed of SEs and new movement in social innovation. Lastly, the active interaction of SEs with other new players, as described above, has brought in and created new language and vocabularies for the SE sector, such as "shared value," "impact ventures," and "shared economy." They act as the basis for the generation and the transformation of organizational practices in SEs and change the discourse of their development.

To conclude, given the historical context under which SEs have been developed, it is understandable that at the present juncture Hong Kong has a relatively strong WISE sector, while the other categories of SEs are still underdeveloped. Moving to the next stage of development, it is apparent that working towards building a more pluralistic sector could enhance the innovativeness and entrepreneurial capacity of the entire social entrepreneurship space. To maximize social value creation on multiple fronts, different approaches could be adopted to support different kinds of SE operators to propel the development of their respective SE categories (Miller, 2010).

Practically, a recent policy report suggests the emergence of four types of SEs.[5] First is the next generation of WISEs; so-called WISE 2.0 strive to enhance their impact through scaling up, scaling deep, and scaling out. Second is SE addressing bottom-of-the-pyramid (BOP) and shunned markets, through instituting the right business models and shrewd business skills. Third is SEs adhering to the collaborative consumption/sharing economy movement. SEs can do so through the sharing of otherwise idle or unused products or productive assets with or without money exchanges (鄒崇銘、黃英琦、阮耀啟，2014). Lastly, SEs adhering to the broader social economy movement can develop communities by engaging different community segments in the process while implementing alternative economic practices. Essentially then, encouraging social innovation for public problem-solving and engendering community building through citizen co-production are two complementary policy goals that the government should proactively pursue in its effort to promote SE in the future.

Notes

1   For detailed policy analysis, please refer to *Research Study on the Social Enterprise Sector in Hong Kong – to Capture the Existing Landscape of Social Enterprises of Hong Kong*, November 2014. It is a consulting research commissioned by the Home Affairs Bureau.
2   SIEDF was renamed from the original Social Enterprise Development Fund.
3   *Promoting the Development of Social Enterprises*, April 2014 (www.aud.gov.hk/eng/pubpr_arpt/subj_socwf.htm).
4   http://efgimpact100.wordpress.com/2014/03/05/thinking-aloud-idea-of-impact-100/
5   Chapter 2, *Research Study on the Social Enterprise Sector in Hong Kong – to Capture the Existing Landscape of Social Enterprises of Hong Kong*, November 2014.

References

阮耀啟 (2008). 重新認識社會企業。*青年研究學報*, 11(1), 3–12。
阮耀啟、陳健民 2014由單一走向多元：前瞻香港社企發展趨勢。法鼓人文關懷與社會實踐學術研討會─社會企業與創2014年10月3日─4日。

鄒崇銘、黃英琦、阮耀啟主編，《共享香港:從社會企業、公平貿易、良心消費到
共享經濟》，印象文字2014

紀治興 （2014）. 社會投資回報。CUP, September.

Au, K., & Birtch, T. A. (2010). "Social Enterprise as an Interactive Process between Entre-
preneurs and the Community: A Social Capital Perspective", in S. H. Ng, Stephen Y.-L.
Cheung, & B. Prakash (Eds.), *Social Capital in Hong Kong – Connectivities and Social
Enterprise*. Hong Kong: City University Press, pp. 279–301.

Au, K., Vertinsky, I., & Wang, D. (2001). "The New Public Management in Hong Kong:
Can Long Marches and Small Wins Lead to a Successful Reform?" in L. Jones, J.
Guthrie, & P. Steane (Eds.), *Learning from International Public Management Reform*.
London: Elsevier-Oxford Press, pp. 311–335.

Chan, K. M., & Yuen, Y.K.T. (2013). "An Overview of Social Enterprise Development
in Hong Kong and China", *Journal of Ritsumeikan Social Sciences and Humanities*, 5:
165–178.

Dacin, M. T., Dacin, P. A., & Tracey, P. (2011). "Social Entrepreneurship: A Critique and
Future Directions", *Organization Science*, 22: 1203–1213.

DiMaggio, P. J., & Powell, W. W. (Eds.). (1991). *The New Institutionalism in Organizational Analysis* (Vol. 17). Chicago: University of Chicago Press.

Galaskiewicz, J., & Barringer, S. N. (2012). "Social Enterprises and Social Categories",
in B. Gidron & J. Hasenfeld (Eds.), *Social Enterprises: An Organizational Perspective*.
New York: Palgrave Macmillan, pp. 47–70.

Giddens, A. (1984). *The Constitution of Society: Outline of the Theory of Structuration*.
Berkeley: University of California Press.

Ho, A.P.Y., & Chan, K. T. (2010). "The Social Impact of Work-Integration Social Enterprise in Hong Kong", *International Social Work*, 53(1): 33–45.

Lounsbury, M., & Strang, D. (2009). "Social Entrepreneurship: Success Stories and Logic
Construction", in D. Hammack & S. Heydemann (Eds.), *Globalization, Philanthropy,
and Civil Society*. Bloomington: Indiana University Press, pp. 71–94.

Miller, E. (2010). "Solidarity Economy: Key Concepts and Issues", in E. Kawano, T. N.
Masterson, & J. Teller-Elsberg (Eds.), *Solidarity Economy I: Building Alternatives for
People and Planet*. Amherst, MA: Center for Popular Economics, pp. 25–42.

Morris, M. H., Webb, J. W., & Franklin, R. J. (2011). "Understanding the manifestation
of entrepreneurial orientation in the nonprofit context", *Entrepreneurship Theory and
Practice*, 35(5), 947–971.

Ng, S. H., Cheung, Stephen Y.-L., & Prakash, B. (Eds.) (2010). *Social Capital in Hong
Kong – Connectivities and Social Enterprise*. Hong Kong: City University Press.

Nicholls, A. (2010). "The Legitimacy of Social Entrepreneurship: Reflexive Isomorphism
in a Pre-paradigmatic Field", *Entrepreneurship: Theory and Policy*, 34(4): 611–633.

Nicholls, A., & Cho, A. (2006). "Social Entrepreneurship: The Structuration of a Field", in
A. Nicholls (Ed.), *Social Entrepreneurship: New Models of Sustainable Social Change*.
Oxford: Oxford University Press. pp. 99–118.

Pache, A.-C., & Santos, F. (2013). "Inside the Hybrid Organization: Selective Coupling as
a Response to Competing Institutional Logic", *Academy of Management Journal*, 56:
972–1001.

Shaw, E., & Carter, S. (2007). "Social entrepreneurship: Theoretical antecedents and
empirical analysis of entrepreneurial processes and outcomes", *Journal of Small Business and Enterprise Development*, 14(3), 418–434.

Thornton, P., Ocasio, W., & Lounsbury, M. (2012). *The Institutional Logics Perspective:
A New Approach to Culture, Structure and Process*. New York: Oxford University Press.

3 Social innovation and entrepreneurship in Hong Kong

A public policy dimension

Jane C. Y. Lee

Introduction

This chapter aims to give macro and micro perspectives to the development of social innovation and entrepreneurship in Hong Kong from a public policy dimension. It will offer a historical overview of the role of the government since 2005, the rise of the civic society movement, the interaction between government and civic society leaders and the political support to advance SE as a new approach to tackle Hong Kong's social problems. It will also lay out relevant policy issues, such as definitions and legal framework, governance and audit, public education and publicity, as well as training and talent development. The chapter will conclude by illustrating the landscape that shapes the evolving ecosystem in Hong Kong and a possible vision of such development for creating new values in Hong Kong's free market system.

The context

The origins of a policy on social innovation and entrepreneurship in Hong Kong must be discussed in the context of a unique environment in which the free market economy and the welfare sector were traditionally bifurcated from each other. While the government and the business sectors aligned clearly to position Hong Kong as a free market economy, corporations' engagement in welfare has been mainly philanthropic and very often, in the Chinese saying, inclined 'to get rich first before contributing back to social good'. For many years, there have been no shortage of financial resources contributed through corporations' philanthropic arms whenever there were needs. Such contributions have also been extended to mainland China since the 1980s, as evident by donations to various key disaster reliefs, such as the large-scale floods in eastern China in the 90s and the earthquake in Szechuan in 2008, to name just a few.

The delivery of social services by nongovernmental organizations (NGOs) had a unique tradition in Hong Kong, which was mainly due to the belief in minimal involvement in welfare services by the then colonial government. For many years, religious organizations such as the Catholic Caritas and Anglican Sheng Kung Hui, as well as community-based Chinese voluntary associations like Tung Wah

Group of Hospitals and Po Leung Kuk, played a key role in taking care of the needs of the Chinese-speaking community, particularly during the social disloca- tions in the pre- and postwar periods in the twentieth century. Government policy on welfare spending began in the 1960s, which became a public-private partner- ship in which government was principally a funder and NGOs were service pro- viders. Looking back, government's financial contribution to the social services sector was relatively substantial, and by the 1990s, many NGOs primarily lived on government subvention.

A new funding model was then developed in 2000, which shaped a new direc- tion of the welfare landscape. A lump sum grant policy was first introduced by the Social Welfare Department with the primary objective of controlling public spending on social welfare. Under a new financial service agreement, NGOs were allowed much greater freedom to deploy the resources within the 'lump sum', although they complained that the government did not provide adequate financial input to the ongoing services. Many NGOs began to proactively revamp their service approach and raise new sources of funding, including seeking sponsor- ships from and/or developing partnership projects with the business sectors. There have been frequent dialogues between NGOs and the Social Welfare Department at various levels, which were coordinated through an intermediary organization, the Hong Kong Council of Social Services (HKCSS) (HKCSS-HSBC landscape study 2014).[1] Over the years, welfare spending was well controlled but continued to increase. By 2014/15, for example, the government budget on welfare spend- ing (excluding housing, health and education) constituted about 15.1 percent of public expenditures. If spending on welfare, public housing, education and health care were also considered as "welfare" in a broader sense, the combined spending accounted for 47.6 percent of public expenditures (HKSAR Government, 2014c)[2] in the same year.

The origins of social enterprise as a policy agenda

The lump sum grant was introduced at a time when Hong Kong was in the process of experiencing a financial crisis and economic recession. Although government controlled the ceiling on welfare spending, it had to recognize that the increasingly emerging poverty problems became a phenomenon. In the few years between 2001 and 2003, chicken flu and severe acute respiratory syndrome (SARS) occurred unprecedentedly, which not only raised the alarm on the potential impact of any public health management issue in a densely populated city like Hong Kong, but also boosted the unemployment rate to a record high of 7.3 percent (HKSAR Government 2003),[3] which was in sharp contrast to the state of full employment in 1997, when Hong Kong was returned to Chinese sovereignty. Some policy initiatives to support training and employ- ment opportunities for the disadvantaged groups began to emerge. Partnerships between NGOs and corporations were also encouraged. An example was the Enhancing Employment of People with Disabilities through Small Enterprise project (3E), which was set up in 2001/02 (Social Welfare Department, 2014)[4] with the aim of enhancing employability of people with disabilities. Another example was the creation of the Community Investment and Inclusion Fund (ICIIF), which was aimed to promote sustainable social capital by encouraging private sector engagement in partnership projects with NGOs.[5] The policy agenda obviously began to shift towards developing rather than feeding those people who were in need.

The Commission on Poverty (CoP) was set up in early 2005 to tackle poverty problems. A key agenda of the CoP was to consider 'social enterprise' (SE) as a possible option to strengthen employment opportunities for disadvantaged groups. At a CoP meeting on 28 June 2005, members agreed on the importance of assisting the unemployed to move back into mainstream employment and that "helping the 'able-bodied unemployed' to move from welfare to self-reliance should be the focus of further work" (Commission on Poverty, 2005).[6] In another meeting, on 12 September 2005, a full discussion paper was set out for the first time on the proposal to develop social enterprises in Hong Kong to enhance the self-concept and employability of the disadvantaged. It was also hoped to promote social capital and encourage the stronger engagement of business corporations in poverty alleviation.[7]

The CoP did not intend to give a definition of social enterprise but categorized its major feature as "enterprise that conducts its activities, in whole or in part, with both a commercial and a social purpose".[8] As such, it did recognize some existing services as 'social enterprises', including (a) subsidiaries of for-profit businesses which ran well-developed corporate social responsibility programs alongside their business operations; (b) services that were run by charities and nonprofit organizations which have become more entrepreneurial and have integrated market approaches with some welfare programs; and (c) enterprises stemming from projects supported by government seed funding with long-term financial self-sufficiency while currently at various levels of cost recovery.[9]

The CoP paper of September 2005 was the first government paper that clearly stated its position to support social enterprise as a new policy move. The paper was well researched and supported by policy models of other countries like the UK, Ireland, Germany, Finland and the US.[10] It was also clear to the government that social enterprise was a new policy area and that it was prepared to facilitate and support SEs as 'businesses'. As anticipated, some skepticism would come from small and medium-sized businesses (SMEs) that were concerned that any funding for social enterprises would give preferential treatment to a special category of 'business' organization, particularly during unfavorable economic environments. Government therefore decided to first focus on funding the SE projects of NGOs at the initial stage. A HK$150 million fund was created after the financial secretary's Budget Speech of 2006/07 for the Enhancing Self-Reliance Through District Partnership Program (ESR) (Home Affairs Department, 2014a),[11] which offered seed money to NGOs starting up a social enterprise for the purpose of creating employment opportunities for the disadvantaged groups in the districts. A similar fund relevant to SE, called Revitalizing Historic Buildings Through Partnership (hereafter the Heritage Fund), was set up in 2008 under the Commission for Heritage's Office of the Development Bureau. Both the ESR and the Heritage Fund gave emphasis to partnership and creation of jobs at the district level (Commissioner for Heritage, 2014).[12] The government made clear that social enterprise was not intended to replace the conventional welfare service delivery but would be an alternative model supplemental to the conventional welfare approach when rendering employment-related support to the disadvantaged.

The policy initiatives to support the development of social enterprise clearly put emphasis on poverty alleviation but represented the beginning of a breakthrough in the traditional 'welfare' and 'service'-oriented delivery model. Through the setup of the few funds mentioned above, government's policy attempted on the one hand to promote entrepreneurial spirit among the NGOs, and on the other to engage business corporations in poverty alleviation, not just by means of philanthropy, but also by means of partnerships. While government advocated an approach to support people to be self-reliant, the policy actually called for a new mindset to dealing with deep-rooted social problems. The thinking was to promote to all parties to jointly help people to help themselves with a focus on increasing employment and reducing intergenerational poverty (Tsang, 2005).[13]

The whole agenda-setting process was able to gain political support, as evident in the two motions and debates discussed in 2006 and 2007 in the Legislative Council (Subcommittee to the Study of Combating Poverty, 2008),[14] whose members principally agreed that the administration should formulate policies to effectively promote and support the development of social enterprises in order to narrow the gap of income disparity and alleviate the hardships of disadvantaged groups. Research was also initiated by the Legislative Council subcommittee on social enterprise policies of the UK and Spain, which drew some references on experiences of other governments and policies (Li & Wong, 2007).[15]

'Social enterprise' was, however, a new idea in Hong Kong at that time, as the concept was unfamiliar to everybody – NGOs, government civil servants and business corporations alike. In other words, the majority of the people in different sectors had very little knowledge of what social enterprise was about and how it would work for them. The discussions of the House Committee meeting of the Legislative Council in 2007 did point out problems like the lack of public understanding of social enterprises, lack of relevant entrepreneurship professional knowhow, lack of appropriate legal and regulatory frameworks to facilitate the development of the SE sector and difficulties in gaining access to financing by SEs. One of the key recommendations of the subcommittee at that time was to establish a high-level cross-bureau task force to formulate overall strategies for developing social enterprise and designate a bureau/department to be responsible for overseeing and promoting the development of and providing assistance to the social enterprise sector (Subcommittee to the Study of Combating Poverty, 2008).[16] Other recommendations included suggestions on creating an enabling market environment for the development of social enterprise, strengthening training and support through cross-sector collaboration and reviewing appropriate regulatory frameworks to cater to the special needs of social enterprises. Naturally, policies related to social enterprise were primarily related to definitions and legal frameworks, awareness building, publicity and marketing and better support for the development of the SE sector.

By 2007 more than one policy bureau and/or department became involved in the social enterprise policy. The ESR program was managed by the Home Affairs Bureau (HAB), the ICIIF was managed by the Labor and Welfare Bureau, the 3E fund was managed by the Social Welfare Department and the Heritage Fund was managed by the Development Bureau. Ultimately, the HAB was asked to be the main policy bureau responsible for setting out the direction of social enterprise policy after a government restructuring exercise. It was in this context that a Social Enterprise unit was set up and the Social Enterprise Advisory Committee (SEAC) was ultimately established in 2010 with members coming from different sectors.[17]

Following the decision of the then Poverty Commission, various efforts have been made by government to generate discussions, training and incubation relating to social entrepreneurship. These efforts included seminars organized by the government's Central Policy Unit in 2006, setting up of the Social Enterprise and Business Center (SEBC)[18] under the HKCSS in 2008 and the organization of the Social Enterprise Summit by the HAB in 2007.

Key problems: definition and misperception

A few challenges could easily be discerned from the above process of agenda setting. Fundamentally, the policy outcome created different interpretations on social enterprise. Would SE be a business or a welfare service? Although government aimed to support SE as a 'business', the ESR fund's eligibility was only confined to NGOs with tax exempt status. The social work professionals working in NGOs were totally unprepared to get involved in 'business' per se, even though they had difficulties with the lump sum grant policy and began to strengthen engagement of the business corporations in their services. The business sector on the other hand perceived SE as part of the poverty alleviation measures and so would not consider it as a policy that supported investment. The misperception was principally shaped by the context of which the SE policy was formed under the auspices of the CoP and the limited eligibility of the ESR fund. Very quickly, SE became a very odd subject both to the welfare and the business sectors.

One of the debates concerned the definition of social enterprise, which also varied both academically and practically in different contexts and in different countries. Generally speaking, academics and practitioners, both locally and internationally, would broadly agree on SE as consisting of 'innovative initiatives to deal with a social issue with entrepreneurial spirit' (Alvord, Brown, & Letts, 2004; Austin, Stevenson, & Wei-Skillern, 2006; Korosec & Berman, 2006; Perrini & Vurro, 2006; Yunus, 2008).[19] Whether they are profit or nonprofit entities, they should be financially self-sustainable, and profit making would not be the primary objective. Similarly, it has been stated on the website of the HAB that SE is defined "as a business to achieve specific social objectives such as providing the services or products needed by the community, creating employment and training opportunities for the socially disadvantaged, protecting the environment, funding its other social services through the profits earned, etc. Its profits will be principally reinvested in the business for the social objectives that it pursues, rather than distributed to its shareholders" (Home Affairs Bureau, 2014b).[20] This definition was similar to that of its official counterpart in the UK, the Office of the Third Sector.[21] The government in Hong Kong, however, refused to consider a regulatory framework for SE similar to the Community Interest Company (CIC) in the UK (Office of the Regulator or CIC, 2012),[22] on the ground that Hong Kong's tax structure should remain simple. Even though the HAB's definition did clearly regard SE as a 'business', eligibility for the ESR fund predominantly affected the perception and the mindset.

Roles of civic society

Civic groups emerged in conjunction with the ongoing discussions within the political system. By 2007/08, some individuals who studied outstanding overseas examples felt that the Hong Kong government's focus on offering grants to NGOs to start social enterprise projects was not adequate. K. K. Tse, a retired business consultant, for example, set up an organization called the Hong Kong Social Entrepreneurship Forum, together with a few other people with business backgrounds. These people were (a) C. H. Kee, formerly Hong Kong managing director of Hewlett-Packard, who became a director of Fullness Social Enterprise, providing haircutting and car repair services to support employment and training opportunities for ex-inmates; (b) Timothy Ma, formerly a social worker, who became the founding CEO of an emergency call service, the Senior Citizen's Home Safety Association, a social enterprise providing emergency services to elders living alone; (c) Yvonne Yeung, CEO of Mental Care, who offered on-the-job training for mentally rehabilitated members through sales of health care products in hospital shops; (d) Patrick Cheung, a former investor and businessman, who founded and served as the first managing director of Dialogue in the Dark Hong Kong, the first social enterprise in the form of shareholding; and (e) Hoi Wai Chua, then policy director of HKCSS who was responsible for overseeing the SEBC. Another platform organization that was set up more or less at the same time was Social Ventures Hong Kong, an organization aiming to incubate and invest in socially entrepreneurial projects, by Francis Ngai with the support of passionate philanthropists and experienced investment bankers. Francis Ngai was named one of the Ten Outstanding Young Persons in Hong Kong in 2011 in recognition of this initiative. Another institution, the Hong Kong General Chamber of Social Enterprises, was established in the same year under the leadership of Alice Yuk.

K. K. Tse quickly emerged as one of the key civic leaders and created impact through publications and shared cases and stories in the monthly newsletters of the Hong Kong Social Entrepreneurship Forum. Soon after he was appointed as a member of the SEAC, he rightly pointed out in an early meeting in 2010 that the public seemed to have the impression that a social enterprise should provide employment or services to disadvantaged groups being operated by NGOs, obtain initial capital from government grants and not distribute dividends even when profits were made.[23] K. K. Tse was one of those who strongly advocated the setup of a regulatory framework similar to the CIC in the UK. He also served as the founding chairman of Dialogue in the Dark Hong Kong, a shareholding company applying the CIC model in practice.

Another nongovernment platform that aggregated civic groups was formed in early 2008 amidst the emergence of the above-mentioned organizations shortly after the Social Enterprise Summit was organized by the Home Affairs Bureau in December 2007. Jane Lee (the author), formerly founding CEO of the Hong Kong Policy Research Institute, the first nongovernment think tank in Hong Kong, called these people together in early 2008 to discuss the possibility of organizing an alternate Social Enterprise Summit led by members of the civic society. They quickly consented to accommodate various interpretations of SEs and used three key words: 'innovation', 'entrepreneurship' and 'impact', to frame the character-istics of a social enterprise. Tactfully, these people decided to adopt the original term, 'Social Enterprise Summit', in English but modify the Chinese name by adding two characters: *min-jan* (nongovernment). After some initial communi-cation, the government positively responded to the nongovernment efforts and agreed to give support financially through the Civic Education Committee. By October 2008, ten civic societies quickly joined hands to organize the first 'non-government' Social Enterprise Summit. Since then, the nongovernment Summit has expanded very rapidly and become the key platform of exchange of con-cepts, ideas and good practices with overseas and local examples. The Summits were delivered in many different formats, such as symposiums, workshops, dia-logues, dinners, book sales, bazaars, exhibitions, awards and competitions. The key organizers made a lot of efforts annually to engage different sectors of people in the events and gradually came up with the consent that cross-sector partnership should be the key direction of the social enterprise movement in Hong Kong. The Home Affairs Bureau gradually found that the civic-led Social Enterprise Summit was in line with its policy objectives and requested in 2010 to join the Summit as a co-organizer; yet, it agreed that the whole event should remain a civic-led activ-ity with a democratic decision-making structure. At this stage, the Summit had already aggregated sixteen co-organizers and was coordinating about one hun-dred organizations each year, which were involved in such different capacities as partners, sponsors or supporting organizations. The annual events were attended by over 1,000 people, with participants from Hong Kong, mainland China, Tai-wan and other parts of the world. In an increasingly politicized society like Hong Kong, the Summit has become one of the very few successful examples of govern-ment effectively working in partnership with the civic society sector. In his speech delivered at the Opening Ceremony of the Social Enterprise Summit of 2012, T. S. Tsang, then secretary of the HAB, openly acknowledged that even though the SE policy was first initiated by the government, its growth and development should be taken up and led by leaders of the civic society.[24] The author, the chair of the Social Enterprise Summit, also mentioned from time to time that officials of the bureau were very supportive of the Summit's decisions (Luk, Lee & Tse, 2012).[25] Through organizing the annual events, a cohesive movement advocating social innovation and social entrepreneurship emerged from 2008 onwards, with the Social Enterprise Summit becoming the annual highlight of the movement.

The successful public-private partnership in Hong Kong mentioned above was not planned deliberately but was achieved in a very particular context. The emergence of the civic society movement happened when the HAB first took up the responsibility to coordinate SE policy in 2010. Tied into the varying arguments on what defined a social enterprise was the low level of public awareness, as pointed out in the Legislative Council discussions mentioned above. It should be noted that when the SE policy was initially kicked off in 2006/07, formal and informal surveys did show that public awareness of 'social enterprise' was very low (Tang et al., 2008).[26] The poor level of public awareness was linked with mindset problems of different sectors. NGOs, for example, felt that their core competence was services, not business and sales. Business leaders, on the other hand, felt that it would not be feasible for them to incorporate social objectives into their daily operations because their businesses were primarily aimed to achieve sales and income targets, and the philanthropy foundations felt that their mandates were bound by what were stated in the organizational mission statement and could not easily offer grants to 'business' projects, even though these businesses would have social goals. Other sectors, like civil servants and school teachers, were inevitably unaware of SE as a policy that was relevant to them. By 2008/09, people of different sectors generally considered that SE was not within their scope of activity.

'Promoting public understanding' and 'fostering an SE-friendly ecosystem'[27] naturally became the focal points of the SE policy led by the HAB and its Social Enterprise Advisory Committee formed in 2010. In the few years after the establishment of the SEAC, a few initiatives were taken to promote the general understanding of SEs, including the launch of some schemes, namely SE Bazaar, SE Award and SE Friend. Training at management and operational levels were initiated by SEAC and sponsored by the HAB to encourage opportunities for SEs to set out strategic directions and learn business skills relevant to their businesses with social objectives. Coupled with the training was a pilot scheme for priority bidding of selected government service contracts by SEs as a means to support SE development. Under the pilot scheme (2008–2011), only when no suitable SEs were identified for the contracts would non-SE service providers be invited to bid (Panel on Welfare Services, 2012).[28] The HAB also sponsored a Social Enterprise Challenge to encourage students at higher-education institutions to submit proposals for competition. Champions would be given awards and recognition as well as opportunities to receive startup seed money. A few awardees did start up interesting businesses after they graduated. The SE Challenge became another annual event and gradually built up interest and awareness among the academics as well as the students. The HAB's involvement in the Social Enterprise Summit was equally important. It not only signified effective public-private partnership

(HKSAR Government, 2014a)[29] but also saw joint efforts with civic society leaders to design tailored programs that encouraged the participation of the business, NGO, public and academic sectors. In addition to these, the emergence of a new platform, Make a Difference (MAD), a program designed for young people by Ada Wong, the initiatives by C. H. Kee to advocate ethical consumption and the Fullness Social Enterprise Society (FSES) were equally important efforts that strengthened general understanding of SEs, particularly among young people. Opportunities arose when liberal education components were strengthened in Hong Kong's education system, SE courses in tertiary institutions gradually emerged and secondary school teachers began to welcome SE programs and activities that suited their students.

Public awareness of social enterprise increased substantially in the seven to eight years after 2008. For example, a 2013 survey conducted by a research team led by Kevin Au of the Chinese University of Hong Kong (CUHK) (Au, 2014) showed that 78.5 percent of the general public claimed that they had either heard of SE or subscribed to services and/or bought products of social enterprises.[30] The percentage was even higher among young people (88.6 percent) and adults (81.3 percent). Among those who purchased SE products/services, 73.6 percent were willing to pay an extra 10 percent for comparable SE products and 12.5 percent were willing to pay an extra 20 percent.[31] The level of public awareness and recognition showed significant improvement compared with a previous public poll conducted by the University of Hong Kong in 2009, which showed that only about 59 percent of the public was aware of SE.[32]

It is fair to comment that the significant growth in general awareness and acceptance in social entrepreneurship in Hong Kong in these few years were the joint efforts of the Home Affairs Bureau and the civic society leaders, with most of the new initiatives coming from the nongovernment sector (see Figure 3.1) Gradual improvements in the branding, quality and image of the SE products also reshaped public perception that purchasing such products was more than philanthropy. Media reports gradually shifted from focusing on SE's lack of financial sustainability to emphasizing socially innovative ideas and good stories that moved people's hearts and minds.

Other policy issues: funding and incubation

Having gone through some initial experiences, the government made some policy adjustments and introduced a few improvements to the ESR scheme in 2011, including extending eligibility to nonprofit organizations without charitable status and introducing mentorship schemes for the project awardees to enhance success rates. Meanwhile, the government decided in 2012 to stop the pilot scheme for priority bidding after a review in 2011/12 because SEs were not able to cope with the multiple contracts, and the prices quoted were too high. SEs, however, found that the contract sizes were too big. The government also considered that the scheme, which accorded preferential treatment to SEs, was not in line with the procurement principles of fairness and open competition.[33]

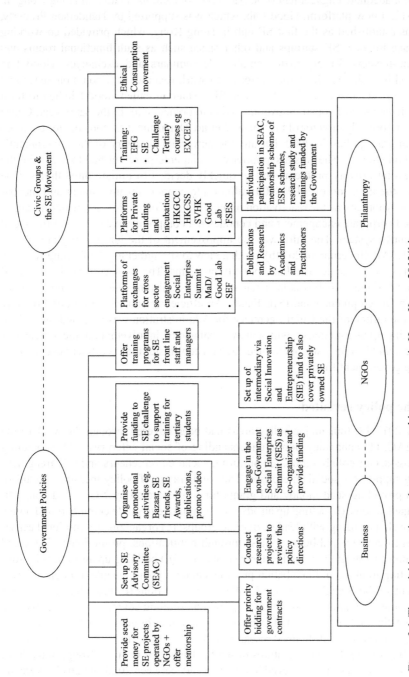

Figure 3.1 The social innovation and entrepreneurship ecosystem in Hong Kong, 2013/14

One of the problems that was commonly discussed among the civic leaders was the inadequate engagement of impact investors and incubators in Hong Kong. In 2012, a new platform, Good Lab, which was supported by Handerson Property, was established as the first SE hub in Hong Kong, which provided co-working space for new SE startups and other space such as multifunctional rooms and mini-theaters for organizing small-scale seminars and exchanges. Good Lab quickly gathered all major platforms to work together in a common space and synergized with a newly established SE restaurant called Good Kitchen to form an iconic site of social innovation and entrepreneurship. In the same year, Carrie Lam, formerly director of the Social Welfare Department responsible for the lump sum grant policy in 2000, became the new chief secretary of the government's administration. She was a supporter of social enterprise but had to deal with the pressing poverty problems and so quickly decided to initiate three things. One was the injection of a HK$500 million into support for investment and incubation. Another was the reactivation of the Commission on Poverty, which strengthened corporate engagement and conducted a comprehensive review of the social security system. The third was the improvement of the lump sum grant system (HKSAR Government 2014b)[34] with a view to strengthening the funding schemes to respond to acute social and poverty problems. The SE sector much welcomed the SE Fund, which was later renamed the Social Innovation and Entrepreneurship Development Fund (SIE Fund). An efficiency unit which reported directly to the Office of the Chief Secretary for Administration was assigned the task of setting up intermediaries with a view to enhancing involvement of the nongovernment and business sectors to incubate and administer the investment decisions of the government fund.[35]

The policy revisited

By 2012/13, four major policy areas had been covered through the work of the SEAC: (1) enhancing public understanding of social enterprises, (2) promoting cross-sector collaboration, (3) nurturing social entrepreneurs and (4) strengthening support for social enterprises. The whole range of policy measures included: (a) providing seed money and grants for SEs operated by NGOs and nonprofit organizations; (b) setting up an advisory committee to invite comments and inputs as well as liaising with leaders of civic groups; (c) organizing promotional activities to enhance public awareness through publications, promotional videos and commitments at the Social Enterprise Summit; (d) building up awareness by supporting training and incubation programs among young people through involvement in the Social Enterprise Challenge competition; (e) providing mentorship schemes through the ESR fund; (f) providing training courses for managerial and front-line staff in SEs; (g) offering priority bidding for government contracts; and (h) supporting a full-fledged research study by 2012/13 to review the SE policy.

What were the major features of the SE landscape in Hong Kong? What have been achieved or not achieved in the few years between 2006 and 2013? Were the policies adequate or not?

According to the landscape survey of the SEBC, there were a total of 406 social enterprises in 2012/13.[36] Most of them were micro-businesses relating to products and services in catering and food manufacturing, medical care, eco/recycling, education and training, domestic cleaning and renovation, fashion and accessories and logistics. The figure had doubled since 2007/08 when about 222 social enterprises were recorded by the same study. It is paradoxical to note that even though there were huge mindset problems among the NGOs, the majority of the social enterprises in Hong Kong belonged predominantly to the category of 'work-integrated social enterprises' (WISEs) established by NGOs with a single source of funding, in the form of either government seed money or grants.

The Audit Commission[37] has conducted a few reviews of the government funds relevant to SEs, and the most updated report was released in April 2014 after a comprehensive audit of the 3E and the ESR schemes. It revealed that grants of about HK$62 million and HK$158 million have been spent via the 3E and ESR schemes, creating 622 and 2,287 jobs respectively. The employees were generally satisfied with the opportunities to enhance their self-reliance.[38] For the ESR scheme, 51 percent of the projects recorded an operating surplus, of which 62 percent operated beyond the funding and monitoring period.[39]

There were some questions about the effectiveness and efficiency of the social enterprises, and many people were concerned about whether SEs had high failure rates with poor business skills. The few research studies done in Hong Kong – by the CUHK, the Bauhinia Foundation Research Center and the Engage Hong Kong project (Bauhinia Foundation Research Centre, 2013)[40] – found that SEs faced a number of challenges, including lack of innovation; lack of marketing, management and business skills; and lack of competitiveness in a highly competitive environment in Hong Kong.

Counter-arguments, however, suggested that the above-mentioned criticisms should be revisited. The new values, like community building and social inclusion, unfamiliar to a business operation, advocated by SEs and NGOs gradually became the trend recognised by the general public. As such, generating business return should not be primarily the value of social enterprises. Their positive externalities (Kee, 2013; Santos. 2012)[41] – including the creation of social capital and the tripartite partnership among the government, civic groups and the business sector – should be recognised. A 2013 study by the Fullness Social Enterprise Society funded by the ESR scheme, for example, showed that 2,287 socially disadvantaged people and their families benefited for 6.4 years from the HK$158 million ESR funding spent during the period on 145 projects, the cost of which was on average much less than the amount spent by Comprehensive Social Security Assistance, a government-funded program that supports people without jobs or who are below the poverty level of income.[42] According to FSES's finding, the survival rate of the social enterprises of the ESR scheme was 77 percent by the end of the fifth year (which was normally the end of the funding period), and the median life of these social enterprises was from 6.4 to 7.2 years (Kee, 2014).[43] The study concluded that the public money through the ESR scheme was well spent. By applying an analytical framework on 'social return on investment'

(SROI), FSES's study also found that the SROI of the social enterprises in Hong Kong were three to seven times that of an average SME,[44] and these benefits were in addition to the dignified way of living provided to the disadvantaged groups of people. The study by the FSES did present a unique line of anti-mainstream criticism and helped justify government's continued efforts to support the development of SEs.

Echoing the findings of FSES, the research study conducted by a CUHK team in 2013 acknowledged that the government's SE policy had contributed to the setting up of a new group of 'businesses' aiming to resolve social problems innovatively and had developed a new approach to social capital creation by facilitating multi-stakeholder participation.[45] Social enterprises in Hong Kong did attempt in a broader sense to address unmet social needs through introducing innovation in the production, distribution or consumption realm of a value creation process. They also brought stakeholders together and redesigned and reconfigured the production-distribution-consumption ties of the value economy chain.[46]

The author considers that despite all challenges mentioned above, the different stakeholders of the SE sector have made substantial achievements since 2007/08. First, the social entrepreneurs in Hong Kong did play a pivotal role in driving and creating new social values in Hong Kong. They have developed the capacity of a 'hidden' sector of people who were previously considered 'unemployable' and merely relied on welfare. The SEs did operate within a highly competitive environment in Hong Kong but made a lot of trials and errors with continuous self-corrections. In this sense, they were proactive, risk taking and innovative within constraints. Second, it is important to acknowledge that a number of SE platform organizations have been established in these few years. Together, they played a significant role in advancing new value creation and maintained frequent formal and informal dialogue with each other. As a result, there have been substantial improvements in the level of public awareness and recognition. Mindset and perception among NGOs, philanthropy, educationists and academics, business and even civil servants also shifted significantly in favor of it.

Towards a blended and hybrid economy for Hong Kong's free market system

The author witnessed the development of the SE policy in the past nine or ten years and the growth of this sector in Hong Kong. Looking back, the social economy landscape has made substantial improvements amidst Hong Kong's dominant mindset in the free market economy. As of 2015/16, although the number of social enterprises continued to grow slowly to about 500, the social and business sectors remained fundamentally truncated from each other, as they were in 2005/06. Social and poverty problems deeply rooted in Hong Kong society continued to enlarge. Why do these problems remain acute with the growth of the SE sector?

By 2013/14, many policy gaps and issues remained. A research report on 'Mind the Gap' prepared by an Engage Hong Kong project team in 2013 pointed out five cross-cutting issues, which were: mindset, definitions, impact investment, governance and accountability, as well as the roles of the government. Inadequate cross-sector collaboration was a key problem mentioned in the report, which was related to a lack of a culture of knowledge sharing and collaboration due to the 'silo' mindset, where 'social' and 'business' could not blend together. Definition is an issue that affects mindset. There may, however, be a major change in government's attitude towards the definitional issue. By 2014, government agreed to make changes on its website relating to the 'description' (not 'definition') of SE and clearly adopted the CIC model of the UK that no less than 65 percent of the SEs' distributional profits should be reinvested in the business for the social objectives that they pursue.[47] Such change leads to further relaxation of the eligibility criteria of the ESR funding schemes to private business agreeing to cap profit distributions.

The author agrees that SE is a challenging business, particularly when it comes into operation. What an SE needs is a driver or a leader with passion and commitment to resolve a social problem, the will to think innovatively and take risks and the ability to execute in a competitive market environment and overcome the dilemmas arising from the balance between social and business objectives. The silo mindset described is the key obstacle. Civic leaders like Ada Wong have been organizing a series of tri-sector training sessions at the Good Lab with a view to creating a new generation of tri-sector leaders. Cross-sector leadership is the kind of personnel, rather than people with business skills, that is needed.

Value creation discussed among academics is another area that needs attention. The advocacy of Michael Porter[48] in creating shared value among the corporations, which fundamentally calls for corporations to create social values for society, not just as philanthropy or social responsibility, are either unattended or addressed superficially by the business sectors in Hong Kong. The 'blended value' concept proposed by Jed Emerson (Bugg-Levine & Emerson 2011)[49] is almost unknown to government officials and business leaders. The general distrust against business corporations, which are increasingly regarded as an important source of creating social, environmental and economic problems (both locally and globally), if unaddressed, would become political hurdles to cross-sector collaboration.

The author considers that the SE landscape has been building up substantially but the ecosystem has yet to be strengthened. Increased awareness and recognition are important elements that facilitate the further engagement of the various sectors – business, NGOs, philanthropy, academics and civil service alike. Now, the new concepts such as 'blended value', 'shared value creation', 'responsible or ethical consumption' and 'social economy' are introduced through the joint efforts of the civic groups complemented by the courses introduced in the academic sector. While the Engage Hong Kong study advocates a blended value approach, the CUHK study puts more emphasis on multi-stakeholder participation and shared value creation. The FSES study, on the other hand, advocates knowledge volunteering and responsible consumption. What is needed further is the development of an impact investing environment, the strengthening of the incubators, as well as a publicly credible impact assessment tool.[50]

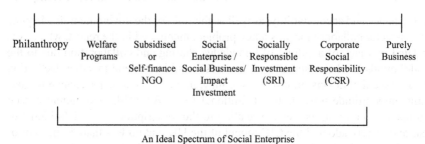

Philanthropy   Welfare   Subsidised   Social   Socially   Corporate   Purely
               Programs   or   Enterprise /   Responsible   Social   Business
                            Self-finance Social Business/ Investment Responsibility
                            NGO   Impact   (SRI)   (CSR)
                                          Investment

An Ideal Spectrum of Social Enterprise

Figure 3.2 Spectrum of social enterprise.

Adapted from: Lee, J., "社企的廣闊光譜與生態" [The Broad Spectrum and Ecology of Social Enterprises], in M. Luk, J. Lee, & K. Tse (Eds.), 我們可以改變世界: 香港社企領袖及創業家文集 [*We Can Change the World: Essays from Social Enterprise Leaders and Entrepreneurs in Hong Kong*], Hong Kong: Cloud Publications, 2012, p. 18.

There has indeed been a growing momentum in the general support for the development of SE. The most critical issue at stake is the mindset change and the grooming of cross-sector participation and collaboration.

As a conclusion, the author envisages that the development of SE policy not only enhances the employment opportunities for the disadvantaged, but also brings about a wealth of new concepts, which will gradually bring solutions to the capitalist economy of Hong Kong society. In view of the positive interactive relationship between the government and the civic groups in Hong Kong, the government should have the capability to further strengthen the engagement of the corporations and articulate shared value creation as a policy vision for Hong Kong with a view to enhancing a blended value in its established free market system. The author hopes to see that most of the business corporations will integrate social objectives into their mission statements and that the boundary of NGOs and business will become blurred with the two sectors collaborating together for social good and financial sustainability (see Figure 3.2)[51]

Notes

1 The Hong Kong Council of Social Service was first established in 1947 as a nongovernmental organization to coordinate refugee relief work. It gradually developed into an umbrella organization for voluntary and community organizations and coordinated NGOs in the name of 'Agency Members', who provided over 90 percent of Hong Kong's welfare services.
2 HKSAR Government, *The 2014–15 Budget*. Hong Kong: HKSAR Government, 2014, http://www.budget.gov.hk/2014/eng/pdf/e_budgetspeech2014-15.pdf, accessed 24 June 2014. Government expenditure is the aggregate of operating expenditure and capital expenditure. Unlike public expenditure, it excludes expenditure by the Trading Funds and the Housing Authority.
3 HKSAR Government, *Hong Kong 2003 – The Economy*. Hong Kong: HKSAR Government, http://www.yearbook.gov.hk/2003/english/append/app6_17.html, accessed 23 June 2014.

4 The objective of the project is to enhance the employment of people with disabilities through a market-driven approach and direct creation of more work opportunities for people with disabilities. Through the grant of seed money to NGOs, the project supports the creation of small enterprises/businesses to ensure that people with disabilities can enjoy genuine employment in a carefully planned and sympathetic working environment. For details, see Social Welfare Department of the HKSAR Government, *Enhancing Employment of People with Disabilities through Small Enterprise Project*, http://www.swd.gov.hk/en/index/site_pubsvc/page_rehab/sub_listofserv/id_enhancinge/, accessed 23 June 2014.

5 The Community Investment and Inclusion Fund is a HK$300 million fund established in 2001 aiming to encourage innovative solutions through cross-sectoral partnerships to build community capacity for mutual help.

6 Commission on Poverty. *From Welfare to Self-Reliance: Social Enterprise Development* (paper for discussion at the Commission's meeting on 12 September 2005, CoP Paper 22/2005 September). Hong Kong: HKSAR Government, 2005, p. 1.

7 Commission on Poverty, *From Welfare to Self-Reliance: Social Enterprise Development* (paper for discussion at the Commission's meeting on 12 September 2005, CoP Paper 22/2005 September). Hong Kong: HKSAR Government, 2005.

8 *Ibid*, p. 1.

9 *Ibid*, p. 1.

10 *Ibid*.

11 The Enhancing Self-Reliance Through District Partnership Programme was set up initially in June 2006 as a five-year HK$150 million fund, which was aimed to strengthen district-based poverty alleviation work and assist socially disadvantaged groups in gaining self-reliance. It provided a maximum of HK$3 million seed money for NGOs with tax exempt status to set up social enterprise projects that fit its objectives. For more details, see Home Affairs Department of the HKSAR Government, *Public Services > Enhancing Self-Reliance Through District Partnership Programme*, http://www.had.gov.hk/en/public_services/en_self_reli/index.htm#a, accessed 24 June 2014.

12 The Commissioner for Heritage's Office of the HKSAR Government. *Revitalising Historic Buildings Through Partnership Scheme*, http://www.heritage.gov.hk/en/rhbtp/about.htm, accessed 24 June 2014.

13 Tsang, D., *The 2005/06 Policy Address: Strong Governance for the People*, Hong Kong: HKSAR Government, 2005, para. 40-41, http://www.policyaddress.gov.hk/05-06/eng/pdf/speech.pdf, accessed 24 June 2014.

14 In November 2004, a subcommittee to study the subject of 'combating poverty' was set up under the House Committee of the Legislative Council. The subcommittee discussed the launch of the ESR program in June 2006 and the development of SEs in July and December 2007.

15 Li, S. & Wong, T., *Social Enterprise Policies of the United Kingdom, Spain and Hong Kong*. Hong Kong: Research and Library Services Division of Legislative Council Secretariat, 2007, http://www6.cityu.edu.hk/projectflame/resources/pdf/2.pdf, accessed 25 June 2014.

16 Subcommittee to Study the Subject of Combating Poverty. *Report on Development of Social Enterprise* (LC Paper No. CB(2)2390/07–08). Hong Kong: Legislative Council of the HKSAR, 2008, para. 4.4, p. 15, http://www.legco.gov.hk/yr07-08/english/hc/papers/hc0627cb2-2390-e.pdf, accessed 25 Jun 2014.

17 The terms of reference of SEAC were (a) to advise the government on the formulation of policies and strategies for supporting the sustainable development of social enterprises in Hong Kong; (b) to advise the government on programs/activities that promote development of social enterprises and to monitor their implementation; (c) to foster better understanding and encourage closer cooperation amongst relevant stakeholders in the development of social enterprises, and (d) to undertake research studies on matters pertaining to the development of social enterprises.

18 The objective of the Social Enterprise and Business Center (SEBC) was to advance social entrepreneurship and social innovation. Its funding came from both private and public (Home Affairs Bureau) funding. For more details, see at http://socialenterprise.org.hk/, accessed 23 June 2014.

19 See Alvord, S. H., Brown, D. L., & Letts, C. W. 'Social entrepreneurship and societal transformation: An exploratory study'. *Journal of Applied Behavioural Science*, 2004, No. 40, pp. 260–282; Austin, J., Stevenson, H., & Wei-Skillern, J. 'Social and commercial entrepreneurship: Same, different, or both?' *Entrepreneurship Theory & Practice*, 2006, No. 30, pp. 1–22; Korosec, R. L., & Berman, E. M. 'Municipal support for social entrepreneurship'. *Public Administration Review*, 2006, Vol. 66, No. 3, pp. 448–462; Perrini, F., & Vurro, C. 'Social entrepreneurship: Innovation and social change across theory and practice', in J. Mair, J. Robinson, & K. Hockerts (Eds.), *Social entrepreneurship*. Basingstoke, UK: Palgrave Macmillan, 2006; Yunus, M. *Creating a world without poverty: Social business and the future of capitalism*. New York: Public Affairs Books, 2008.

20 Home Affairs Bureau of the HKSAR Government. *Social Enterprise, Introduction > What Is Social Enterprise*, http://www.social-enterprises.gov.hk/en/introduction/whatis.html, accessed 23 June 2014

21 SE in the UK is defined as business with primarily social objectives whose surpluses are principally reinvested for that purpose in the business or community, rather than being driven by the need to maximize profit for shareholders and owners. See Department of Trade and Industry of UK Government, *A Progress Report on Social Enterprise: A Strategy For Success*, UK: Department of Trade and Industry, 2003, p. 6, http://www.uk.coop/sites/storage/public/downloads/strategyforsocialenterprise_progressreport_2003.pdf, accessed 23 June 2014.

22 The Companies (Audit, Investigations and Community Enterprise) Act was passed in 2004 in UK (CAICE Act 2004), which set up a regulatory framework for SE, a Community Interest Company (CIC). CICs are companies with limited shares or a guarantee with a statutory 'Asset Lock' to prevent the assets and profits being completely distributed to shareholders or guarantees. For more details, see Office of the Regulator of Community Interest Companies, "Chapter 1 – Introduction", in *Community Interest Companies: Guidance Chapters*, UK: Department for Business Innovation & Skills of UK Government, 2012, https://www.gov.uk/government/publications/community-interest-companies-how-to-form-a-cic, accessed 24 June 2014.

23 Based on the author's participation as a member of the Social Enterprise Advisory Committee

24 Tsang, T. S., *Speech at the Opening Ceremony of the Social Enterprise Summit 2012* (video clip). 29 November 2012, Hong Kong.

25 Lee, J., "香港社企發展的趨勢" [The Development Trend of Social Enterprises in Hong Kong], in M. Luk, J. Lee, & K. Tse (Eds.), 我們可以改變世界:香港社企領袖及創業家文集 (We Can Change the World: Essays from Social Enterprise Leaders and Entrepreneurs in Hong Kong), Hong Kong: Cloud Publications, 2012, p. 111.

26 A pilot survey was conducted by SEBC in 2006, which showed that 70 percent of the respondents (SEs) said the public had a poor understanding of SEs. In another survey conducted with the general public, 75 percent did not understand what an SE was. See Tang, S. K., Ho, L. F., Au, K.Y.F., Lee, J.K.C., & Ko, L.S.F., *Social Enterprises in Hong Kong: Toward a Conceptual Model*. Hong Kong: Central Policy Unit of the HKSAR Government, 2008, p. 12, http://www.cpu.gov.hk/doc/en/research_reports/20080421%20Social%20Enterprises%20in%20Hong%20Kong.pdf, accessed 24 June 2014.

27 These two items were regular agendas of the subsequent SEAC meetings.

28 The pilot scheme was rolled out in three phases in 2008, 2009 and 2011, which altogether covered 132 service contracts comprising 120 cleaning and 12 gardening contracts. About 75 contracts valued at HK$ 30 million were awarded to SEs involving

570 jobs. See Panel on Welfare Services, *Background Brief Prepared by the Legislative Council Secretariat for the Meeting on 9 January 2012: Social Enterprise development in Hong Kong*, LC Paper No. CB(2)717/11–12(05). Hong Kong: Legislative Council, 2012, http://www6.cityu.edu.hk/projectflame/resources/pdf/5.pdf, accessed 25 June 2014. See also: Audit Commission of HKSAR. "Chapter 7: Home Affairs Bureau, Home Affairs Department and Social Welfare Department – Promoting the Development of Social Enterprises", in *Report No. 62 of the Director of Audit (April 2014)*. Hong Kong: Audit Commission, 2014, p. 79, http://www.aud.gov.hk/pdf_e/e62ch07.pdf, accessed 25 June 2014.

29 Government support for the Social Enterprise Summit became a policy and was included in the "Policy Agenda" booklets of the Policy Speech of the Chief Executive in 2014. The HAB also adopted "Cross Sector Partnership" as one of their policy focus, which was similar to the key objective of the Social Enterprise Summit. See HKSAR Government. *The 2014 Policy Address: Policy Agenda*, Hong Kong: HKSAR Government, 2014, p. 64, http://www.policyaddress.gov.hk/2014/eng/pdf/Agenda_Ch3.pdf, accessed 25 June 2014.

30 Au, K. et al. *Research Study on the Social Enterprise Sector in Hong Kong – to Capture the Existing Landscape of Social Enterprises in Hong Kong*. Hong Kong: CUHK Center for Entrepreneurship & HKCSS-HSBC Social Enterprise Business Center, 2014, para 5.6(9), p. 37 and A4–3.

31 *Ibid.*

32 Public Opinion Programme, the University of Hong Kong. *Survey on Knowledge and Attitude towards Social Enterprise in Hong Kong* (commissioned by Baptist Oi Kwan Social Service and DBS Bank (Hong Kong) Limited). Hong Kong: Public Opinion Programme, the University of Hong Kong, 2009, http://hkupop.hku.hk/chinese/report/socialEnterprise09/index.html, accessed 25 June 2014.

33 Audit Commission of HKSAR. "Chapter 7: Home Affairs Bureau, Home Affairs Department and Social Welfare Department – Promoting the Development of Social Enterprises", in *Report No. 62 of the Director of Audit (April 2014)*. Hong Kong: Audit Commission, 2014, para. 5.11–5.15, pp. 79–80, http://www.aud.gov.hk/pdf_e/e62ch07.pdf, accessed 25 June 2014.

34 The Funding Scheme was enhanced and executed on a step-by-step basis since the 2013/14 and 2014/15 financial year. See HKSAR Government. *Address by the Chief Executive the honorable CY Leung at the Legislative Council Meeting on 15 January 2014*. Hong Kong: HKSAR Government, 2014, para. 84, p. 27, http://www.policyaddress.gov.hk/2014/index.html, accessed 24 June 2014.

35 The objectives of the Social Innovation and Entrepreneurship Development Fund (SIE Fund) are to establish or support schemes and experiments with a view to attracting, inspiring or nurturing social entrepreneurship to develop innovations that aim at creating social impact and build social capital for supporting poverty relief in Hong Kong. See more at http://www.sie.gov.hk/en/, accessed 25 June 2014. At the time of completing this paper in 2015, a few intermediaries were just announced with a view to piloting matching grants to strengthen business engagement.

36 The number of social enterprises grew from 222 in 2007/08 to 406 in 2012/13. See HKCSS – HSBC Social Enterprise Business Centre (SEBC). *Hong Kong social enterprise landscape study 2012–13*. Hong Kong: HKCSS – HSBC Social Enterprise Business Centre (SEBC), 2013, http://www.socialenterprise.org.hk/sites/default/files//general/powerofgood_72%28dpi%29_0.pdf, accessed 25 June 2014.

37 The Audit Commission is one of the government departments of the HKSAR Government. The Director of Audit is appointed by the Chief Executive and reports to the Chief Executive. Its main functions are to provide independent, professional and quality audit services to the Legislative Council and public sector organisations in order to help the government enhance public sector performance and accountability in Hong Kong. http://www.aud.gov.hk/eng/home/home.htm, accessed 25 June 2014.

38 Based on the questionnaire developed by Home Affairs Department for the employees, it was found that 78 percent of the employees agreed that their jobs let them learn more working skills and 82 percent agreed that they were more confident with their future employment. See Audit Commission of HKSAR. "Chapter 7: Home Affairs Bureau, Home Affairs Department and Social Welfare Department – Promoting the Development of Social Enterprises", in *Report No. 62 of the Director of Audit (April 2014)*. Hong Kong: Audit Commission, 2014, para. 3.48, pp. 52–53, http://www.aud.gov.hk/pdf_e/e62ch07.pdf, accessed 25 June 2014.

39 As expected, the audit also pointed out inefficiency in the bureaucratic procedures in handling applications as well as the need to improve the cost effectiveness of the scheme. See *Ibid*. para. 3.18–3.23, pp. 40–42.

40 The Bauhinia Foundation Research Centre. *Social Enterprises in Hong Kong*. Hong Kong: The Bauhinia Foundation Research Centre, 2013, http://www.bauhinia.org/document/doc163eng.pdf, accessed 25 June 2014. Au, K. et al. *Research Study on the Social Enterprise Sector in Hong Kong – to Capture the Existing Landscape of Social Enterprises in Hong Kong*. Hong Kong: CUHK Center for Entrepreneurship & HKCSS-HSBC Social Enterprise Business Center, 2014. Alto, P. & Wong, P.M. *Adopting the London Principles: Policy Considerations to Grow Impact Investing in Hong Kong*. Hong Kong: Asia Community Venture, 2014, http://www.asiacommunityventures.org/wp-content/uploads/2013/01/Adopting-the-London-Principles-Growing-Impact-Investing-in-Hong-Kong-July-2014.pdf, accessed 21 August 2014. Alto, P. & Wong, P. M. *Mind the gap: Lessons and findings from EngageHK*. Hong Kong: Asia Community Venture, 2013, http://www.asiacommunityventures.org/wp-content/uploads/2013/08/EngageHK_Final_Webversion.pdf, accessed 25 June 2014.

41 Filipe Santos (2012) proposes a positive theory on social entrepreneurship and suggests that social entrepreneurship is the pursuit of sustainable solutions to neglected problems with positive externalities. See Santos, F. "A positive theory of social entrepreneurship". *Journal of Business Ethics*, Vol. 111, No. 3 (2012), pp. 335–351. See also Kee, C. H. *Social Return On Investment (SROI) of Enhancing Self-Reliance (ESR) through District Partnership Projects* (unpublished paper). Hong Kong: Fullness Social Enterprises Society (FSES), 2013, https://www.fses.hk/ourdb/files/ourdb@fses.hk/fses_June_Article.pdf, accessed 25 June 2014.

42 *Ibid*, p. 5

43 *Ibid*. See also Kee, C. H. *Social Return on Investment (SROI) of Enhancing Employment of People with Disabilities through Small Enterprise Project (3E)* (unpublished paper). Hong Kong: Fullness Social Enterprises Society (FSES), 2013, https://www.fses.hk/ourdb/files/ourdb@fses.hk/fses_august_Article.pdf, accessed 25 June 2014.

44 It was claimed that 70 percent of the new commercial firms survived by the end of second year and 50 percent survived by the end of the fourth year. The median life expectancy of a firm was 4 years. *Ibid*. p. 4.

45 Au K. et al. *Research Study on the Social Enterprise Sector in Hong Kong – to Capture the Existing Landscape of Social Enterprises in Hong Kong*. Hong Kong: CUHK Center for Entrepreneurship & HKCSS-HSBC Social Enterprise Business Center, 2014, para 1.6(b), p. 3.

46 *Ibid*, pp. 8–9.

47 Based on the author's participation as a member of the Social Enterprise Advisory Committee.

48 Porter, M. E., & Kramer, M. R. "Creating shared value", *Harvard Business Review*, Vol. 89, No. 1/2 (2011), pp. 62–77.

49 Jed Emerson has built up a "Blended Value Framework", which calls for blending of social and business values. The first book that was published on the topic was *Impact Investing Transforming How We Make Money While Making a Difference* by Antony Bugg-Levine and Jed Emerson in 2011. See Bugg-Levine, A. & Emerson, J. *Impact Investing Transforming How We Make Money While Making a Difference*.

San Francisco: Jossey-Bass, 2011. See also Porter, M. E., & Kramer, M. R. "Creating shared value", *Harvard Business Review*, Vol. 89, No. 1/2 (2011).
50 Hong Kong General Chamber of Social Enterprises (HKGCSE), with the sponsorship of the Standard Chartered Bank 150th Anniversary Foundation, has entrusted the Project Flame @ City University of Hong Kong to conduct a joint study into the development of a Social Enterprise Endorsement (SEE) System in Hong Kong since October 2013.
51 Lee, J., "社企的廣闊光譜與生態" (The Broad Spectrum and Ecology of Social Enterprises), in M. Luk, J. Lee, & K. Tse (Eds.), 我們可以改變世界: 香港社企領袖及創業家文集 [We Can Change the World: Essays from Social Enterprise Leaders and Entrepreneurs in Hong Kong], Hong Kong: Cloud Publications, 2012, p. 18.

References

Alvord, S. H., Brown, D. L., & Letts, C. W. (2004). "Social Entrepreneurship and Societal Transformation: An Exploratory Study", *Journal of Applied Behavioural Science*, 40: 260–282.
Au, K. (2014). *Research Study on the Social Enterprise Sector in Hong Kong – to Capture the Existing Landscape of Social Enterprises in Hong Kong*. Hong Kong: CUHK Center for Entrepreneurship & HKCSS-HSBC Social Enterprise Business Center.
Austin, J., Stevenson, H., & Wei-Skillern, J. (2006). "Social and Commercial Entrepreneurship: Same, Different, or Both?" *Entrepreneurship Theory & Practice*, 30: 1–22.
Bugg-Levine, A., & Emerson, J. (2011). *Impact Investing Transforming How We Make Money While Making a Difference*. San Francisco: Jossey-Bass.
Commission on Poverty. (2005). *From Welfare to Self-reliance: Social Enterprise Development*. Paper for discussion at the Commission's Meeting on 12 September 2005, CoP Paper 22/2005 September. Hong Kong: HKSAR Government.
Commissioner for Heritage. (2014). Revitalising Historic Buildings Through Partnership Scheme, http://www.heritage.gov.hk/en/rhbtp/about.htm, accessed 24 June 2014.
HKCSS – HSBC Social Enterprise Business Centre (SEBC). (2013). *Hong Kong Social Enterprise Landscape Study 2012–13*. Hong Kong: HKCSS – HSBC Social Enterprise Business Centre, http://www.socialenterprise.org.hk/sites/default/files//general/powerofgood_72%28dpi%29_0.pdf, accessed 25 June 2014.
HKSAR Government. (2003). *Hong Kong 2003 – The Economy*. Hong Kong: HKSAR Government, http://www.yearbook.gov.hk/2003/english/append/app6_17.html, accessed 23 June 2014.
HKSAR Government. (2014b). *Address by the Chief Executive the Honorable CY Leung at the Legislative Council Meeting on 15 January 2014*. Hong Kong: HKSAR Government, para. 84, p. 27, http://www.policyaddress.gov.hk/2014/index.html, accessed 24 June 2014.
HKSAR Government. (2014a). *The 2014 Policy Address: Policy Agenda*. Hong Kong: HKSAR Government, p. 64, http://www.policyaddress.gov.hk/2014/eng/pdf/Agenda_Ch3.pdf, accessed 25 June 2014.
HKSAR Government. (2014c). *The 2014–15 Budget*. Hong Kong: HKSAR Government, http://www.budget.gov.hk/2014/eng/pdf/e_budgetspeech2014-15.pdf, accessed 24 June 2014.
Home Affairs Bureau. (2014a). Public Services > Enhancing Self-Reliance Through District Partnership Programme, http://www.had.gov.hk/en/public_services/en_self_reli/index.htm#a, accessed 24 June 2014.

Home Affairs Bureau. (2014b). Social Enterprise, Introduction > What Is Social Enterprise, http://www.social-enterprises.gov.hk/en/introduction/whatis.html, accessed 23
June 2014.

Kee, C. H. (2013). Social Return on Investment (SROI) of Enhancing Self-Reliance (ESR)
Through District Partnership Projects (2013, unpublished paper). Hong Kong: Fullness
Social Enterprises Society (FSES), https://www.fses.hk/ourdb/files/ourdb@fses.hk/
fses_June_Article.pdf, accessed 25 June 2014.

Kee, C. H. (2014). Social Return on Investment (SROI) of "Enhancing Employment of
People with Disabilities through Small Enterprise Project" (3E) (2013, unpublished
paper). Hong Kong: Fullness Social Enterprises Society (FSES), https://www.fses.hk/
ourdb/files/ourdb@fses.hk/fses_august_Article.pdf, accessed 25 June 2014.

Korosec, R. L., & Berman, E. M. (2006). "Municipal Support for Social Entrepreneurship", *Public Administration Review*, 66(3): 448–462.

Li, S. & Wong, T., (2007). *Social Enterprise Policies of the United Kingdom, Spain and
Hong Kong*. Hong Kong: Research and Library Services Division of Legislative Coun-
cil Secretariat, http://www6.cityu.edu.hk/projectflame/resources/pdf/2.pdf, accessed 25
June 2014.

Luk, M., Lee, J., & Tse, K. (Eds.) (2012). 我們可以改變世界: 香港社企領袖及創業家
文集 [We Can Change the World: Essays from Social Enterprise Leaders and Entrepreneurs in Hong Kong], Hong Kong: Cloud Publications.

Office of the Regulator of Community Interest Companies. (2012). "Chapter 1 – Introduction", in *Community Interest Companies: Guidance Chapters*. UK: Department for
Business Innovation & Skills of UK Government, https://www.gov.uk/government/
publications/community-interest-companies-how-to-form-a-cic, accessed 24 June 2014.

Panel on Welfare Services (2012). Background Brief Prepared by the Legislative Council
Secretariat for the Meeting on 9 January 2012: Social Enterprise Development in Hong
Kong, LC Paper No. CB(2)717/11–12(05). (2012). Hong Kong: Legislative Council,
http://www6.cityu.edu.hk/projectflame/resources/pdf/5.pdf, accessed 25 June 2014.

Perrini, F., & Vurro, C. (2006). "Social Entrepreneurship: Innovation and Social Change
Across Theory and Practice", in J. Mair, J. Robinson, & K. Hockerts (Eds.), *Social
Entrepreneurship*. Basingstoke, UK: Palgrave Macmillan, pp. 57–86.

Porter, M. E., & Kramer, M. R. (2011). "Creating Shared Value", *Harvard Business Review*,
89(1/2): 62–77.

Public Opinion Programme, the University of Hong Kong. (2009). *Survey on Knowledge
and Attitude Towards Social Enterprise in Hong Kong (Commissioned by Baptist Oi
Kwan Social Service and DBS Bank (Hong Kong) Limited)*. Hong Kong: Public Opinion
Programme, the University of Hong Kong, http://hkupop.hku.hk/chinese/report/social
Enterprise09/index.html, accessed 25 June 2014.

Santos, F. (2012). "A Positive Theory of Social Entrepreneurship", *Journal of Business
Ethics*, 111(3): 335–351.

Social Welfare Department. (2014). 'Enhancing Employment of People with Disabilities
through Small Enterprise' Project', http://www.swd.gov.hk/en/index/site_pubsvc/page_
rehab/sub_listofserv/id_enhancinge/, accessed 23 June 2014.

Subcommittee to Study the Subject of Combating Poverty. (2008). *Report on Development of Social Enterprise (LC Paper No. CB(2)2390/07–08)*. Hong Kong: Legislative
Council of the HKSAR, 2008, http://www.legco.gov.hk/yr07–08/english/hc/papers/
hc0627cb2-2390-e.pdf, accessed 25 June 2014.

Tang, S. K., Ho, L. F., Au, K.Y.F., Lee, J.K.C., & Ko, L.S.F. (2008). *Social Enterprises in
Hong Kong: Toward a Conceptual Model*. Hong Kong: Central Policy Unit of the HKSAR

Government, p. 12, http://www.cpu.gov.hk/doc/en/research_reports/20080421%20
Social%20Enterprises%20in%20Hong%20Kong.pdf, accessed 24 June 2014.

The Bauhinia Foundation Research Centre. (2013). *Social Enterprises in Hong Kong.*
Hong Kong: The Bauhinia Foundation Research Centre, http://www.bauhinia.org/docu
ment/doc163eng.pdf, accessed 25 June 2014.

Tsang, D. Y. (2005). *The 2005/06 Policy Address: Strong Governance for the People.* Hong
Kong: HKSAR Government, http://www.policyaddress.gov.hk/05–06/eng/pdf/speech.
pdf, accessed 24 June 2014.

Yunus, M. (2008). *Creating a World without Poverty: Social Business and the Future of
Capitalism.* New York: Public Affairs Books.

4 The blank spots and blind spots on Hong Kong SE policies

Kee Chi-Hing

Introduction

Objectives of the chapter

This chapter aims to evaluate the effectiveness of the social enterprise (SE) policies of the Hong Kong government, which consist of the Enhancing Employment of People with Disabilities Through Small Enterprise (3E) Project approved in 2001, and the Enhancing Self-Reliance Through District Partnership (ESR) Program approved in 2006. Both schemes fund work-integration social enterprises (WISEs), which create job opportunities for the powerless segments of the population.

There are 75 SEs in the 3E Project. They create jobs for the disabled people, including the physically disabled, mentally retarded, and mentally ill. There are 144 SEs in the ESR Program. They create jobs for socially disadvantaged people, including elderly, low skilled people, deviant youth, ethnic minorities, and ex-offenders. Together with about another 10 SEs funded by Community Investment and Inclusion Fund (CIIF), the total number of government-funded SEs account for 56 percent of the 406 social enterprises listed in the 2013 SE Directory[1] compiled by Hong Kong Council of Social Services.

The development of social enterprises in Hong Kong

The Hong Kong government has introduced the policy of "welfare-to-work", or simply workfare, to empower able-bodied but disadvantaged groups with work. It is because one third of safety net beneficiaries are able-bodied. This is to be realized through the jobs created by SEs which were recommended by the Commission on Poverty in 2007. In fact, the 3E Project had already been set up in 2001. In 2013, 71 percent of the 406 SEs listed in the SE Directory employed the disabled or socially disadvantaged.

According to Stephen Fisher (Chan et al., 2010),[2] the then Secretary of the Commission on Poverty, the intention of the government was to have social enterprises to solve "problems that the market fails to resolve or the government cannot resolve satisfactorily". He recalled that back in 2007 there were 32 percent of households on Comprehensive Social Security Assistance (CSSA), but the adults in the households were employable, including single parents who had small children, people with low incomes, and people unemployed. They suffered from structural unemployment which resulted from Hong Kong's transformation of the manufacturing economy to a service economy that usually required highly educated staff.

Fisher further explained that while SEs can help alleviate the poverty problem, the government's consideration is more than just social cost saving or reduction of wastage of human resources, but helping the disadvantaged to have a dignified way of living because work is an important element in the core value of Hong Kong (Chan et al., 2010).[3]

In Hong Kong, there is worry that social enterprises operated by non-government organizations (NGOs) may have great challenges in business performance. In 2008, the Central Policy Unit (Tang et al., 2008)[4] reported constraints faced by NGOs in running social enterprises:

a   Some SE managers pointed out the indecisiveness in NGOs – social workers from NGOs do not always follow decisions, particularly relating to the discipline of workers.
b   There is some difficulty in changing the mentality of NGOs that pay too much attention to social mission.
c   Social workers working for SEs lack the business knowledge and related mindset, and they may not be able to survive in open-market competition after the first two years of using all the seed money.
d   The specific abilities these NGOs lack include expertise in running a business, managing skills and knowledge in formulating market strategies.

The former chief executive of the Hong Kong Special Administrative Region Government, Donald Tsang, had SE policy in his annual Policy Address from 2007 to 2010. However, the success rate of SE was considered not up to expectation. The prevalent opinion was that most SEs operated by social workers need more training to cope with the business challenges. He had not covered the SE policy in his last Policy Address in 2011, in which he concluded his contributions for his role as the chief executive.

The development of the definitions of social enterprises in academia

However, there is a growing appreciation of SE overseas. In the 2013 survey commissioned by Social Enterprise UK, 78 percent[5] of SEs used the SE status in their marketing, as compared with only 53 percent doing so in 2011. The concept of "Buy Social" in the UK has increased the commercial value of the SE label. As SE is going to the mainstream and the number of SEs keep increasing, scholars found that definitions of SE as business setups for a social missions or as having double bottom lines were insufficient as a stringent definition.

Back in 1972, banks[6] first coined the term "social entrepreneur" as one "who saw the possibility of using managerial skills directly for socially constructive purposes". Not much has been discussed since then.

In 1998, Dees[7] proposed that social entrepreneurs can be defined as change agents in the social sector by:

- adopting a mission to create and sustain social value (not just private value).
- recognizing and relentlessly pursuing new opportunities to serve that mission.
- engaging in a process of continuous innovation, adaptation, and learning.
- acting boldly without being limited by resources currently in hand.
- exhibiting heightened accountability to the constituencies served and for the outcomes created.

In 2006, Dees (Dees & Beth, 2006)[8] proposed how to differentiate social enterprise from social innovation. While business income generation is a must for social enterprises, it is not the case of social innovation which focuses on "systemic changes". But, while the US practitioners talk much about social innovation, 69 percent (Mair et al., 2012)[9] of the projects are in developing countries where "systemic changes" are more likely to be achieved.

In 2011, Massetti[10] proposed how to differentiate social enterprise from corporate social responsibility (CSR). Social enterprises focus on social impact maximization as long as sustainability is achieved, while companies with CSR still focus on profit maximization. This helps screen out commercial enterprises with CSR as SEs in the US.

Santos (2012)[11] proposed a positive theory of social enterprise that "social entrepreneurs address the neglected problem in the society, with sustainable solutions based on empowerment, which generates positive externalities to the powerless segments of the population". This is a much improved criterion to distinguish between the selfless social enterprises aimed at the common good and the limited selfish enterprises which capture most of the values created, although they claim to be social enterprises.

Research question

Four stages of knowledge development

Knowledge is developed through four stages. First, cases in a new phenomenon are studied and followed by landscape surveys. Second, tentative theories are proposed based on imaginations of the phenomenon. They are then criticized and debated based on existing data. Third, the relatively better theories are validated on the accuracy of their prediction by large-scale surveys. Even those theories that survive through the validation are not necessarily the truth but only the better theories in explaining and predicting the phenomenon. They may be replaced by newer theories later. Finally, practical values of the new knowledge are exploited by applied research.

Problem in concluding the ineffectiveness of SEs in stage 2

But SE research in Hong Kong has been stuck at stage 2 ever since 2006, when the Commission on Poverty first showed interest in SEs. One of the tentative, but prevailing, theories is that NGOs are not good at running social enterprises, which in turns implies that the 3E Project and ESR Program are not successful. These opinions had been reflected in the rhetoric of Policy Addresses from 2007 to 2010 as the lack of entrepreneurial skills and mindset or as training and supporting measures. These claims have been taken for granted. But there are blank spots and blind spots (Kamler & Thomson, 2006).[12]

No evidence on who can run SEs better than NGOs

Critical examination is absent before concluding the validity of the statement. For example, there is not any examination and discussion on the success rate of social enterprises run by non-social workers. Hence there is not any benchmark. Social workers are not good at business, but the conclusion cannot be drawn that they are worse than non-social workers in running business, as there is no evidence provided. In fact, most people are not good at starting and running businesses, hence most people are employees instead of business owners.

Absence of accounting for the cost to generate social impact in SEs

Moreover, the primary purpose of social enterprise is the creation of social value, but there is not any study on the achievement of their social impacts. The social mission requires additional resources to make it happen. In fact, those SEs which employ mentally retarded or physically disabled people have to consume a lot of energy and resources, not only to teach these employees the technical skills but also have to take care of their psychological conditions and their family problems. Relatively, those employing seniors or low-skilled people are easier to manage. However, there is not any study to account for the cost of these extra resources for delivering the social impact. Without a proper accounting, an apple to apple to comparison to similar commercial enterprise is not possible.

Blended return on investment

Instead of accounting for the extra costs, another approach is accounting for returns. Some scholars proposed the concept of blended return on investment (BROI), which includes both the value of traditional financial returns and the social impact in the denominator. However, the quantification of the social impact in financial terms is still not yet mature. Unlike financial impact of businesses, work in social science always has the problem of evaluation. The problem has not been faced directly. Scattered answers are merely assumed without critical analysis (Mills, 1959, 2000).[13]

The value of this chapter

These issues are seldom seriously debated or researched through comparative studies. The major blind spot is ignorance of benchmark data like SE data in the UK, the commercial enterprise data in the US, and Hong Kong data from those NGOs that have both a welfare arm and an SE arm, and hence comparative results can be found.

In Santos' proposal, there are four elements of social entrepreneurship: sustainable solutions, logic of empowerment, positive externalities, and benefit for the powerless segments of the population. Since government funding schemes require job creation for the powerless, the logic of empowerment is already built in.

Therefore, the research questions covering the remaining three elements are:

• Are social enterprises run by NGOs and funded by the Hong Kong government as sustainable as commercial enterprises?
• Are the positive externalities generated by these social enterprises at least as cost-effective as those generated by traditional welfare approaches, or even better?
• How much positive externality benefits the powerless segment of the population, and how much positive externality benefits those not in the powerless segment?

Methodology

A pragmatic view (Creswell, 2013)[14] is taken for the strategy of inquiry, because the purpose is to criticize the prevailing tentative theory that NGOs are not good at running social enterprises. Within the pragmatism, the data are treated in a post-positive manner which is reductionistic, logical, and deterministic based on *a priori* theories. A comparative study[15] is adopted to criticize the prevailing theory. The dependent variables are the cost-effectiveness of similar social impacts and the median life spans of the social enterprise and commercial enterprise. The independent variable is whether it is a social enterprise or not. The former is the test group and the latter is the benchmark group.

The dependent variables and independent variables

The two dependent variables are the median life span and cost-effectiveness of social impact. The independent variable is the grouping – either the SE group or the benchmark group.

Since local social enterprises are not listed companies, it is difficult to get audited financial reports to check their profitability. Hence, an objective measure is the survival rate and the median life span, which are objective facts that can be observed. Self-reported profitability from social enterprise, although biased, is collected but only as supplementary data. In fact, it is even more difficult to get the audited financial reports of commercial enterprises. Though audited reports of listed companies are available, the size and complexity of SEs are not comparable.

A way to empower the powerless segments of the population is job creation. Hence, the wage taken by the employees with disabilities or socially disadvantaged employees is a good proxy for workfare, which is the intended social impact. The benchmark is the cost for generating similar workfare through the traditional welfare approach, that is, the local sheltered workshop.

Social enterprises are set up for the social mission. Sustainability is a way to increase the total social value created through their life spans. The longer the life span, the more social value is created. Sustainability is a condition for increasing social value. Sustainability can be achieved by financially breaking even through business income or a mix of business income and donations. That is, sustainability does not equal business financial breakeven. The benchmark is the survival rates or median life spans of commercial enterprises.

Research design

Table 4.1 is how the social impact and business performance of social enterprises are to be compared.

The test group comprises SEs funded by government, except item (5), which contains two SEs from the 3E Project and two SEs from the ESR Program, plus one SE which is run as a limited-by-share company by businesspeople. All of them are profitable. The purpose is to demonstrate the ratio of revenue to investment and the ratio of workfare to investment.

Table 4.1 Design of a comparative study to evaluate social enterprises

	Test Group		Benchmark Group	
Enterprise performance	1)	Median life span of SEs funded by 3E Project	2)	Comparison with US commercial enterprises on median life span
	3)	Percentage of profitable SEs funded by ESR Program	4)	Comparison with the UK on percentage of profitable SEs
Social impact	5)	Workfare/year generated by selected SEs, plus reference on selected NGOs' funding allocated to generate social impacts	8)	Comparison with Stewards[16] on cost-effectiveness on workfare generation in sheltered workshop
			9)	Comparison with UnLtd[17] on cost-effectiveness on funding social entrepreneurship
	6)	Workfare/year generated by 3E Project	10)	Comparison with the social capital project of CDA[18] on comprehensiveness of measurement of social return on investment
	7)	Workfare/year generated by ESR Program		

For item (1), the 3E Project is used for estimating the median life span because the 3E Project has data for eleven years, while the ESR Program has only five years of data. Moreover, since the survival rates of year 4 and year 5 of the two scheme is quite close, showing the 3E Project data is quite representative for the ESR data. For item (3), the 3E Project had not collected the profitability data. Only ESR has. Items (6) and (7) show the assumptions and calculations to derive the total workfare received by the disabled or socially disadvantaged over the median life span as a ratio of the one-time investment (or grant) received.

The cases in the benchmark group are selected for comparison on different aspects of the SEs.

Data collection

Median life span of social enterprises funded by the 3E Project

In August 2013, the data on the 3E Project was received from the Social Welfare Department of the Hong Kong government. The survival pattern of all the approved ventures is listed Table 4.2. Up to now seventy-six ventures were approved and seventy-five of them were set up.

Since 69 percent (52/75) of the social enterprises still survive, the median life span has to be projected from the annual "dying" trend of the SEs; especially the younger batches of SEs by referencing the trend of those with longer histories. This is done up to year 8 in Table 4.2. It is because in year 9, the size of the reference sample (i.e., the batches of 2003, 2004, and 2005) drops to 36 percent[19] of the total number of SE ventures. Hence, a more conservative dying rate[20] is used – so is the case for year 10. The resulting median life span is between

Table 4.2 The survival pattern of social enterprises funded by the 3E Project up to 2013 (HK$)

Year	Accumulative No. of Ventures	Accumulative Funding Amount Approved	Years in Operation										
			Y1	Y2	Y3	Y4	Y5	Y6	Y7	Y8	Y9	Y10	Y11
2003	10	$6,196,945	10	10	10	9	9	9	8	8	8	8	7
2004	20	$9,960,925	10	10	9	8	8	7	7	6	6	6	
2005	27	$14,084,250	7	7	7	7	7	7	7	6	6		
2006	35	$18,269,906	8	8	7	6	4	4	4	3			
2007	42	$21,723,978	7	7	7	6	6	6	5				
2008	45	$24,762,997	3	3	3	3	3	2					
2009	52	$30,355,414	7	6	5	4	3						
2010	60	$34,481,387	8	8	7	5							
2011	66	$41,104,545	6	6	6								
2012	70	$45,828,331	4	4									
2013	75	$52,346,580	5										

Table 4.3 The projected survival rate of the SEs funded by the 3E Project

Year	Y1	Y2	Y3	Y4	Y5	Y6	Y7	Y8	Y9	Y10
Survival	100%	99%	93%	81%	75%	71%	67%	59%	52%	45%

Table 4.4 Survival rates and self-sustainability rate of ESR projects

	End of Funding[22]	Year 3	Year 4	Year 5
Projects ceased	0%	13%	20%	23%
Survival rate	100%	87%	80%	77%
–Project at loss	–81%	–51%	–30%	–24%
–Project not at loss	–19%	–36%	–50%	–53%

years 9 and 10. It is calculated to be 9.3 years. This is not the actual median of survival years but the best available estimate (Miller, 1985)[21] based on those ventures with long histories (see Table 4.3).

Percentage of profitable social enterprises funded by the ESR Program

In 2013, the ESR team in the Home Affairs Department of the Hong Kong government provided their 2012 survey data, as shown in Table 4.4. ESR was approved in 2006, hence the longest duration of operation is only five years. The start dates of the social enterprises were aligned.

The survival rate at the fifth year of projects is 77 percent, of which 24 percent is at loss and 53 percent is either breakeven or profitable. Since the survival rates in years 4 (80 percent) and 5 (77 percent) are very close to that of 3E's years 4 (81 percent) and 5 (75 percent), and the contexts of these two schemes are very similar, it is assumed that the median life span of ESR is similar to that of 3E at 9.3 years.

As a reference, in the Hong Kong Council of Social Services 2013 report, a sample of 48 SEs out of the total of 406 surviving SEs, 24 of them indicated profitability and the other 24 indicated loss. However, the sample contains surviving SEs with varying years in operation.

Comparison with US commercial enterprises on median life span

In the US, 70 percent of new commercial firms survive by the end of their second year and 50 percent survive by the end of their fourth year (Barringer & Ireland, 2010).[23] Hence, the median life expectancy of commercial firms is four years. In another survey, only 40 percent of commercial firms survived after six years, and only 18 percent after ten years (Marcum & Smith, 2002).[24] Hence, the median life span is also less than six years.

Comparison with the UK on percentage of profitable SEs

According to a 2013 report[25] by Social Enterprise UK, 55 percent of the social enterprises were profitable, 18 percent breakeven, and 22 percent at a loss; 5 percent did not respond. But the sample contain only surviving SEs and with varying years in operation.

Workfare generated by selected social enterprises

The following are data obtained from four individual social enterprise organizations, which operate a total twenty-two SEs, 5 percent of the total SE population (see Table 4.5). The percentages of the annual revenue on total investment and the percentages of the annual workfare on total investment are listed. The median revenue on investment is 324 percent by taking the average between Stewards and HKTS (Hong Kong Translingual Service), which rank second and third in the numbers.

As a reference, the percentages of the income of the charities allocated to the service programs are collected from iDonate,[26] a charity rating agency. Examples of big charity organizations which have to publicize their financials and do not have significant business income are Oxfam, which spent 80 percent of its total expenditure on service programs, World Vision 95 percent, MSF (Medicines sans Frontiers) 80 percent, and Community Chest, which only allocates 82 percent of the donation income to other charities, after deducting its own overhead. The median of these four organizations is 81 percent.

Table 4.5 Ratio of revenue on investment and ratio of workfare on investment

Name of SE Organization	Years in Operation	Funding Source	Investment (HKD, 000)	Revenue (HKD, 000)	Workfare (HKD, 000)
Number of SE Units			Investment/ Investment	Revenue/ Investment	Workfare/ Investment
Mental care, 14	11	3E Project grant + donation	11,570 100%	70,700 611%	6,860 59%
HKTS, 1	3	ESR Program grant	700 100%	2,700 **386%**	1,170 167%
Stewards, 6	9	3E Project grant + donation	2,510 100%	6,580 **262%**	2,730 109%
My concept, 1	6	ESR Program grant + donation	1,300 100%	1,700 131%	430 33%
Total, 22 units				Median 324%	

Workfare generated by the 3E Project

The social mission of the ESR Project is to enhance the employment of people with disabilities. The main component of workfare (work-to-welfare) is the wage, which is a good proxy for the social impact. First, it can be monetized to calculate the ratio between the investment and the social impact. Second, it is much better than using the number of employees, as most SEs cannot provide the full-time-equivalent (FTE) number of part-time employees. In 2013, there were 541 disabled employed with an average income of HK$6,245/month; the total workfare is HK$40,542,540/year.[27]

As the total amount granted to the seventy-five ventures was $52,364,580, each dollar granted generates workfare valued at 77.4 cents/year.[28] In short, each dollar granted will lead to $7.2[29] over the median life span of 9.3 years. The social return on investment (SROI) of the 3E funding is very good.

Workfare generated by the ESR Program

The social mission of the 3E Project is to enhance the self-reliance of socially disadvantaged (SD) people through employment. Hence the concept is also workfare. Up to 2012, there have been 144 projects funded with HK$156 million. Half of them had responded to the survey. The 144 ESR projects employ 2,370 people, of which 604 employees are full-time and the remaining 1,766 are part-time. These numbers include 2,064 SDs, of which 368 are full-time and 1,696 are part-time.

A proxy of the workfare is the wage earned by the SDs. Though we use the wage as a proxy, the actual values received by the SD are more than money, but "a dignified way of living", as recalled by Fisher. At present the total annual workfare to the 2,064 SDs is HK$64 million. The accumulated ESR grant is HK$156 million. That means that each ESR grant dollar leads to 41 cents of SD wage. In 9.3 years, the total workfare generated is 3.81 dollars.[30]

The ratio in six years of ESR is 0.41 and that in twelve years 3E is 0.77. The level of workfare for the same dollar of investment will grow over the years. It is because the level of workfare is proportional to the business revenue, which in turn is a function of the years of operation due to the learning curve of the business knowledge and the accumulation of the customer base. The Social Enterprise UK survey[31] also reported the revenue of social enterprises with different ranges of years in operation. The longer the years of operation, the bigger he size of the revenue (see Table 4.6).

Table 4.6 The correlation between the revenue size and years of operation

Years of Operation of the SEs	<3 Years	4–5 Years	6–11 Years	>11 Years
Medium annual revenue size	£ 44,000	£ 89,000	£ 205,000	£ 360,000

Comparison with Stewards on workfare generated in sheltered workshops

In 2009, Stewards commissioned a comparative study from KEEP Consulting Ltd[32] on the SROI of the two sheltered workshops and that of their five social enterprises, such as catering service in schools and car beauty service with the purpose for providing job opportunity for disadvantaged groups.

Sheltered workshops aim to provide persons with disabilities with appropriate vocational training and enhance their working capacity in order that they can move on to supported or open employment. Various training and activities are provided to them, such as training in work habits, training allowance, and activities to meet the services users' developmental/social needs. In this study, focus is on the comparison of the workfare between the sheltered workshop and the social enterprise because they are "numerically comparable" on the economic impact to the society.

In the first sheltered workshop, for $1/year of workfare, the ongoing funding needed was $6.4/year. In the second workshop, the funding needed was $5.0/year. At that time, the portfolio of SEs consisted of some profitable ones and some at losses. But the overall number was still at loss. For $1/year of workfare, Stewards had to inject $1.7/year to maintain all social enterprises. Therefore, the cost to maintain the same amount of workfare is less through social enterprises. The ratio between sheltered workshop and the SEs was $5.0 to $1.7.

After the comparison, Stewards tuned its social enterprises portfolio based on the blended return on investment, which consisted of two measures: the financial return and the workfare (as the social impact). Both of them can be expressed in dollar value.

For continuous improvement of the enterprise, Stewards closed down those social enterprises with negative BROI and shifted the people and resources to other social enterprises. After the tuning, the portfolio was still at a loss at the first place. But within months, for $1/year of workfare the funding needed to cover the loss significantly reduced to $0.7/year. The ratio between sheltered workshop and the SEs was widened to $5.0 to $0.7.

Later, the profitability of portfolios of social enterprises was turned around. The portfolio is self-sustainable financially. Now for $1/year of workfare, Stewards does not need to inject funding. The ratio between sheltered workshop and the SEs is $5.0 to $0.0. Moreover, each dollar of investment in SEs generates $2.79 of annual revenue, and $1.08 workfare/year. [33]

Comparison with UnLtd on cost-effectiveness of funding SEs

UnLtd[34] is a charity founded in 2000 for developing social entrepreneurs. It was selected as a reference because it provides insights on the difference between a charity and an SE.

One of its programs, the Higher Education Funding Council for England (HEFCE) (UnLtd, 2013),[35] reveals its operation data. It partnered with 70 higher education institutions (HEIs) to realize the potential of social entrepreneurship. Out of the £1 million total cost, £625,000 was given out as awards to 200 students and HEI staff to set up 200 social ventures. There were 191 awardees at level 1 with a startup fund amounting to £2,500 (HK$30,200). The most promising 5 percent (i.e., 9 persons) were awarded at level 2 with a scale-up fund amounted £15,000 (HK$181,200). The most popular businesses included:

- Training local people and raising aspirations of young people under eighteen, both of which helped to increase access to higher education.
- Services to students within their HEIs to improve their experience and success.
- Creating volunteer opportunities to improve students' employability prospects.

The average awarded amount is £3,125. From their business, they generated an additional £5,800 income. Each has 540 beneficiaries, which means 540 customers paying £5,800 for services which cost £8,925.[36]

The HEFCE program used £1 million to develop 200 awardees, each costing £5,000 (HK$60,400/person). As most could not break even, they were at-loss businesses which were not generating positive externalities for the powerless people but benefiting the students and HEI staff. As a result of these entrepreneurship experiences, 90 percent of awardees felt better able to run a social venture and they intended to continue.

As a reference, the 2012 the total expenditure of UnLtd[37] is shown in Table 4.7. Since there were 1,000 awardees, the average cost per awardee was £8,764 (HK$106,000), of which only 37 percent was directly to go to the awardees. Since 2000, there have been at least 7,000 awardees. If its survival rate is similar to the 3E Project, close to 5,000 of their ventures should still exit. Unfortunately, the survival data cannot be found on its website.

Comparison with the Community Development Association on SROI measurement

The Community Development Association (CDA) is a small NGO which had a social capital project in Hong Kong's Tin Siu Wai called Dawn Market in 2008 to 2012. Oxfam Hong Kong had provided HK$1.5 million over three years to fund CDA's effort to help the marginalized families in Tin Shui Wai. The services

Table 4.7 Breakdown of 2012 UnLtd expenditure

Cost of Supports to Awardees	Awards	Cost of Fund Generation	Governance	Trading Activities in Subsidiary	Total Expenditure
£5,010,253	£3,268,496	£127,692	£121,531	£79,122	£8,764,059

of CDA to those families soon evolved from assistance to getting welfare supports and counseling only to helping them increase family incomes through being hawkers in main pedestrian paths in the district, which was not intended for commercial activities. The number of hawkers increased from around twenty in 2008 to more than eighty in 2012. The average income per hawker increased from HK$126/day to HK$253/day. By the end of 2013, the Hong Kong government had built a new market in another location in the same district to house all these hawkers.

The accumulative results of this CDA project over three years in the Donald Kirkpatrick[38] model are as follows.

- Cost: The total financial input is the HK$1.5 million from Oxfam.
- Cost: Volunteers contributed 5,040 man-hours: 144 man-hours from two scholars, 1,440 man-hours from five social workers, and 3,456 man-hours from other volunteers.
- Level 1 Satisfaction: The overall current life satisfaction is 3.61 on a scale of 1 to 5, with 5 being the best. When asking the hawkers to assess their life satisfaction before being hawkers, the average satisfaction was 2.40.
- Level 2 Knowledge: The overall median daily income increased from HK$126/day to HK$253/day. This was echoed by their self-assessment on business knowledge improvement from 2.6 to 4.5 on a scale of 1 to 5.
- Level 3 Behaviour: The median on number of new good friends is 9.94, of which they can ask 2.26 friends to borrow a sum of money equal to the hawkers' monthly income.

	Receive from Others	*Provide to Others*
Help between good friends	87.5%	83.3%
Helps on taking care of the "shop"	79.2%	75.0%
Initiate chats	62.5%	62.5%
Borrow goods or tools	37.5%	25.0%
Ask to help buy things	25.0%	12.5%

- Level 4 Impact: The total income of the hawkers over three years was HK$8.9 million, the residents' benefit from the lower prices of the hawkers was HK$1.3 million, and the possible saving of government CSSA cost was HK$3.7 million.

A point to note is that in an SE project, SE organization is the primary driver of the social impact and financial impact. But in this social capital project, CDA's role was that of a trigger and enabler. The financial impact was driven by the hawkers themselves.

Discussion

The data collected are summarized and organized in the Table 4.8.

Table 4.8 Results of the comparative study to evaluate social enterprises

	Test Group		Benchmark Group	
Enterprise performance	1)	Median life span of SEs funded by the 3E Project is 9.3 years.	3)	Median life span of the US commercial enterprises is four years. This matches another survey in which the median is less than six years.
	2)	At the fifth year, 53% of social enterprises funded by the ESR Program self-reported as profitable. If those ceased in operation are taken out from the denominator, the percentage is 66%. By the way, the more years in operation, the higher the likelihood of being profitable.	4)	Profitability of SEs in the UK was 73%. The denominator does not include those that already ceased to operate.
Social impact	5)	The median annual revenue of the four selected SEs is 386%, and the median annual workfare is 64%. In the four selected major NGOs in Hong Kong, for each $1 of donation or grant received, $0.81 is used in service programs, including direct benefits to the beneficiaries and administrative costs of the specific service program.	8)	In Stewards, $1/year of workfare required at least $5/ year of grant or donation. That is $0.2 workfare/ year for $1/ year of grant or donation. But the benefits received by the beneficiaries are more than $0.2, such as the welfare supports and counselling services to the beneficiaries and their families.
	6)	Workfare/year generated is $0.41/year/dollar granted by ESR, which is in operation for 6 years. Assuming the median life span is the same as 3E, the total workfare over 9.3 years is $3.8 workfare/ year for $1 of one-time grant.	9)	The expenditure of UnLtd in 2012 was £8,607,094 for 1,000 award recipients. That means the average expenditure per recipient was £8,607 (HK$103,972). The actual money to the awardees was £3,268,496, i.e., 37% of the total cost.
	7)	Workfare/year generated is $0.77/year/dollar granted by 3E, which is in operation for 11 years. So the total workfare over 9.3 years is $7.2 workfare/year for $1 of one-time grant	10)	In CDA, a more comprehensive measurement covering monetized impacts, behavioural statistics, skills improvement reflected by income changes, and pre and post overall satisfaction score.

Social enterprises have much longer median life span than commercial enterprises

The median life span of SEs is about double that of commercial enterprises in the US. So, they have a relatively much better sustainability (see Table 4.9). The better business of SEs as compared with commercial enterprises was also found

Table 4.9 Comparison of revenue growth between SEs and SMEs in the UK

	% of Social Enterprises	% of Small-Medium Enterprises
Revenue increased in past twelve months	38%	29%
Revenue decreased in past twelve months	22%	31%

Table 4.10 Correlation between revenue size and years of operation

Years of Operation of the SEs	<3 Years	4–5 Years	6–11 Years	>11 Years
Medium annual revenue size	£ 44,000	£ 89,000	£ 205,000	£ 360,000

in the Social Enterprise UK 2013 survey.[39] It shows that SEs have higher revenue growth rates compared with small to medium-sized enterprises (SMEs). A possible explanation is the bigger social capital owned by SEs. Because the primary motive of social entrepreneurs is to generate benefits for the powerless people instead of for themselves, their selflessness earns the respect and voluntary support from others.

Moreover, if a SE is at loss, but the amount of loss is still less than the cost for delivering similar social impact, then the existence of the social enterprise is still worthwhile and the SE is kept. The case of Stewards which compares the two approaches shows the superiority of the SE approach, as long as for those only mildly mentally handicapped.

The social return on investment of social enterprises is well justified

The SROI of the ESR Program is about 380 percent, which means $3.8 per $1 granted, as calculated by the average annual workfare generated times the median life span.[40] The SROI of the 3E Project is about 720 percent.[41] The difference in the two SROIs is due to the difference in workfare. The 3E Project has a higher one because annual workfare is proportional to annual revenue, which in turn is affected by years of business experience and accumulation of customer a base.

The Social Enterprise UK survey[42] also reported the revenue of social enterprises with different ranges of years in operation. The more years of operation, the bigger the size of the revenue (see Table 4.10).

The traditional welfare approach operates in a subtraction equation. The resource allocated to the service program is the money input minus the overheads. So in the best case, one dollar becomes 81 cents only. But the SE approach operates in a multiplication equation due to the business operation. The money input will be multiplied to become the annual revenue, and not once but for years again and again. So one dollar becomes 7.2 dollars over 9.3 years.

Comparison between the 3E Project and UnLtd on cost-effectiveness in funding SEs

The similarities between UnLtd and the 3E Project include the following.

- Both started around 2001.
- Both are funders of social entrepreneurship ventures.
- Both have measures to support the grantees.

The differences between them are as follows.

- The 3E Project focuses on the beneficiaries of the SEs funded, with a very specific requirement that the beneficiaries should be the people with disabilities. UnLtd focuses on the potential social entrepreneurs and only has a generic social mission requirement.
- The average cost per grant of the 3E Project is more than ten times the UnLtd award, but the average number of grant/year of the 3E Project is only 7 while that of UnLtd is 1,000.
- The sustainability of the ventures funded by the 3E Project is much better than UnLtd.
- The 3E Project collects data about social impact, which is the level 4 measure of the Donald Kirkpatrick[43] model, while UnLtd is the lower three levels, as show in Table 4.11.

Table 4.11 Comparison between UnLtd's 2009–11 HEFCE Program and the ESR Program

Measure	UnLtd's HEFCE	3E Project
Level 4: Impact	Create 2 paid jobs, and 12 volunteer jobs, and sell to 540 clients for a total of £5,800.	Generate HK$540,567/year of workfare to 7.2 disabled employees, over 9.3 years
Level 3: Behaviour	After three years, 76% of the ventures still exist.	After three years, 93% of the ventures still exist.
	No data on survival rate after five years.	After five years, 75% still exist.
Level 2: Learning	No data	No data
Level 1: Reaction	Ninety percent feel better able to run SE.	No data
	Eighty percent intend to run the SE after graduation; 62% feel better in leadership skills.	
Cost	Each get £3,125 (HK$37,750) on average,	Each SE granted HK$697,941 on average.
	or cost £5,000 (HK$60,400)[44] if included overhead cost.	No data on the 3E Project overhead cost.

Conclusion

The better cost-effectiveness of SE echoed J. A. Banks, who defined social entrepreneurship in 1972 and emphasized the "managerial" skill as the main driver of the intended results.

The SE funding schemes of the Hong Kong government performs very well in meeting their objectives as reflected by the SROI. It is because unlike the traditional welfare approach, which has a subtraction effect on the funding due to overhead costs, SE has the multiplying effect from the revenue-generating business, which in turn leads to workfare provided to the disabled or socially disadvantaged year after year.

One of the grantees of the 3E Project is Stewards, which had a favourable evaluation on the cost-effectiveness of its SEs as compared with its sheltered workshop in workfare generation. While a sheltered workshop needs injection of funding as long as it is in operation, SE has the opportunity of breakeven, and no more funding is required, while the operation still keeps going. The limitation is that SE can only handle those people with minor disabilities only.

On the other hand, though both the 3E Project and UnLtd fund social entrepreneurial ventures, they cannot be compared, as the focus of UnLtd is developing social entrepreneurs, not social enterprises. Since the cost per award is close to the price of self-funded masters degree programs, UnLtd's effectiveness is better compared with the mindset changes, knowledge gained, and new behaviour developed of a formal education program.

Finally, this chapter demonstrates a way to evaluate the SROI of the SEs in two funding schemes of the Hong Kong Government, together with the survival trend of about 200 SEs over ten years of operation, and change of the mix consisted of those SEs ceased, those profitable, and those still at a loss. The assumptions and estimations in deriving the results are listed so that future research can improve them to get more accurate results. It also argues against prevailing theories or opinions in conferences, media, and the public impression that NGOs funded by government are not good at running SEs. Finally, though the number and sizes of SEs are smaller compared with the UK and some developed countries, the ecosystem developed in Hong Kong is a forerunner in terms of the SE performance and the way to measure the performance.

Recommendation

Many evaluation methods have been proposed for SEs. Actually, the trick is how to monetize the intangible social benefits. In business, similar problems on monetizing intangible benefits were encountered during the days of Total Quality Management (TQM) in the 1980s. Hence, the job should borrow the knowledge from multinationals with rich practical experience in the rhetoric articulating TQM benefits.

The case of CDA demonstrates a more comprehensive way to reflect the social impacts of SEs, based on the Kirkpatrick model, covering affective, cognitive, behavioural, and financial dimensions. In fact, CDA had also collected narratives from the hawkers in its qualitative study, together with the surveys to quantify the changes, and the monetized impacts. CDA set an example of communicating the social impact.

Notes

1 Hong Kong Council of Social Services (2013), *2013 Social Enterprise Directory.*
2 Chan, K. K. Allan; Chen, Y. Y. Amy; and Young, N. Michael (2010), *Social Enterprises for a New Age: Six Case Studies in China,* Hong Kong Baptist University, pp. 11–12.
3 Chan, K. K. Allan; Chen, Y. Y. Amy; and Young, N. Michael (2010), *Social Enterprises for a New Age: Six Case Studies in China,* Hong Kong Baptist University, p. 15.
4 Tang, Kwong-Leung; Fung, Ho-Lup; Au, Y. F. Kevin; Lee, Kin-ching James; and Ko, S. F. Lisanne (2008), *Social Enterprise in Hong Kong: Toward a Conceptual Model,* Central Policy Unit of the Government of the Hong Kong Special Administration Region of the People's Republic of China, pp. xiv–xv.
5 Social Enterprise UK (2013), *The People's Business: The State of Social Enterprise Survey 2013*, p. 26.
6 Banks, J.A. (1972), *The Sociology of Social Movements*, London: Macmillan, p. 53.
7 Dees, J Gregory (1998, revised in 2001), *The Meaning of "Social Entrepreneurship".*
8 Dees, J. Gregory and Anderson B. Beth (2006), "Framing a theory of Social Entrepreneurship: Building in Two Schools of Practice and Thought", *REDF*, can be retrieved on 22 August 2013 from http://www.redf.org/from-the-community/publications/457.
9 Mair, Johanna; Battilana, Julie; and Cardenas, Julian (2012), "Organizing for Society: A Typology of Social Entrepreneuring Models", *Journal of Business Ethics* (2012) 111: 353–373.
10 Massetti, Brenda (2011), "The Duality of Social Enterprise: A Framework for Social Action", *Review of Business*, Vol. 33, No. 1.
11 Filipe M. Santos (2012), "A Positive Theory of Social Entrepreneurship", *Journal of Business Ethics*, 111: 335–351.
12 Kamler, Barbara; and Thomson, Pat (2006) *Helping Doctoral Students Write: Pedagogies for Supervision*, Oxon: Routledge, p. 4. What we do not know well enough to even ask about or care about are blind spots. What we know enough to question but not answer are blank spots.
13 Mills, C. Wright (1959, 2000), *The Sociological Imagination*, Oxford: Oxford University Press, p. 76.
14 Creswell, John (2013), *Research Design: Qualitative, Quantitative, and Mixed Methods Approach* (4th Ed.), Los Angeles: SAGE, pp. 10–11.
15 Creswell, John (2013), *Research Design: Qualitative, Quantitative, and Mixed Methods Approach* (4th Ed.), Los Angeles: SAGE, p. 12.
16 Stewards, http://www.stewards.org.hk/index_en1.php
17 UnLtd, http://unltd.org.uk/
18 "CDA" is Community Development Association, which is a small NGO with only two social workers as employees.
19 The total number of ventures is 75. The sample sizes for calculating the overall annual dying rate are: 70 samples in the second year, 66 in the third year, 60 in the fourth year, 52 in the fifth year, 45 in the sixth year, 42 in the seventh year, 35 in the eighth year, and 27 in the ninth year over the total 75 ventures, which means 27/75 = 36 percent sampling rate only.
20 The annual dying rates are: second year 98.6 percent, third year 93.8 percent, fourth year 87.3 percent, fifth year 93.0 percent, sixth year 94.6 percent, seventh year 93.9 percent, and eighth year 88.5 percent. Hence, the worst annual dying rate is 87.3 percent.

This rate is used to estimate survival rate for the ninth year, which is 52 percent, the tenth year is 45 percent, and the eleventh year is 39 percent. So the median is between the ninth and tenth years.

21 Miller, David (1985), *Popper Selection*, Princeton, p. 30: "We do not know, we only guess . . . if you criticize my guess, and if you offer counterproposals, I in turn will try to criticize them".

22 In year 2011, the Funding Period of ESR was changed from two years to three years. Hence, the data in the column "End of Funding" include both projects with two years of Funding Periods and projects with three years of Funding Periods. However, since the survey was in 2013, the data in the column "Two Years after [Funding]" were all at their fourth years, and the last column were all at their fifth years or even longer.

23 Barringer, Bruce; and Ireland, Duane (2010, 3rd edition), *Entrepreneurship: Successfully Launching New Ventures*, Upper Saddle River, NJ: Prentice Hall.

24 Marcum, Dave; and Smith, Steve (2002), *businessThink: Rules for Getting It Right – Now and No Matter What!*, New York: Wiley.

25 Social Enterprise UK (2013), *The People's Business: The State of Social Enterprise Survey 2013*, p. 30.

26 The website of iDonate is http://www.theidonate.com/

27 Five hundred forty-one disabled employed with an average income of $6,245/month. Hence the total workfare is 541 disabled × $6,245/month × 12 months = $40,542,540/year.

28 $40,542,540 / $52,364,580 = 77.4%.

29 77.4 cents/year × 9.3 years = 7.2 dollars.

30 Calculated by $0.41 × 7.2 years = $2.95.

31 Social Enterprise UK (2013), *The People's Business: The State of Social Enterprise Survey 2013*, p. 16.

32 KEEP Consulting's website http://www.keep-consulting.com/index.html

33 This part of the chapter was extracted from *FSES Research Report 2013 August*, "SROI of 3E of SWD" by Kee, Chi-Hing; and Chiu, Jimmy.

34 The website of UnLtd is http://unltd.org.uk/

35 The HEFCE program is documented in a report "Unlocking the Potential of Social Entrepreneurship in Higher Education", which as of 25 August 2013 could be retrieved from http://unltd.org.uk/wp-content/uploads/2012/11/Unlocking-the-potential-of-social-entrepreneurship-in-HE.pdf

36 £3,125 +, £5,800 = £8,925, i.e., HK$114,240.

37 The UnLtd 2012 Report can be retrieved on 26 August 2013 from http://unltd.org.uk/wp-content/uploads/2012/07/UnLtdAnnualReview_2012_no_crops_compressed.pdf

38 Wikipedia on "Donald Kirkpatrick", can be retrieved from http://en.wikipedia.org/wiki/Donald_Kirkpatrick

39 Social Enterprise UK (2013), *The People's Business: The State of Social Enterprise Survey 2013*, p. 16.

40 For the ESR Program, average annual workfare is $0.41. The median life span used is 9.3 years.

41 For the 3E Project, average annual workfare is $0.77. The median life span is 9.3 years.

42 Social Enterprise UK (2013), *The People's Business: The State of Social Enterprise Survey 2013*, p. 16.

43 Wikipedia on "Donald Kirkpatrick", can be retrieved from http://en.wikipedia.org/wiki/Donald_Kirkpatrick

44 For HEFCE, the cost for each award is about the price of an average self-funded masters degree provided by universities in Hong Kong. But it does not seriously assess the knowledge gained like a formal education.

References

Barringer, Bruce, & Ireland, Duane (2010). *Entrepreneurship: Successfully Launching New Ventures*, 3rd edition. Upper Saddle River, NJ: Prentice Hall.

Chan, K. K. Allan, Chen, Y. Y. Amy, & Young, N. Michael (2010). *Social Enterprises for a New Age: Six Case Studies in China.* Hong Kong: Baptist University.

Creswell, John (2013). *Research Design: Qualitative, Quantitative, and Mixed Methods Approaches*, 4th edition. Los Angeles: SAGE.

Dees, J. Gregory, & Anderson B. Beth (2006). "Framing a Theory of Social Entrepreneurship: Building in Two Schools of Practice and Thought", *REDF*, http://www.redf.org/from-the-community/publications/457, accessed 22 August 2013.

Filipe, M. Santos (2012). "A Positive Theory of Social Entrepreneurship", *Journal of Business Ethics*, 111: 335–351.

Kamler, Barbara, & Thomson, Pat (2006). *Helping Doctoral Students Write: Pedagogies for Supervision*. Oxon: Routledge.

Mair, Johanna, Battilana, Julie, & Cardenas, Julian (2012). "Organizing for Society: A Typology of Social Entrepreneuring Models", *Journal of Business Ethics*, 111: 353–373.

Marcum, Dave, & Smith, Steve (2002). *BusinessThink: Rules for Getting It Right – Now and No Matter What!* New York: Wiley.

Massetti, Brenda (2011). "The Duality of Social Enterprise: A Framework for Social Action", *Review of Business*, 33(1): 50–64.

Miller, David (1985). *Popper Selections*, Princeton University Press, p. 30: "We do not know, we only guess . . . if you criticize my guess, and if you offer counterproposals, I in turn will try to criticize them.

Mills, C. Wright (1959, 2000). *The Sociological Imagination*. Oxford: Oxford University Press.

Villenueve-Smith, F., & Chung, C. (2013). The People's Business: The State of Social Enterprise Survey 2013. Social Enterprise UK. Downloaded from: http://www.socialenterprise.org.uk/uploads/files/2013/07/the_peoples_business.pdf (accessed 8 January 2016).

Tang, Kwong-Leung, Fung, Ho-Lup, Au, Y. F. Kevin, Lee, Kin-ching James, and Ko, S. F. Lisanne (2008). *Social Enterprise in Hong Kong: Toward a Conceptual Model,* Central Policy Unit of the Government of the Hong Kong Special Administration Region of the People's Republic of China.

UnLtd (2012). "Unlocking the Potential of Social Entrepreneurship in Higher Education", http://unltd.org.uk/wp-content/uploads/2012/11/Unlocking-the-potential-of-social-entrepreneurship-in-HE.pdf, accessed 25 August 2013.

UnLtd (2012). http://unltd.org.uk/wp-content/uploads/2012/07/UnLtdAnnualReview_2012_no_crops_compressed.pdf, accessed 26 August 2013.

5 Public policy measures and promotion of social enterprises in Taiwan

Yu-Yuan Kuan and Shu-Twu Wang

Introduction

Since the beginning of the 1990s, Taiwanese society has experienced rapid transformation in politics, economy, population structure and social needs in the last two decades; various non-profit organizations (NPOs) had thus flourished under such circumstances. Yet, due to the resource competitions among different organizations, as well as the government's incentives to attract NPOs to assist her to respond to the severe unemployment and perplexed social issues, many Taiwanese NPOs have attempted to start up social enterprises (SEs) to realize social philanthropic practices and develop these organizations in accordance with the market and industry needs. Such ideas have existed in both concepts and practices, as several NPOs have emerged in the early 1990s and adopted business or venture approaches to operate, such as the bakeries and restaurants operated by the Children Are Us Foundation, the wheelchair business operated by the Eden Social Welfare Foundation, the car wash and gas stations operated by the Sunshine Social Welfare Foundation, the restaurants, gas stations, key-in services and glaze factory operated by the Taipei Victory Potential Development Centre for the Disabled, sales of books and cards on wilderness and paid eco-tours operated by the Society of Wilderness, and so on.

The term "social enterprise" has been widely discussed in the social and public arena in Taiwan. In the mainstream discourse, the goals of social enterprises include creation of employment and related training opportunities, which are especially important for so-called marginalized people (those who risk falling into poverty, the disadvantaged or physically disabled; see Kuan, Chen, Lu, & Wang, 2012). Since the 1990s, the idea of de- institutionalization has been incorporated into the social care policies prompted by the European welfare states, the emphasis being on community care and design policies that will drive the society to accept more minority groups to join the workforce and diminish social exclusions with paid training or all forms of short-term/ long-term employment opportunities. The functions of such a welfare participation model will not only increase the incomes and resources of the marginalized groups, but also enhance their social experiences and confidence and develop their working skills, which will encourage the mainstream society to accept and include them (Defourny, 2001).

Kuan (2007) indicated that the factors that led to the emergence of the social enterprises in Taiwan included: (1) the response to social needs; (2) the search for financial stability and autonomy; (3) the promptness of the privatization and purchase of social welfare services; (4) government's policy incentives and grants; and (5) the increasing interest in the practice of corporate social responsibility (CSR). Moreover, the activities of social enterprise in Taiwan include the following five categories: (1) affirmative (or work-integrated) business; (2) local community development business; (3) service provision and product sales; (4) venture capital business; and (5) social cooperatives. Each of the social enterprises mentioned above has its specific organizational characteristics and target groups. For instance, the organizations that are engaged in local community development aim to assist the local communities to develop their cultures and business, while the affirmative businesses[1] tend to focus on solving the unemployment issues for those who are socially excluded. The venture capital businesses, on the other hand, stress use of the ventures and profits of the for-profit enterprises to support the philanthropic activities of NPOs. However, the characteristics and components of these five types of social enterprises do not contradict one another; there could be certain characteristics that are shared among several types of social enterprises.

One of the major factors that could explain the rise of social enterprises in Taiwan would be the various policy measures adopted by the Taiwanese government (Chan, Kuan, & Wang, 2011; Kuan, 2007; Kuan & Wang, 2010a, 2010b). For example, Kuan and Wang (2010a, 2010b) indicated that though the Taiwanese government did not enact specific laws for regulating the formation and operation of social enterprises, there indeed exist certain laws and decrees that lure and encourage non-profits to engage in social enterprise activities. For example, the Law for Protecting the Disabled People stipulates: "The cost of goods produced and services provided by all institutions or organizations for disabled people and shelter workshops must be reasonable and kept low. All levels of government agencies, public schools, public utilities agencies receiving government grants, institutions, and private schools are called on to prioritize the abovementioned groups in making their purchases." This method mandates that all levels of government agencies, public schools, public utility organizations and other institutions put the NPOs that mainly provide services to the disabled people at the top of their list of suppliers, and at least 5 percent of the total purchases must be acquired from them. This particular decree encouraged certain non-profits to establish their own social enterprises. As a consequence, part of this policy contributed to offering many opportunities to establish social enterprises for those NPOs that provide services for the disabled people.

In addition, from the end of the 1990s till now, Taiwan's public sector, in an effort to alleviate the social impacts of rising unemployment rates, began to roll out relevant policies like the Social Welfare Industrialization Policy, the Multi-Employment Service Program launched by the Council of Labour Affairs (CLA),[2] and the Industrialization of Long-Term Care Services jointly launched by the Council for Economic Development, the Health Department and the Social

Affairs authority.[3] As a result, many NPOs started to incorporate for-profit, commercial activities into their regular operating plans. This approach in essence is similar to the social economy and social enterprise policies launched in continental Europe (Kuan, 2007).

In accordance with the discussion above, this chapter intends to address the roles and functions of the Taiwanese government in promoting the development of social enterprises along with an analysis of how the recent public policy measures prompted by the Taiwanese government have impacted the development of social enterprises. As for the empirical data utilized for analysis, this chapter will include the results obtained from the three waves of surveys conducted by the authors on social enterprises in Taiwan (Kuan, 2007; Kuan & Lu, 2004; Kuan & Wang, 2010a, 2010b; Kuan et al., 2012)[4] and analyze the roles and functions of the Taiwanese government in social enterprise development with the perspectives provided by the interviewed organizations (Chan et al., 2007; Kuan, Chan, & Wang, 2011; Kuan & Wang, 2013). Afterwards, the analysis will be given to how it has happened that public policy measures on helping social enterprises in Taiwan have been transformed gradually in recent years from not only sustaining to provide grants for personnel expenditures but also to the provision of educational programs and consulting services, etc.

Theoretical frame – institutional theory

Theoretically thinking, the development of social enterprises has undergone a close relationship with its political context, especially the institutional changes in the environment, which will profoundly affect the operational efficiency of NPOs' engagement in the activities of social enterprises. According to the perspectives of institutional theory, an organization's life chances are improved greatly by organizational demonstrations of conformity to the norms and social expectations existing in the institutional environment (Meyer & Rowan, 1977). Consequently, NPOs engaged in the operation of social enterprises are not able to remain outside the public policy circumstances. In addition, as for the actual situation of the current social environment, the government is not only the largest funder for many non-profit organizations, but also the most important institutional actor with its laws and legal mandates (Guo, 2005).

The debate on NPOs' involvement in the operation of social enterprises is of great significance. On the one hand, the operation of social enterprise is based on the legitimacy of the legal structure; on the other hand, it is attracted by various incentives provided by the government's related policies, which then results in the financial stability for NPOs and their input of resources into the operation of social enterprise. For instance, the former emphasizes that social cooperatives in Italy have confined their operations strictly on the legal requirement, underscoring that cooperatives must operate "in the general interest of community and for the social integration of citizens" (Borzaga & Santuari, 2000). The latter may take into account the financial incentives offered by the government, for instance, by utilizing outsourcing as a way of bringing in the government's authority to ensure social enterprise in the provision of products and services. In western Europe, as Kerlin (2009) indicates, the importance of such societal support through public subsidies or public contracts, as well as through private donation and volunteer work, may lead non-profit providers to develop social enterprises.

Kerlin (2006: 254–256) further argues that the institutional environments for social enterprise in the United States and western Europe tend to reflect a focus more on private business in America and a focus more on government and social service in Europe. In western Europe, the institutional environment for strategic support of social enterprise is much more tied to government and the European Union's support. Though the first wave of European social enterprises emerged without any specific public support, the 1990s saw the emergence of the development of specific public schemes in many countries. Government support includes new legislation and the coordination and policy work of specific public authorities and programs. In a word, "social enterprises are embedded in the political context. Public policies in the field of social enterprises are the result of interactions between their promoters and representatives of public bodies." The dynamic of institutionalization "could lead to the development of innovative public schemes and at the same time to a movement of 'isomorphism' on the part of social enterprises, towards public organizations or for-profit enterprises" (Nyssens, 2006: 319).

Social enterprises in Taiwan – role of government

In this section, based on the empirical data obtained from the three surveys on the social enterprises in Taiwan (Kuan, 2007; Kuan & Lu, 2004; Kuan & Wang, 2010a, 2010b; Kuan et al., 2012), we are going to analyze the roles and functions of the Taiwanese government in the development of social enterprises with the perspectives provided by the interviewed organizations.

Income resources of social enterprises

The result of the 2006 survey (Chan et al., 2007) revealed that the major income resources of SEs in Taiwan were "grants and commission fees from the government" (100 percent), followed by "public donation" (88.1 percent), "sale of products and services" (76.2 percent) and "membership fees" (57.7 percent). In 2010 (Kuan, Chan, & Wang, 2011), 77.2 percent of the SEs in Taiwan indicated that their income came from grants and commission fees from the government, followed by sale of products and services (70.2 percent), public donation (30.7 percent) and membership fees (22.8 percent). In 2013 (Kuan & Wang, 2013), 80 percent of the SEs received their income from grants and commission fees from the government, followed by sale of products and services (70.9 percent), public donation (40 percent) and membership fees (20.9 percent) (see Figure 5.1).

In terms of income, the survey revealed that grants and commission fees from the government and sale of products and services were the two major financial resources for Taiwanese social enterprises. It is worthy to note that sale of products

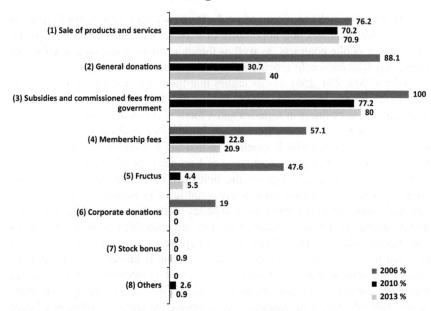

Figure 5.1 Sources of funding of Taiwanese SEs in 2006, 2010 and 2013.

(percentage of enterprises citing each source)

*Multiple choice questions

Sources: Chan et al., 2007; Kuan, Chan, & Wang, 2011; Kuan & Wang, 2013

and services ranked right after grants and commission fees from the government, which fully demonstrated the ambitions of Taiwanese social enterprises in seeking financial independence and continuous development. Such results explained that the public sector had played a rather important role in their organizational expansion and management.

Revenue of social enterprises

In terms of the overall revenue of Taiwanese social enterprises (see Table 5.1), the survey conducted in 2006 found that the financial resources received were insufficient; about 48.8 percent of the interviewed organizations had experienced deficit, while 27.9 percent of those had met their balance and 23.3 percent of those had generated surplus, which indicated that Taiwanese social enterprises had experienced difficult financial situations in 2006.

The result of the 2010 survey indicated that the general revenue of the social enterprises had improved: 47.4 percent of interviewed organizations had received surplus, while 28.9 percent of those reached balanced and 23.7 percent experienced deficit (see Table 5.1). However, after excluding the government's public grants, 52 percent of the organizations would experience deficit, while 23 percent of those would meet their balance and only 25 percent of those would receive surplus (see Figure 5.2). As a result, it was found that the operation of Taiwanese social enterprises were still in the developmental phase. Given the facts of the current operation of social enterprises in Taiwan, without the financial measures from the governments, it would be difficult for them to operate on a long-term basis.

The result of the 2013 survey indicated that 36.7 percent of the interviewed social enterprises had received surplus, while 33.91 percent met their balance and 29.4 percent experienced deficit (see Table 5.1). However, the gap in the differences did not matter much. After excluding the government's public grants, 63 percent of the organizations would experience deficit, while 21 percent of those would meet their balance and only 16 percent of those would receive surplus (see Figure 5.2.1). Such phenomena not only manifests the importance of the governmental resources to social enterprises, but also reflects the current business environment as less favorable for Taiwanese social enterprises.

Table 5.1 SE overall revenue in Taiwan in 2006, 2010 and 2013

	2006		2010		2013	
	f	%	f	%	f	%
(1) Surplus	10	23.3	54	47.4	40	36.7
(2) Deficit	21	48.8	27	23.7	32	29.4
(3) Balanced	12	27.9	33	28.9	37	33.9
N	43	100.0	114	100.0	109	100.0

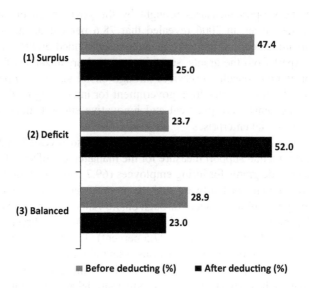

■ Before deducting (%)   ■ After deducting (%)

Figure 5.2 SE overall revenue in 2010.

(before and after deducting public subsidies)

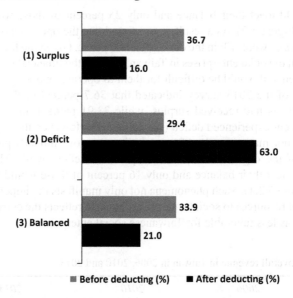

Figure 5.2.1 SE overall revenue in 2013.

(before and after deducting public subsidies)

Support measures brought by the Taiwanese government

In terms of the support measures brought by the government of Taiwan (see Figure 5.3), the survey in 2006 revealed that 78.6 percent of the interviewed organizations indicated that the governments had provided grants for the social enterprises. Apart from the grants, some interviewed organizations further indicated that providing consulting services through onsite visits (50.0 percent) and setting up of relevant websites from government for integrating marketing information (42.9 percent) were practical and innovative support measures for the development of social enterprises.

When it came to the survey in 2010, the result also revealed that the most effective governmental support measure for the management of social enterprises would be to provide grants for hiring employees (69.7 percent), followed by support from government for hardware such as premises and equipment (31.2 percent), providing consulting services through onsite visits (30.3 percent), providing grants for business operation and training (28.4 percent) and direct purchase of goods and services from government (27.5 percent). The data elaborated that the provision of grants for hiring employees was essential for the operation and development of social enterprises in Taiwan. In addition, the Taiwanese government had also provided these social enterprises some material and non-material support measures, such as initiating product endorsement or other marketing help, providing consulting services through onsite visits and other related grants for operation and training. Furthermore, sometimes the governments purchased the products or services provided by the social enterprises; thus, the support measures come in various forms.

Once again, the most recent survey (2013) reemphasized the importance of all types of grants, including providing grants for hiring employees (74.5 percent), followed by providing grants for business operation and training (37.3 percent) and support from government for hardware such as premises and equipment (36.4 percent), providing consulting services through onsite visits (32.7 percent), setting up of relevant websites from government for integrating marketing information (31.8 percent) and direct purchase of goods and services from government (30.0 percent). As a matter of fact, these governmental support measures were quite similar to those provided in the 2006 and 2010 surveys, which were mostly about grants, software/ hardware facilities, usage of the equipment and premises (whether with or free of charges), consulting services through onsite visits and vocational training, the support in marketing through local authorities and setting up websites to integrate marketing information on products and services.

Generally speaking, the enabling context facilitated by the government on the development of social enterprise includes the following characteristics: (1) a well-developed legal framework; (2) provision of financial assistance; (3) provision of consulting and training to enhance the capacity of the social enterprises; (4) fostering cooperation among varied organizations and business

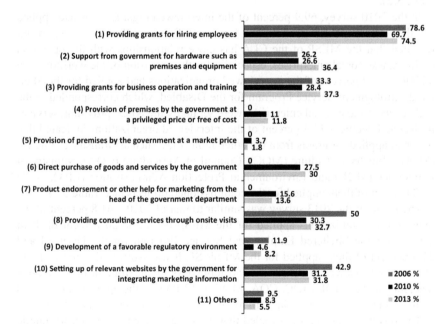

Figure 5.3 Support measures implemented by the Taiwanese government.

(data from the 2006, 2010 and 2013 surveys)

* Multiple choice Questions

fields and; (5) developing marketability (UNDP, 2007; United Nations, 2012). If the above five characteristics were adopted to analyze the support measures of the Taiwanese government on the operation of social enterprises, the most effective measures would be financial measures, followed by capacity building of business operation through consulting services or training and developing marketability. On the other hand, governments dedicated less attention to shape a legal framework for the social enterprises and fostering cross-organizational and cross-sectoral cooperation.

Most frequently applied public grants program for social enterprises in Taiwan

As the Taiwanese government had provided the most support measures for the development of social enterprises, especially financial measures, the researchers would like to explore which public grants programs Taiwanese social enterprises would apply for the most. In terms of public grants, the 2006 survey indicated that about 55.8 percent of the interviewed organizations had applied for the Sheltered Employment Service Program for the Disabled, while 37.2 percent applied for the Multi-Employment Service Program–Economic Plan (MESP-EP), 30.2 percent for the Multi-Employment Service Program–Social Plan (MESP-SP) and 30.2 percent for the commissioned projects entrusted by the local authorities (see Table 5.2).

In the 2010 survey, 69.9 percent of the interviewed organizations had applied for the MESP-EP, followed by 27.4 percent for the MESP-SP; such result revealed that the MESP of the CLA has close relationships with the operation of Taiwanese social enterprises, especially for the provision of the workforce. In addition, 23.9 percent of the interviewed organizations had applied for the Sheltered Employment Service Program for the Disabled, which corresponded to the reality where most social enterprises were set up by the NPOs providing services to disabled people – 13.3 percent of the interviewed organizations indicated that they had applied for grants from the other authorities, such as Ministry of Interior (MOI), Ministry of Culture (MOC), Council of Agriculture (COA), Ministry of Economics (MOE) and Environmental Protection Administration (EPA), while 13.3 percent of them applied for the commissioned projects (see Table 5.2).

The result of the 2013 survey was similar to that of 2010 – 61.8 percent of the interviewed organizations applied for the MESP-EP, while 30 percent of them applied for the Sheltered Employment Service Program for the Disabled and 21.8 percent of those applied for the MESP-SP. It was worthy of note that more and more interviewed organizations had applied for grants from the other authorities (such as the MOI, MOC, COA, MOE and EPA), as the application rate had increased from 13.3 percent in 2010 to 29.1 percent in 2013 (see Table 5.2).

The results of the survey revealed that the most frequently applied-for public grant programs during the mid-2000s to 2013 were the Multi-Employment Service Programs (both social and economic plans), followed by Sheltered Employment Service Program for the Disabled. However, in the recent years, grants

Table 5.2 Most frequently applied-for public grants program for social enterprises in 2006, 2010 and 2013

	2006	2010	2013
	%	%	%
1. Sheltered Employment Service Program for the Disabled	55.8	23.9	30.0
2. Multi-Employment Service Program–Social Plan	30.2	27.4	21.8
3. Multi-Employment Service Program–Economic Plan	37.2	69.9	61.8
4. Multi-Employment Service Program–Fostering Plan	NA	NA	7.30
5. Grants from other authorities (e.g., MOI, MOC, COA, MOE, EPA)	NA	13.3	29.1
6. Commissioned projects	30.2	13.3	12.7
7. Specially authorized usage of premises, equipment and buildings	11.6	1.8	2.7
8. Independent operation without the application of public grants	20.9	7.1	9.1
9. Others	4.7	0.9	0.9
N	43	113	110

* Multiple choice questions

NA: The choice option was not included in the questionnaire of that year.

provided by the other authorities (such as the MOI, MOC, COA, MOE and EPA) were also very appealing for Taiwanese social enterprises. Furthermore, the 2013 survey indicated that 7.3 percent of the interviewed organizations had applied for the Multi-Employment Service Program (Fostering Plan), which was proposed by the CLA in 2010 as a capacity-building program for increasing the employability of those families and industries that were affected by Typhoon Morakot; the program was later enlarged in 2012 and aimed to transform into an action plan to enhance the capacity of Taiwanese social enterprises (Shih, 2013).

Policy context transformation concerning the support for social enterprises in Taiwan

The previous section attempted to analyze the roles of the Taiwanese government in enhancing the capacity building of social enterprises from the mid-2000s to nowadays. This section will elaborate what active policy measures the Taiwanese government has taken in promoting the development of social enterprises, their implications and how they differ from the policy measures fostered before the mid-2000s.

Transformation of the CLA's Multi-Employment Service Program

Since early 2000s, two types of policies have been carried out by the Taiwanese government for the promotion of social enterprises in Taiwan. One type of policies focused on the employment services rendered to physically and mentally disabled individuals, while the other emphasized the employment service policies for the jobless (Kuan & Wang, 2010a). Concerning the latter, the Multi-Employment Service Program (MESP) promoted by the CLA was a joint effort of the private and public sector to promote employment partnerships through creative inquiries, local development plans and guiding the unemployed in joining the civil society work. It was highlighted that the common efforts made by the public and the private sector ought to create employment opportunities, nurture the abilities of the unemployed and relieve the unemployed disadvantaged minorities affected by the crisis and pressure. After the grants terminated, it was hoped that they would be able to carry on with their life, expand their capabilities and continue providing employment channels to the jobless. Thus, the MESP was considered as an important public policy dedicated to the development of social enterprises.

The MESP was initiated in 2002, focusing on the collaboration between the CLA and the NPOs in the creation of local employment opportunities. After the project application was accepted, the project could receive the subsidy for a maximum of three years. In 2008, the MESP had integrated a "relative subsidy" measure to encourage the grantees to sustain themselves for sustainable operation. After the project had been subsidized for three years, the grants used for subsidizing hiring renewed and new employees would decrease gradually every year to prompt the NPOs to sustain themselves for sustainable operation. The MESP encompassed both social and economic goals, encouraged the entrepreneurship of social innovation and social business and prompted the vertical and horizontal integration and transformation of the industries with public support measures to develop social enterprises. The expenditure of the MESP was averagely 1 billion TWD per year, and the total expenditure had exceeded 12 billion TWD (about 400 million USD) during the period from 2002 to 2012. Table 5.3 presents the total number, types and the distribution percentage of the NPOs that had received grants from the MESP from 2009 to 2012. On average, 616 NPOs received grants each year; among those, 82.7 percent of them were community-based, followed by work-integrated (15.1 percent) and "social cooperatives" (2.2 percent).

After five or six years of implementation of the MESP, the Bureau of Employment and Vocational Training (BEVT) observed that whether the NPOs were engaged in the service or economic value-added industries, they were in need of professional management knowledge and consulting services to achieve

Table 5.3 Types of NPOs that received grants from the MESP, 2009 to 2012

Year	No. of NPO (a + b + c)	Community Based (a)	Social Cooperative (b)	Work Integration (c)
2009	675 (100.0%)	564 (83.1%)	15 (2.3%)	96 (14.6%)
2010	557 (100.0%)	450 (80.8%)	15 (2.7%)	92 (16.5%)
2011	637 (100.0%)	530 (83.2%)	11 (1.7%)	96 (15.1%)
2012	593 (100.0%)	497 (83.8%)	13 (2.3%)	83 (13.9%)
Average %	616 (100.0%)	82.7%	2.2%	15.1%

Source: Shih, 2013, p. 6

sustainable development. Thus, BEVT started to reflect on the term "social enterprises" and decided that it should support the NPOs in this direction. Mr. Lin, a senior employee of BEVT, indicated in the personal interview:

> The Multi-Employment Service Program had carried a top-down guiding characteristic since its developmental stage. Apart from coordinating a Review Committee, providing guidelines for the NPOs with the review regulations, the BEVT had also provided consulting services. In the earlier times, BEVT would draft the content of the consulting services and designate the focused issues and consulting services. As a matter of fact, at that time, the NPOs did not specify the types of consulting services they needed, thus, the guidance of BEVT was rather important.[5]

However, after the mid-2000s, BEVT had modified its working methods; the hierarchical relationship had shifted from a top-down model to a bottom-up model. Section Chief Huang, serving at the Employment Service Center of Yunlin-Chiayi-Tainan Region of BEVT, observed the transformation.

> We would investigate the needs of the NPOs whom were our grantees, consulted them with resource proposition and we would conduct evaluations afterwards. We would apply an initial analysis where we would bring in the experts to accompany the NPOs with professional analysis and recommendations. Based on the result of the expert's diagnosis, we would then provide the related resources. As we the public authorities would accompany the NPOs on a long-term basis, we would attempt to analyze the needs of the NPOs and discuss with them to identify what the public authorities could do for them, along with the assistance of the experts and resources. In the meantime, the NPOs could also bring in their own requests.[6]

Such bottom-up consulting models had prompted the NPOs to evolve as well-organized social enterprises; this was especially true with the emergence of the MESP–Fostering Plan in 2010. The original fostering plan intended to support post–natural disaster reconstruction work (especially in the regions affected by Typhoon Morakot), regional revitalization and development and innovative projects such as social venture or employment support systems. After the fostering plan was put into practice, the MESP expanded its service scale to disaster-affected regions all over Taiwan. The program aimed to stress the importance of industrial transformation or innovation, social venture entrepreneurship and revitalization of the region for development and prompt the vertical and horizontal integration of services and industries.

The grants of the MESP–Fostering Plan provided for the NPOs include staffing cost (salary for hiring employees and their health insurance cost), administrative cost, training cost for the hired employees[7] and consulting cost. Thus, the MESP–Fostering Plan not only provides more flexibility in subsidizing the staffing cost, but also subsidizes training and consulting cost; this is because the concept of the Fostering Plan was to accompany the NPOs to stay in line with the industrial trends. The cost for training and consulting took part almost 40 percent of the staffing cost.[8]

In general, the roles of the CLA or the MESP have gone through obvious transformation in the recent years. During the early 2000s to mid-2000s, the support measures tended to endorse the human resources of the NPOs; yet, in the recent years, the focus has shifted to upbringing the capacity of the NPOs for the capacity building of social enterprises instead of solving only the employment issues. In addition, the CLA also dedicated its efforts to improving the marketability of social enterprises. On the official website of CLA, there exists a webpage (Go Fun, http://gofun.evta.gov.tw/se.aspx) featuring social-enterprise products from all over Taiwan and successful stories of Taiwanese social enterprises.

Establishment of the Office of Social Economic Development

When the CLA first introduced the MESP, it had paid much attention to the development of social enterprises in Japan, South Korea, Singapore, Hong Kong, the USA and Europe. The CLA was especially interested in the roles of government in the development of social enterprises, thus the CLA had also visited social enterprises in the above regions several times. Whether it is necessary to formulate legal acts for supporting and regulating social enterprises or not, the Taiwanese government had taken some references from the Social Enterprise Promotion Act that was enacted in South Korea in 2007.

In December 2011, CLA officially launched the Office of Social Economic Development (OSED) to draft and promote policies related to the development of social enterprises, construct resource integration platforms and diminish the possible obstacles. In the short term, it was hoped that the goals of employment promotion would be implemented; in the long term, it was hoped that the OSED would ascertain the spirit of social innovation. To put it simply, the mission of the OSED is to promote the NPOs to transform into social enterprises; in the near future, the OSED intends to dedicate its efforts to advocacy and policy planning and construction of communication and interaction platforms and to assist the NPOs to develop social enterprises. It is hoped that the OSED will put the social economy into practice and realize the goals of creating an "economy that benefit[s] the people" and promotes "social justice" (Lee, 2012; Shih, 2013).

Integrating social enterprises into the guiding principles for Taiwanese social welfare policy

"Guiding Principles for Taiwanese Social Welfare Policy" is the most important reference for the Taiwanese government in regards to social welfare policy promotion; the Executive Yuan of Taiwan would review and announce the latest version of the guiding principles every ten years. Such principles were announced in 1994 and 2004, yet the term "social enterprises" had never been included in the past. In January 2012, the Executive Yuan announced the "Guiding Principles for Taiwanese Centenary Social Welfare Policy—Towards a New Society with Equity, Inclusion, and Justice". In the foreword, it was clearly stated that "the government should promote public-private partnerships and should encourage collaborations by the private sector. Moreover, the government should be committed to creating the environment for the development of non-profit organizations and social enterprises in order to provide perfect service for citizens."

In addition, in December 2011, the Executive Yuan announced the "Guiding Principles for Gender Equality Policy". In the section "Employment, Economics and Welfare", specific action measures were emphasized, such as "establishing programs and support measures to encourage social enterprises, amend legal acts that would influence the development of social economy or cooperative economy (such as the public procurement measures and the Cooperative Act) . . . develop marketing channels and opportunities; in the meantime, amend the related legal acts to create an environment favorable for social enterprises to operate cooperative business".

These two important guiding principles both reaffirmed that social enterprises will be highlighted in Taiwanese social welfare policy and gender equality policy in the future during the policy-making and execution procedure.

GONGOs as the supportive platform for social enterprises

So-called government organized non-governmental organizations (GONGOs) are quasi-nongovernmental organizations that are set up by the government; their major goals are to assist the government to advance its public policy. GONGOs are frequently used by governments in the Western or developed countries for assisting public authorities to conduct domestic or international public affairs, such as international humanitarian or social development missions (Kuan & Lu, 2004). The Taiwanese government has also utilized some GONGOs to assist social enterprises to mature; examples include the Foundation for Women's Rights Promotion and Development (FWRPD; governed by the MOI), the Taiwan Textile Federation (governed by the MOE), the National Culture and Arts Foundation (NCAF; governed by the MOC), and so on. These organizations have also proposed certain projects to promote the healthy operation and the organizational development of social enterprises. For instance, since 2012, the NCAF has been actively engaged in the Arts Up Project, which aims to foster collaboration between art and business sectors (website of NCAF, 2013/05/15). Moreover, the FWRPD has functioned as a platform to support the development of social enterprises operated by women and aboriginals since the late-2000s (website of FWRPD, 2013/04/30)

Conclusions

As a result of the three surveys on social enterprises in Taiwan, the interviewed social enterprises indicated that the most effective support measures provided by the Taiwanese government since mid-2000s were financial measures, followed by capacity building of business operation through consulting services or training and development of marketability. On the other hand, the Taiwanese government dedicated less attention to shape the legal framework for social enterprises and foster cross-organizational and cross-sectoral cooperation.

When the authors attempted to examine the transformation of the Taiwanese government's policy measures on the development of social enterprises since mid-2000s, it was discovered that though the government continued to underscore the importance of financial measures, it has shifted its core goals from being employment centered to the capacity building of social enterprises, and thus came the policy measure on providing consulting services to develop healthy social enterprises and the emergence of the Multiple Employment Service Program–Fostering Plan in 2010. In other words, the provision of consulting and training services and the enhancement of marketability will further develop the business operational capacity of social enterprises as the core policy measures that the Taiwanese government has adopted for promoting their development.

Although the Taiwanese government does not intend to enlist special legal acts for the promotion of social enterprises, it has been included as a concerned party in the policy address. On the level of the public authorities, social enterprises have been enlisted in the "Guiding Principles for Taiwanese Social Welfare Policy" and the "Guiding Principles for Social Gender Equality Policy", emphasizing the importance of collaboration between the government and the NPOs and the creation of an environment favorable for the development of social enterprises.

In terms of the administrative framework, although the Taiwanese government does not actually have a designated bureau like the Social Enterprise Unit under the Department of Industry and Trade in the United Kingdom to promote the development of social enterprises, or a legal framework like the Community Interest Companies Law to regulate the organizations (Defourny & Nyssens, 2010), CLA had launched the OSED under the BEVT to formulate and promote policies related to the development of social enterprises, construct a platform to integrate the related resources and exclude the obstacles for such development. However, it is a pity that the OSED is still not an official bureau under CLA's organizational structure and the Executive Yuan does not have the intention to formalize its status so far.

In terms of fostering cross-ministerial and cross-sectoral cooperation, the above analysis has revealed that under the influence of the CLA, other public authorities (such as the MOI, MOE, COA, CEPD, MOC) have gradually recognized the importance of the integration of public resources to support the NPOs to develop social enterprises. In the meantime, local governments in Taiwan have also supported social enterprises and the public authorities in terms of the operation of social enterprises. This is especially true with GONGOs in Taiwan, as they have functioned as the platforms to support the development of social enterprises.

Despite encouraging the development of social enterprises, government policies and subsidies also represent an obstacle. Social enterprises in Taiwan still need to pay attention to the following two disadvantages. The one is the possibility for social enterprises to play the residual complement-type role, helping the government to make up insufficient employment services. The other is the acquisition of related resources for social enterprises to rely excessively upon government grants, resulting in the 'institutional isomorphism' phenomenon. From the points of view of institutional theory, the governmental supports in the finance and relevant legal norms sometimes benefit social enterprises' conductive business and development. In the meantime, the occurrence of 'institutional isomorphism' may also inhibit social enterprises from doing the possible; therefore, to manage sustainability for the organizations, social enterprises shall assess the potential advantages and disadvantages from the dependence on the government's financial support.

Notes

1 At the moment, social enterprises that are engaged in "affirmative business" and "service provision and product sales" are most commonly seen in Taiwan. Some medium or large-scale NPO social enterprises fall into at least one of these categories, such as those operated by the Eden Social Welfare Foundation, the Children Are Us Foundation, the Sunshine Social Welfare Foundation, the Syin-Lu Social Welfare Foundation, the First Social Welfare Foundation and the Yu-Cheng Social Welfare Foundation.
2 The Council of Labor Affairs was withdrawn and became the Ministry of Labor in February 2014.
3 The Council for Economic Development was reorganized as the National Development Council in January 2014, and the Health Department and Department of Social Affairs were combined into the Ministry of Health and Welfare in July 2013.
4 The total number of the samples and the response rate of these three surveys are detailed as the following. In terms of the surveys conducted in Taiwan, the research team sent out surveys to 124 social enterprises (including 91 social enterprises that offer sheltered employment for the disabled, 24 social enterprises that work on community development and 9 social cooperatives) in Taiwan in May, 2006; 43 social enterprises responded via phone calls and emails, which provided a response rate of 34.7 percent. In 2010, the total sample number was 426 social enterprises (including social enterprises that offer sheltered employment, social enterprises for community development, social cooperatives, social enterprises that engage in service provision and product sales, venture philanthropy organizations and other types of social enterprises) and the response rate was 27.2 percent (116 social enterprises responded). In the survey conducted in April 2013, the total sample number was 430 social enterprises (including social enterprises that offer sheltered employment, social enterprises for community development, social cooperatives, social enterprises that engage in service provision and product sales, venture philanthropy organizations and other types of social enterprises) and the response rate was 25.6 percent (110 social enterprises responded).
5 Lin, Chia-Wei, personal interview in Taipei, 2013/01/21.
6 Huang, Yao-De, personal interview in Tainan, 2013/05/20.
7 For instance, NPOs that receive public grants could host the training programs by themselves; the relevant cost would be subsidized in accordance with the standards of training cost enlisted by BEVT.
8 Huang, Yao-De, personal interview in Tainan, 2013/05/20.

References

Borzaga, C., & Santuari, A. (2000). *Social Enterprise in Italy: The Experience of Social Co-operatives*. ISSAN Working Papers no. 15.

Chan, K. T., Kuan, Y. Y., & Wang, S. T. (2011). "Similarities and Divergences: Comparison of Social Enterprises in Hong Kong and Taiwan", *Social Enterprise Journal*, 7(1): 33–49.

Defourny, J. (2001). "Introduction: From Third Sector to Social Enterprise," in C. Borzaga, & J. Defourny (Eds.), *The Emergence of Social Enterprise*. London and New York: Routledge, pp. 1–28.

Defourny, J., & Nyssens, M. (2010). "Conceptions of Social Enterprise and Social Entrepreneurship in Europe and the United States: Convergences and Divergences", *Journal of Social Entrepreneurship*, 1(1): 32–53.

Guo, C. (2005). "Understanding Collaboration among Nonprofit Organizations: Combining Resource Dependency, Institutional, and Network Perspectives", *Nonprofit and Voluntary Sector Quarterly*, 34(3): 340–361.

Kerlin, J. A. (2006). "Social Enterprise in the United States and Europe: Understanding and Learning from the Difference", *Voluntas*, 17: 247–263.

Kerlin, J. A. (2009). *Social Enterprise: A Global Comparison*. Medford, MA: Tufts University Press.

Kuan, Y. Y., & Wang, S. T. (2010a). "The Impact of Public Authorities on the Development of Social Enterprises in Taiwan", *Journal of Public Affairs Review*, 11(1): 1–23.

Kuan, Y. Y., & Wang, S. T. (2010b). "Taiwanese Social Enterprises: Characteristics, Development Trend, and Effect", paper presented at the 2010 International Conference on Social Enterprises in Eastern Asia: Dynamics and Variations, Taipei, 14–16 June 2010.

Kuan, Y. Y., Chan, K. T., & Wang, S. T. (2011). "The Governance of Social Enterprises in Taiwan and Hong Kong: A Comparison", *Journal of Asian Public Policy*, 4(2): 149–170.

Meyer, J., & Rowan, R. (1977). "Institutionalized Organizations: Formal Structure as Myth and Ceremony", *American Journal of Sociology*, 83: 340–363.

Nyssens, M. (2006). "Social Enterprise at the Crossroads of Market, Public Policy and Civil Society", in M. Nyssens (Eds.), *Social Enterprise: At the Crossroads of Market, Public Policy and Civil Society*. London and New York: Routledge, pp. 313–328.

United Nations (2012). *Fostering Innovative Entrepreneurship: Challenges and Policy Options*. New York and Geneva: United Nations Economic Commission for Europe.

United Nations Development Programme (UNDP) (2007). *Capacity Assessment Methodology: User's Guide*. Capacity Development Group Bureau for Development Policy, UNDP.

Literature in Chinese

Chan, K. T., Kuan, Y. Y., Fan, M. L., Mak, P. S., Wang, S. T., and Lam-Yeung, K. S. (2007). *Exploratory Study on Social Enterprises in Hong Kong, Taiwan and Shanghai*. Kowloon: Hong Kong Polytechnic University.

Kuan, Y. Y. (2007). "Social Enterprise Development in Taiwan", *China Nonprofit Review*, 1, 146–182.

Kuan, Y. Y, Chen, J. T., Lu, W. P., & Wang, S. T. (2012). *Social Enterprises in Taiwan and Hong Kong: A Comparison*. Taipei: Chuliu Publisher.

Kuan, Y. Y., & Lu, W. P. (2004). "The Governance of Governmental NGOs: A Case Study of the Foundations for Agricultural Affairs in Taiwan", *Third-Sector Review*, 1, 127–168.

Kuan, Y. Y. and Wang S. T. (2013). "Social Impacts of Social Enterprises in Taiwan Since the Mid-2000s: An Initial Exploration", *Journal of Community Development*, 43: 51-67.

Lee, K. F. (2012). "Develop Social Enterprises with Taiwanese Features", *TALENT,* 16, 38–41.

National Culture and Arts Foundation (NCAF). http://www.ncafroc.org.tw/news_show. asp?tp=1&id=2234, accessed May 15, 2013.

Shih, S. H. (2013). "The Past and Future of the Government's Promotion of Social Enterprises: With the Perspective of the Council of Labor Affairs", presentation at the International Conference on Social Enterprise and Social Impact: Employment Promotion and Poverty Alleviation, Taipei, 24–25 May 2013.

The Foundation for Women's Rights Promotion and Development (FWRPD), from http:// www.womenweb.org.tw/wrp.asp, accessed 30 April 2013.

6 Social entrepreneurship in Taiwan

Opportunities and challenges

Jennifer H. Chen and Ji-Ren Lee

Introduction

Social entrepreneurship has become a growing trend that has swept the world over the past several decades, with different countries taking unique approaches to match their local cultures (Kerlin, 2006). In Taiwan, "social enterprise" remains a new term subject to separate interpretations. As a relatively new phenomenon still working on finding its place in the local culture, social entrepreneurship has received unprecedented popularity and media attention over the past few years; public and private sectors and academia have held symposiums, conferences, and workshops discussing related topics, and new legislature to promote social enterprise (SE) has been contemplated. At the same time, more and more new entities labeled social enterprises are finding solid footing in operations; generally, 2014 has been regarded as the "Year of the Taiwanese Social Enterprise."

The trends in Taiwan seem to indicate a growing number of individuals and groups enthusiastically taking part in social causes via a business mechanism. Today, people unwilling to stand on the sidelines and pass the buck are taking action themselves in an attempt to use the limited power of the individual to improve society as a whole. From an optimistic perspective, this is a sign of people reflecting on the meaning of modern capitalism and the power of citizen engagement; yet the fragmented approaches in the midst of hype might threaten to call into question the identities, legitimacy, and implementation of the endeavors (Cheng & Wang, 2010).

Generally speaking, the term "social enterprise" refers to an organization that employs commercial methods (revenue generating for products or services) to address societal and environmental problems. However, Taiwanese laws do not yet take account of the concept of social goals achieved through such measures, and no legislation to date includes the term "social enterprise." This leaves unanswered a huge number of questions as to what exactly qualifies an organization to take on this moniker, such as whether it can accept donations and pay dividends, among many other operational issues. While there are strong advocates to seek legal status for a new type of organizational form, in today's Taiwanese context, "social enterprise" is not yet a specific term, nor can the concept behind it be called a new type of organization. Instead, it is helpful to think of this in terms of spirit: the manifestation of social entrepreneurship. At its center is the idea of addressing social issues and pursuing more than private gains, all set against a backdrop of balancing financial, social, and environmental objectives, regardless of operational models.

This paper thus presents an overview of the development of social enterprises in Taiwan with a comprehensive perspective of a wide spectrum of initiatives: from non-profit organization turned enterprising, co-operatives, enterprise-driven new venture, and community-based informal organizations. We will take up the conceptual divergence in the fair trade movement as a window into two major directions taken in the local development of social enterprise. We then address the challenges faced in management and operations before closing with a look at some unique characteristics of Taiwanese social enterprises and future trends in theory and practice. Through these, this general overview aims to bridge different orientations and spur further dialogue of the topic.

A macro framework of existing social enterprises: multifaceted activities

"Social enterprise" is a new term for an old concept. The prototype for this idea is the co-operative, which began taking root in Taiwan during the period of Japanese occupation. Traced further back in history, there were also organizations providing common goods through sustainable supports rather than simply giving charity or offering one-time assistance. For example, in 1865, in the mountainous Nantou area, there was once an initiative by local elites to collect funds to launch for the peasants affordable ferry service. The money collected was used to buy boats and rice fields which provided annual crops to fund for ferry operators and maintenance fees. In a similar vein, Yishu (義塾), privately funded schools available for the commons, were able to support themselves primarily through agricultural harvests.

Today, influenced and inspired by global trends, such as the dual emphasis on profit-making and resolving social problems, as well as the spirit of communal ownership, Taiwan's social enterprise landscape has grown into a diverse environment that cannot be portrayed neatly in any particular framework. As Ramirez (2012) advocated, a transparent and inclusive mindset is beneficial for the field, and as long as the accountability could be upheld, "let priorities guide the trade-offs". Looking at the general evolving process of social enterprises, we could draw up an overview as in Figure 6.1.

Social Needs are what inspire/propel **social entrepreneurs** to identify **opportunities** and select suitable **vehicles** to realize those opportunities. In the process, the entrepreneurs/vehicles would need **funding resources** and **growing enablers,** which can come from government, venture capitalists, citizen sector, and education.

Social needs

Social entrepreneurship in Taiwan began with a focus on employment for the disadvantaged, such as the early bakeries of a foundation dedicated to Down

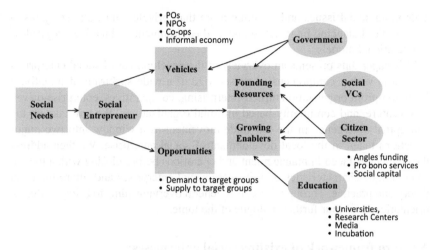

Figure 6.1 Social enterprise landscape

syndrome children; the scope has diversified in recent years to cover a wide range of issues, including agricultural product marketing, fair trade, health care, underprivileged groups, learning and education, environmental conservation, food safety, care for the homeless, rights for the disabled, and community development, among others. Social needs inspire motivation to make change, and these needs are tightly related to the developmental trajectory of a society. In Taiwan, social enterprises have a strong local embeddedness.

Entrepreneurs

Once social needs propel change makers to take initiative, some undertake "intrapreneurship" by starting a new unit of an existing organization with a new approach to issues of concern, while others manifest social entrepreneurship by launching entirely new ventures. What might differentiate a social enterprise's weight on public values is often the breadth of entrepreneurs' prior participation and experience with charitable causes (Chen, C., 2014). In general, those with a background in non-profit or charity work tend to focus on issues related to disadvantage (employment, poverty, social inclusion, etc.) and public goods.

Opportunities

From an entrepreneurial standpoint, social needs and problems can be seen as market or social opportunities. Market development and business opportunity are generally defined by an organization offering paid-for goods or services to meet the demands of society (whether they are as-yet unsatisfied needs or new demands created by social change). The key question is how to draw a distinction between the opportunities of social enterprises and those of traditional business.

Table 6.1 Four broad types of social entrepreneurial opportunities

Opportunity Types	Characteristics	Relation with Target Group
Creating employment for the disadvantaged	Designing innovative employment systems or job type to make a supportive and stable work environment for groups of people with difficulty finding employment; offering chances both for work and for building professional skills. Example: Dialogue in the Dark	Demand of target group's service
Purchase from local or smallholder providers	Establishing fair-trade partnerships, empowering producers or service providers with limited access to resources, including smallholders, minorities, marginalized communities, and the disabled. Example: Homemakers Union Consumers Co-op	Demand of target group's product
Serve underserved market/ customer	Fulfilling disadvantaged people their unsatisfied needs, usually caused by a lack of willingness on the part of corporations to provide products or services to them because the market is too small or the cost too high, limiting profits. Example: Duofu Care and Services Co.	Supply service or product to target group
Reinvent value chain for sustainability	Redefining or revitalizing the value chain to make more effective or efficient use of resources, particularly integrating idle and discarded resources (including power, water, and environments). Example: Rejoice Community Supported Agriculture Group	Advocating sustainable environment

In his definition of social entrepreneurship, Dees (1998) suggests that social entrepreneurs play the role of change agents as "those who target an unfortunate but stable equilibrium that causes the neglect, marginalization, or suffering of a segment of humanity". Subsequent discussions also stress the unique opportunities for social enterprise, including the "inherently unjust equilibrium" of "the exclusion, marginalization, or suffering of a segment of humanity", an endeavor which "releases trapped potential or alleviates the suffering of the targeted groups", and anything that ensures "a better future for the targeted group and even society at large" (Martin & Osberg, 2007).

With the rise of the notion of the "triple bottom line", advocates feel the third line – environment – is another vulnerable category, or target group of concern. Environmental sustainability is regarded as directly linked to social sustainability.

The four broad types of social entrepreneurial opportunities in Taiwan are suggested as Table 6.1.

Vehicles

Entrepreneurs must choose one vehicle, or type of organization, to realize opportunities identified, and different choices mean they will face different legal or external structural environments. Taiwanese social enterprises can largely be divided into four vehicles.

Not-for-profit organization

Jobs creation has been a key aim of social enterprises. From Europe's Third System and Employment Project to Taiwan's Multi-Employment Promotion Project, these approaches try to alleviate unemployment problems by creating new jobs or encouraging the unemployed to begin new initiatives.

Taiwan's Council of Labor Affairs promulgated in 2002 two measures related to sheltered workshops to aid the mentally and physically challenged who otherwise could not find work. As NPOs play the vital role of employers, commercialization was expedited and shelter workshops became pilots of social enterprise. Typically, work integration or affirmative business is the most visible social enterprise model in Taiwan (Kuan & Wang, 2010). Statistics show that the majority of the registered sheltered workshops operate in the small-scale services sector – mostly catering and cleaning businesses but also gas stations, retail outlets, and manufacturers (WDA, 2014). These organizations are regulated by local governments, which issue their business licenses. There remains a clear disparity in the resources available to workshops in urban areas and those in rural areas.

The financial independence of sheltered workshops is inhibited by a lack of professional management, the absence of specialized operations, and the conflicting roles in which administrators find themselves. Even so, a number of employment promotion organizations have shown impressive results. Among them is the Children Are Us Foundation, which opened its first bakery in Kaohsiung, southern Taiwan, in 1997 and now runs twenty-nine sheltered workshops around the country that manage to bring in over 60 percent of revenues from earned income. Another prominent example is the Victory Potential Development Centre for the Disabled, founded in 2000 to develop new job types and to establish and manage sheltered workshops. Victory has found success in providing jobs to the disabled while also turning a profit, and it has branched out from the traditional industry of baked goods into running convenience stores, and even to the making of specialized *liuli* glassware, giving more opportunities to the disadvantaged while increasing their chances to interact with a larger group of people.

Social co-op

The first social enterprises in Taiwan were social co-operatives, which organize internal stakeholders to pursue collective interests. Co-ops help members overcome economic difficulties, leading the Taiwanese government to define them as charitable corporate entities. They also improve the lives of the disadvantaged and, as dedicated welfare organizations, ease the government's burden in providing welfare services (Chiu, 2009)

Since their origins during the Japanese rule of Taiwan (1895–1945), local social co-ops have developed into eleven different categories, mostly industries in the primary sector. Ministry of the Interior data show that there are more than 4,000 co-ops in total, with agricultural and consumer co-ops having a significant share. While those numbers are high, the long history of co-ops without up-to-date policy support has led to a common lack of real operations, resulting in few nowadays that make an actual difference in terms of resolving social problems.

The Homemakers Union Consumers Co-op is one exception. Founded in 1995, it promotes benefiting both producers and consumers through the power of collective buying. Different from the group buying websites popular today, the idea behind the Homemakers Union is to build mutual trust between producers and consumers through long-term partnership. It solves logistics problems through a wide array of techniques to promote sharing and educational outreach, including tours to farm sites and meeting directly with the producers behind what is being sold.

For-profit organization

Taiwan's social enterprises gave rise to a diverse landscape since 2006. Inspired by Nobel Prize laureate Muhammad Yunus, many local social enterprises shifted from a non-profit model to a company form, making them legally identical to commercial corporations.

This model is different from the prior two in various ways: a stronger focus on commerce, a diversity of interests, and a high ratio of young participants. The importance of commercial management is based on the ineligibility of corporations to enjoy the tax-free status, subsidies and grants, and fund raising pursuits allowed for non-profits. In other words, all cash flow comes from the market, so the fate of a corporate social enterprise is based on the judgment of consumers; it cannot survive without healthy profits.

In contrast to the traditional focus on the underprivileged and employment opportunities, corporate social enterprises benefit from the freedom to pursue a wider range of goals, which allows them to use the market mechanism to improve fields that the first and third sectors cannot. Many of the prominent, highly visible social enterprises are in this category, such as, Aurora, Okogreen, Buy Nearby, and Townway. Additionally, at present, the broader environment and legal factors have left the majority of corporate social enterprises in Taiwan agriculture related.

In the absence of social enterprise as a new corporate class, there has been a new trend since 2015 to advocate the movement of Benefit Corporations, with the hope that through a certified label of B-Corp, there could be a systematic and collective approach to pursue stakeholder management, particularly via consumer engagement and brand awareness to bring about long-term values for multiple stakeholders.

Informal economy

The informal economy generally refers to community cultural and creative endeavors and community-supported agriculture or economic activities which cannot easily be categorized, as well as informally established unofficial units.

The development of local culture and industry is one of the major strategies for creating jobs and invigorating local economies around Taiwan. A culture of self-reliance and independence took root in particular after the destructive 1999 earthquake in central Taiwan, when local industries became a conduit for addressing social problems; a similar response came from local industries after the onslaught of Typhoon Morakot through southern Taiwan in 2009. Amid reconstruction efforts, many embraced the idea of community regeneration as they developed unique tourism industries built on culture, ecology, and history. Along with development of local specialties, this provided locals with a new source of income outside of traditional industries, producing more jobs and working to reduce the trend of young people heading to big cities to find work.

The possibility of wide-spanning development of the informal economy is generally limited by the lack of professional knowledge, financial instability, and local politics. However, over the past few years, more and more communities have seen their efforts bear fruit, such as the prominent example of the Nantou Taomi Eco-Village, which was once a depressed aged community struck by a severe earthquake, but after a decade of empowerment processes and relentless entrepreneurial efforts, the community has built its resilience and developed vibrant economic activities, sprouting several formal social enterprises (Liao, 2014).

Founding resources and growing enablers

Government

In terms of the law, the sheltered workshops and the multi-employment promotion program are two public sector policies providing both funding and training facilities aimed at broadening employment opportunities and transforming sheltered workshops into social enterprises, which in turn could become a new employer for the disadvantaged. Draft bills introduced in 2014 aim to further the cause by allowing lawmakers to "give social enterprises a legal stand". The government is also mulling a cabinet-level Social Enterprise Development Committee, a Social Enterprise Fund, with deductions on operational expenses (such as rent) to create a preferential environment for development.

Aside from promulgating rules and regulations, various governmental agencies, such as the Ministry of Labor, Ministry of Economic Affairs, Ministry of Education, and Ministry of Culture, have endorsed the trend of social enterprise development and provided funding to programs and initiatives to promote the setup of new social ventures or the transformation into becoming social enterprises. While there is a divergence in directions, most of the programs and initiatives are short-term in nature, and are oriented toward market solutions, trading income, operational models, celebration of the visionary entrepreneurs, and entrepreneurial competitions.

Social venture capital

Currently, there are a handful of venture capital firms dedicated either solely or partially to social impact investing. Flow Inc., established in 2007, is the first Taiwanese company designated as a social venture capital firm. Though originally intended to provide venture capital to and incubate social enterprises, Flow has ceased from operating social-based venture capital, and instead launched the Charity Innovator Project, which concentrates on employment issues for the disabled. Another company, B Current Impact Investing, opened its doors in 2014 to bridge the gap between social entrepreneurs and potential impact investors as well as mainstream business. B Current offers industry knowledge and networking along with management training and advising to help spur social enterprise development to reach critical mass.

The Gre Tai Securities Market meanwhile launched the Go Incubation Board for Startup and Acceleration Firms in 2013 to support low-capital companies issuing stocks to raise funds. The board, which now lists seventeen companies, eliminates the expense of public offerings and provides managerial consultation. One firm, Duofu, is registered as a social enterprise and has seen success in fund raising; a fair trade firm Okogreen Co., though registered under the farming and forestry category, is also by essence a social enterprise. Both cases mark an important milestone in public awareness of the social enterprise sector.

Education

Since 2010, Taiwan has sprouted a few research institutes for social enterprises and several university research centers covering related topics. The number of student groups focused on social innovation and enterprise has meanwhile steadily grown into a major platform for promoting the idea among young people, and there are a number of civic groups focused on providing resources and assistance for social entrepreneurs. Some groups hold lectures and events to offer guidance on benchmarks and how to replicate success; others emphasize international experience and giving local social enterprises a chance to interact with their counterparts abroad to expand horizons, lessen the distance between different generations of entrepreneurs, and even provide access to real resources.

Social Enterprise Insights, the first Chinese-language information platform in the field in Taiwan, has become one of the most important forces nudging forward local development of social enterprise. Established in 2012, it is an Internet media site focused on networking by introducing the idea of social enterprise through interviews and case studies centered on local efforts as well as features columns written by experts in various fields. As a result, it plays an important role in bringing the latest global developments in social enterprise into Chinese, which to date has relatively little literature on the topic. By overcoming linguistic barriers, Social Enterprise Insights lays an indispensable foundation for future local development in the sector.

Citizen sector

The nature of social enterprises gives them unique access to "social capital": volunteers, donations, and free use or below-market prices for certain venues, to name a few, that helps them overcome the constraints of limited resources. Social capital comprises the trust and connection built between individuals. Among the ethnic Chinese societies, Taiwan has a very high percentage of population getting involved in voluntary actions, whether on a regular or ad hoc basis (SRDA, 2013). Thus, along with the social fiber of trust and connection, there are potentially abundant resources if there is a good cause calling for the need. Volunteers offer not only their time, effort, and money, but also their experience, knowledge, services, and business connections, making them a vital component and real asset (Hsieh & Jiang, 2014).

Conceptual challenges: emphasis on "social" vs "enterprise"

As with many emerging concepts, the hybrid language and focus of social enterprise have changed over time and across space. With its tradition of social economics and co-operative enterprise, Europe saw work integration as the major developmental node of the 1990s, followed by increasing emphasis on governance structure and stakeholder participation as the core for the "social" aspect of social enterprise (Cheng, 2007). The United States, on the other hand, saw a fusion of different values, such as blended value (Emerson, 2003), shared value (Porter & Kramer, 2011), and ethics and social responsibility (Johnson, 2008), with the underlying idea of putting markets to work for both profit and the common good.

Taiwan has adopted a mesh of both the European and the American streams of thought, which has inevitably given rise to some conceptual challenges, namely the balance for the weight of the social aspect versus the enterprise aspect. Alter (2003) suggested consolidating various types of social enterprise on a spectrum, distinguished by major elements such as motivation, objectives, and accountability. While that typology can help in understanding social enterprises, it is also important to look further at the divergent ethos behind the differences.

By examining the fair-trade movement, some insights into the multifaceted nature of social enterprising activities can be obtained. In 2011, the two major fair-trade advocates Fair Trade USA and Fairtrade International announced their breakup. Fair Trade USA uses a plantation model because of its primary focus on growth in sales and with the belief that scalability yields impact. On the other hand, Fairtrade International, which built itself around small producers' organizations and first came up with the ethical certification mark, espouses a producer-focused approach and empowerment policies as its core values.

We could infer from the split between the two major fair-trade players the different ways of building around the concept of social enterprise, and each reflects a specific cultural orientation (Modelo, 2014). Conceptually, social enterprises can flourish by achieving both social and business objectives; in practice, however, tensions can emerge between those in the movement who emphasize the "social" part of social enterprise (for them, the social missions are paramount) and those who emphasize the "enterprise" part (for them, the competitiveness of the enterprise and the scalability of the business is essential to carry out concerns for social issues).

The environment that creates a necessity for social enterprise offers insight into two divergent approaches. One orientation holds that social injustice is inherent in the current economic system, and the distribution of resources is ineffective, putting some at a disadvantage from the start. This perspective seeks a more humane model for handling the market system. Proponents of this view accept the system and its rules, but they seek to alter it with the new idea that people come before profits.

The other side would argue that the power of the market manifests free will because the market system can respond to any given demand – including the "demand" for social goods. This position comes from within the market system itself, and as such, the end goal is full market participation. Proponents argue that despite the number of systematic imperfections in need of improvement, the market nevertheless represents the most effective allocation of resources. From the perspective of this cultural orientation, scaling up (by growing and expanding the market) is the equivalent of establishing impact. Inspired and revised from the Modelo (2014) framework, Table 6.2 compares and contrasts these two different approaches.

Table 6.2 Two communities of approach

	Mission-Focused with Income Generation Activities	*Business-Focused with Social Issues in Mind*
Contextual assumption	Social injustice	Free will
Emphasis	**SOCIAL** Enterprise	Social **ENTERPRISE**
	Social purpose as the end	Social purpose as the means, the by-products, or the bi-focus
Target group	Specific, tightly coupled	Non-specific, loosely coupled
Identity	Collectivism (cooperative)	Individualism (competitive)
Mode of thinking	Synthetic (aiming to integrate multiple factors)	Analytic (focusing on concrete solutions)
Locus of sustainability	Community; environment	Enterprise
Major concerns	Lack of business acumen	Legitimacy
Example	C-Are-Us Workshop	Greenvines
	Aurora Social Enterprise	iHealth

While vibrant growth in social entrepreneurship is something to be celebrated, it is important to keep in mind what Dees (1998) once cautioned: "the indiscriminate use of the term (social entrepreneurship) may undermine its significance and potential importance to those seeking to understand how societies change and progress". While Taiwanese society should certainly be open to all variety of social enterprises, we need meaningful variations, not overly generous definitions.

In the philosophy of Laozi, *Dao* and *Shu* are two important notions. *Dao* (道, literally "the way") is the central idea and principle, and in terms of social enterprise, the mission and value system. If we deviate from Dao, we have only *Shu* (術, literally "the tactic"), which focuses on handling technical matters like planning or acquiring resources, and as soon as you just have that, it's all over. The way we organize a social enterprise is rooted in our underlying belief about the purpose of enterprise and about making social change.

As the debates would persist regarding "what's the boundary of the social enterprise sector?" and "what's the nature of social entrepreneurship?" (Harding, 2004), we believe, without understanding what is rooted in our underlying beliefs about people, the purpose and nature of social organization, and bringing social change, any technical discussion such as the retention or the distribution of surpluses is only trivial. Table 6.2 offers a way to understand the diversity found within the sector, because our philosophical belief leads to our approaches to enterprise.

Operational challenges: critical building blocks

While different types of social enterprises have different goals and features, they face common challenges which, if not overcome, will hamper the future of their development.

Figure 6.2 Critical building blocks of social enterprises.

Innovation

Social enterprises exist to tackle problems while maximizing market potential to create impact. To keep a single bottom line is already challenging enough in today's competitive market, and to maintain double or even triple bottom lines would be an even more daunting task. Therefore, it is imperative for social enterprise to be innovative, to find a niche given the apparent lack of commercial opportunities. Especially oftentimes, they cannot rely on regular commercial mechanisms because the targets of most social issues are disadvantaged groups, who have an inherently weaker ability to produce and consume. That is the main reason why the OECD has since 1999 defined the basic difference between social enterprises and traditional NPOs as an entrepreneurial outlook, a degree of autonomy from the state, and the provision of innovation services (OECD, 1999).

However, the basis and development of innovation remain overlooked by many social enterprise advocates and practitioners in Taiwan. For example, when NPOs targeting physically disadvantaged begin enterprising, they tend to set up car washes and gas station programs, while those aimed at serving people with mental disabilities almost universally turn to food services, cleaning, or craft work, and the blind are stereotypically employed as masseuses. Scholars have noted that the lack of unique organizational characteristics presents the biggest obstacle for NPOs seeking to transform into social enterprises (Leu, 2013). Concentrating commercial pursuits on a limited set of products or services leads to an oversaturation and a highly competitive market with little distinction between different organizations, raising concerns about each one's sustainability.

Substantive innovation would have to start from a new way of looking. In the spirit of Albert Einstein's quote: *"The significant problems we face cannot be solved at the same level of thinking we were at when we created them"*, J. Lee, founder of Aurora Social Enterprise, advocated "creative redefining", through the lenses of innovative approach to provide new identity of an existing state, or a new connection of the existing resources to the external environment (Lee, 2013). For instance, many businesses traditionally overlook people of disability for employment on the misguided belief that their productivity cannot match "regular" employees and would thus cause operational costs to rise. By contrast, an innovative social enterprise would tend to focus on the capabilities, not the limitations, of the disadvantaged and offer a new employment model that is not only a potential market advantage because of its uniqueness but also works to positively change public opinions. One highly successful example is Dialogue in Dark, which breaks the boundary of what blind people could do, turning disability into a basis for developing distinctive experiential goods. Its model not only alters the roles for those to be helped and those to help, but also proves to be financially viable.

Innovation is not a one-time endeavor, but rather a continuous and dynamic process. The objective of fulfilling multiple bottom lines means that if a social enterprise is only able to draw sympathetic customers earlier on but overlooks product and service improvement, it will have trouble maintaining customer loyalty. As a result, innovation is the key to keeping any social enterprise afloat and thereby increasing its impact.

Professional resources

Pelchat (2004) found that when NPOs start enterprising, they tend not to have professional management skills mainly for two reasons: a lack of funds to hire people with the professional skills and the clash of existing organization culture with commercial operation.

In addition to intangible appeals, attractive salaries and benefits are ways to drawing talented professionals to keep things running smoothly. Since they are often in short supply at social enterprises, there is a constant dilemma when personnel needs are not met. Many are left asking themselves: is it a lack of employees that is hurting business, or a lack of resources preventing the organization from hiring more people? This is where social enterprises need to take a page from their NPO cousins and recognize the potential volunteers and social capital outside an organization's scope that are available (Putnam, 2000).

Employment-centric social enterprises face a unique human resources challenge in that their employees play a dual role. An organization focused on training and employment, for example, finds that disadvantaged people are both employees and an "internal customer," i.e. the targets of the organization's mission (Chang, 2014). A tug-of-war between costs and investments is inevitable when more people are needed, which means management must do everything in its power to integrate and synergize different bottom lines.

Business development

Next to professional resources, the execution or business development is the major building block for social enterprises. Many may rely on compassion in the beginning, but sympathy and moving stories only work to win customers over once. While supporters are drawn to social enterprises because of their mission, it takes a quality product or service to bring them back time and time again. All NPOs and for-profits have the common need to focus on administration, finances, sales, production, and customer service along with making smart choices to keep things on track. This is a test of how sensitive social entrepreneurs are to the market and how well they utilize the limited resources on hand because they face the same challenges and risks of any commercial endeavor.

Inevitably, some social enterprises are by nature less agile in the face of changing markets when compared with their NPO counterparts. Sometimes they cannot take advantage of plummeting cost at markets when making purchases because ensuring smallholders guaranteed or fair prices is part of their social mission. In the same vein as the fair trade, once the commitment could be consistently upheld, stable support from the consumers might just follow. A good example is the Homemakers Union Consumers Co-op, which shows that winning public trust can provide the advantage needed to build a stable and robust support system.

Governance/accountability

Because of their social causes, social enterprises often are crowned with halos that subject them to close public scrutiny. Put under the microscope, transparent operations and an internal and external accountability system are musts in order to win trust and credibility (Chen, R., 2014). Governance is far more important for social enterprises than for traditional businesses because they must constantly consider the interests of relevant parties, which are needed for their supporting and participating roles. For these organizations, the role of governance is not just monitoring, but energizing, protecting, and supporting. Different types of social organizations need different board structures based on their ages, missions, personnel makeups, and professional needs. It is important for them to find appropriate directors with complementary skills and resources to ensure that a diversity of voices and needs is included in strategic decisions.

The majority of social enterprises rely upon cause-related marketing (CRM), which is based on cross-organizational cooperation (PO and NPO). However, there are no such typical checks and balances when social enterprises are promoting their products or services in the ethical market, which makes disclosure and financial transparency all the more important to avoid loopholes. The critical question then becomes which stakeholder has the right to demand and the ability to ensure this transparency.

At present in Taiwan, this major concern is left up to self-discipline and good governance. Current practices include self-reporting of profit distribution policies and practices (Leu, 2013), as seen with Luku Tea; promulgating measures to achieving common goods, as seen with News & Market; or designing schemes to encourage public oversight, like membership and sponsorship, as seen with Taiwan Rice Farmer. In general, when self-disciplinary management is not enough to hold the public's trust, government compliance measures or independent third-party assessment are alternatives to keeping legitimacy viable.

Funding

No social enterprise can possibly achieve its vision without the necessary financial capital, the fuel for starting its engines and keeping them running. Basic financing options in Taiwan include funding from family and friends, equity, credit, and bonds, but more and more options are showing up on the scene;

in addition, Taiwan has seen a rise in crowdfunding through online platforms such as Flying V and Red Turtle, together with three newly established national social enterprise awards. Angel investors and traditional funding from charity groups and the government (Lin, 2014) could also be seen in this light. While venture capitalists at the present seem a rarity, the rise in the visibility of credible social enterprises coupled with a clear legal status for them in the future will prove an important resource when seeking funding resources and growth enablers. In the early stage of establishing a venture, entrepreneurs' personal networks, credibility and business models are the basic resources available, but when the venture is aiming for the next milestone in expansion or diversity, social entrepreneurs are likely to find they need more capital. For the next stage of fund raising, a sound governance structure and accountability become the keys to convincing investors.

Conclusion

Looking at Taiwan's social enterprise development over the past several years, it is clear that agriculture dominates the category of newly founded companies, with the value chain activities ranging from production to brand building and particularly promotion for smallholders. Such a phenomenon gives a glimpse into society trends and a developmental trajectory.

Local agriculture has seen a major decline over the past decade under unfavorable public policies that have seen grain self-sufficiency levels plummet and the controversies over farm land appropriation from smallholders intensify. Facing these problems, the young generation has chosen, instead of conventional political advocacy, to take commercial means in a bid to draw society's attention to the agriculture sector by promoting eco-friendly practices, organic production methods, and systems like fair trade, and guaranteed purchasing. In the meantime, a spate of food safety problems over recent years has driven consumers to view agriculture products more than as just a commodity, propelling consumers to reflect and become more conscious about the cultural and health implications. Together, the supply and demand factors pushed the impetus for change and revitalization.

If the essence of social entrepreneurship is to address social issues that are overlooked or even created by the market, government policy, and the welfare system, it is fair to say that wherever problems arise, there is an opportunity for social enterprises to develop and flourish. This perspective indicates that health care, elderly care, and higher educational challenges faced by Taiwan society might be fertile grounds for future organizations to make a strong impact. To tap the potential of market size and scalability, it is paramount for social entrepreneurs to seek the underlying root causes of each social issue of concern rather than just tackle directly the problems appearing on the surface. By looking into the initiating or fundamental cause of a causal chain which leads to the apparent undesirable social outcome, social entrepreneurs would be less likely to be constrained by the specific target groups or locality of concern, but be more likely to come up with innovative solutions to invoke substantive changes that could further be diffused.

Although there is plenty of interest in Taiwanese society toward social enterprise, it is not a panacea. Not every issue is well suited to social entrepreneurship, nor can these organizations fully replace the conventional role of non-profits. The social entrepreneurship model brings risks and challenges, and asking the vulnerable to jump onto the bandwagon and start a business requires careful consideration (Hu, Chang, & Wong, 2012). Instead, social enterprises should be seen as one answer to changes in society, and not the only answer. However, the spirit of social entrepreneurship – creating social value and espousing social innovation – is suitable for any organization to promote.

It takes a wealth of concerned citizens with the spirit of social entrepreneurship to create new approaches in changing the world. From the central government to local city and township administrations, the public sector in Taiwan is putting great efforts into encouraging development with the expectation that it could be a cure for many social ailments. But scholars and social entrepreneurs themselves largely oppose any rush to set the idea of social enterprise into a rigid legal framework. Some are open to legislation to define what constitutes a social enterprise, but many are disinclined to set up a certification system and grading criteria as a basis for preferential or tax-exempt status, as is the case in Korea. The prevailing concerns are that social enterprises are still in an embryonic state and are subject to constant evolution even as they seek to establish legitimacy, making it difficult to come up with one broad standard to certify all of them. Any rigid system at this stage will only stem the growth of the very organizations that the government wants to encourage. On the contrary, it is suggested that citizen engagement gives these organizations the base to boom; all that is needed from the government is the creation of a friendly, encouraging atmosphere that forgoes the preventive presumptions in favor of the positive approach of embracing civic awareness and grassroots support (Chen, 2012).

Given their social mission, size and scale are not the end goal for social enterprises. By nature, they focus on solving the problems of specific communities or specific groups of people (often marginalized) and thus a small sector of society, meaning that scaling up may never be a realistic option. But since social change in theory outweighs market dominance, this does not mean success is unattainable.

As for whether any single organization can achieve its goals, none can expect to tackle the complicated variety of outstanding social problems single-handedly. Recent discussions on the notion of *collective impact* (Kania & Kramer, 2011) could perhaps shed light on future social enterprise development, in terms of more effectively mobilizing and leveraging resources. What makes social enterprise different is the tendency of socially aware organizations to work together on common issues of concern, the opposite of how traditional businesses see others in the same sector as rivals. For social enterprises, competition is a chance to establish and improve an organic, multilevel union of common interests. In the process of doing so, they will undoubtedly see their cooperative networks expand to cover all walks of society, from non-profits to governments and communities and all types of organizations (Chen, J., 2014). Given the relative abundant social capital in Taiwan, platform strategy along with cross-sector communication and coordination (Selsky & Parker, 2005) are promising concepts to develop into practical mechanisms in aiding social enterprises. Additionally, the concept of collaborative governance well rooted in the public administration field or the more recent advocacy of "pluralist forms of governance" might shed further light in providing proactive response to social issues. For the latter, it's been suggested that organizations that tackle social exclusion on both fronts – embracing a trading purpose that addresses the perceived needs of socially marginalized groups, and allowing participation by them in decision-making and wealth creation processes – are most likely to make enduring impacts (Ridley-Duff, 2007). In Taiwan, we have seen operations of such similar spirit, such as the regenerated Taomi Eco-Village supported by the Newhomeland Foundation, and the empowered tribal communities in developing organic farming within the alliance network of Aurora Social Enterprise. These conceptual issues and ongoing cases are well worth further study and exploration for both academic and managerial interests.

References

Alter, K. (2003). Social Enterprise Typology, http://www.4lenses.org/setypology/print, accessed 10 August 2014.

Chang, Ying-Shu (2014). What Can We Do? What Can't We Do? To Figure Out the Brand New Value of Disability Employment. *The 12th NPO Management Conference*, Chiayi, Taiwan.

Chen, Chiu-Cheng (2014). "Preliminary Study of Social Enterprise Legislation and the Fulfillment of SE's Public Value", *Journal of NPO Management*, 16: 28–36.

Chen, Jennifer H. (2012). Social Entrepreneurship in East Asia, presented in SEES Colloquium on Global Perspectives of Social Entrepreneurship: The State of the Field. *The 41st ARNOVA Annual Conference*, USA.

Chen, Jennifer H. (2014). "The Power of the Collective", *Journal of NPO Management*, 16: 120–131.

Chen, R. (2014). "Governing: the Explicit Part of Organization's Soul", in *Power of Good: How Social Enterprise Is Shaking the World*. Taipei: Reveal Books, pp. 267–269.

Cheng, Sheng-Fen and Wang, Zhi-Ya (2010). "The Development of Social Enterprises in Taiwan", *China Nonprofit Review*, 6: 32–59.

Cheng, Sheng-Fen (2007). "The Conception of Social Enterprises", *Policy Research*, 7: 65–108.

Chiu, Chi-Hao (2009). "Research on Job Markets for Rehabilitators: Labor Cooperative Suggested", *Da-Yeh Journal of General Education*, 3: 109–124.

Dees, G. (1998). The Meaning of "Social Entrepreneurship". Draft. https://www.fuqua. duke.edu/centers/case/documents/Dees_SEdef.pdf, accessed 31 July 2014.

Emerson, J. (2003). "The Blended Value Proposition: Integrating Social and Financial Returns", *California Management Review*, Summer, 45(4): 35–51.

Harding, R. (2004). "Social Enterprise: The New Economic Engine?" *Business Strategy Review*, Winter: 49–55.

Hsieh, Bang-Jun and Jiang, Hsiao-Yu (2014). *The First Three Years of Practicing Social Enterprise: Dialogue in the Dark for 1000 Days*. Taipei: Taiwan Foundation for the Blind.

Hu, Jer-San Hu, Chang, Tzu-Yang, & Wong, Haw-Ran (2012). "The Relations of Social Entrepreneurship Models and Resources Integration in Social Enterprise", *Journal of Entrepreneurship Research*, 7: 1–25.

Johnson, D. (2008). " 'Doing Well by Doing Good' Garners Broad Appeal for Academy of Management Conference", *Equal Opportunities International*, 27(7): 646–653.

Kania, J., & Kramer, M. (2011). "Collective Impact", *Stanford Social Innovation Review*, Winter: 36–41.

Kerlin, J. (2006). "Social Enterprise in the United States and Europe: Understanding and Learning from the Differences", *Voluntas,* 17: 247–263.

Kuan, Yu-Yuan, & Wang, Shu-Twu (2010). "The Impact of Public Authorities on the Development of Social Enterprises in Taiwan", *Journal of Public Affairs Review*, 11(1): 1–21.

Lee, J. (2013). *Facilitating Social Changes, Social Enterprise Insights*, http://www.sein sights.asia/story/507/794/1190, accessed 24 August 2014.

Leu, Chao-Hsien (2013). "Social Enterprise: Operational Models & Ethical Market", *Community Development Journal,* 143: 78–88.

Liao, Chia-Chan (2014). "The Transformational Process of Turning a Community-based Initiative into a Social Enterprise", *Journal of NPO Management,* 16: 1–27.

Lin, Yi-Han (2014). Raising Funds: To Activate the Social Enterprises, in *Power of Good: How Social Enterprise Is Shaking the World*. Taipei: Reveal Books, pp. 291–294.

Martin, R., & Osberg, S. (2007). "Social Entrepreneurship: The Case for Definition", *Stanford Social Innovation Review*, Spring: 29–39.

Modelo, M. (2014). "The Paradox of Fair Trade", *Stanford Social Innovation Review,* 12(1): 40–45.

OECD (1999). *Social Enterprise*. Paris: OECD Publishing.

Pelchat, M. (2004). *Enterprising Asian NPOs: Social Entrepreneurship in Taiwan*. Taipei: Himalaya Foundation.

Porter, M., & Kramer, M. (2011). "Creating Shared Value", *Harvard Business Review*, 89(1): 62–77.

Putnam, R. (2000). *Bowling Alone: The Collapse and Revival of American Community*. New York: Simon & Schuster.

Ramirez, K. (2012). "Verifying Social Enterprise: Applying Lessons from Fairtrade and other Certifications", in J. Kickul & S. Bacq (Eds.), *Patterns in Social Entrepreneurship Research*, London: Edward Elgar.

Ridley-Duff, R. (2007). "Communitarian Perspectives on Social Enterprise", *Corporate Governance: An International Review*, 15 (2): 382–392.

Selsky, J. & Parker, B. (2005). "Cross-sector Partnerships to Address Social Issues: Challenges to Theory and Practice", *Journal of Management*, 31: 849–873.

SRDA (2013). 2013 Taiwan Social Change Survey (Round 6, Year 4): Risk Social, https://
srda.sinica.edu.tw/group/sciitem/1/1697, accessed 31 July 2014. Survey Research Data
Archive.
WDA (2014). 2014 Taiwan General Statistics, http://www.wda.gov.tw/home.jsp?page
no=201111160019, accessed 30 August 2014. Workforce Development Agency.

7 The entrepreneurship process in high-performing hybrid organizations

Insights from Diamond Cab

Yanto Chandra

Introduction

Despite the burgeoning research on social entrepreneurship (SE), the majority of research in this domain has been dominated by *Anglo-Saxon* perspectives (Dacin, Dacin, & Tracey, 2011; Defourny & Nyssens, 2010; Kerlin, 2006; Teasdale, 2011) and, to a smaller extent, *African* (Rivera-Santos, Holt, Littlewood, & Kolk, 2015) and *Asian* perspectives (Defourny & Kim, 2011). As predicted by *social origins theory* (Kerlin, 2010; Salamon & Anheier, 1998), different institutional contexts lead to different ways in which social change makers make, give sense to and organize responses to societal challenges. Different institutional contexts are also likely to give rise to different *institutional voids* (London & Hart, 2004; Mair & Marti, 2009) to which entrepreneurial actors can respond as a way of filling those voids. To date, we do not know whether and how social entrepreneurial practices and strategies in the Anglo-Saxon and South Asian contexts diverge or converge with those emerging from the Chinese context.

Research on SE in the Chinese context, where *the state* has historically played a large role in the provision of social services and welfare (Defourny & Kim, 2011) and where SE is not well understood due to linguistic, cultural, economic and political differences (Zhao, 2012; Yu, 2011), is critical. China and other countries embracing *East Asian welfare regimes* have been characterized as societies with a Confucian culture, state-driven development strategy, weak civil society, hierarchical relationships and gender inequality (Defourny & Kim, 2011). Since the early 1990s, however, civil society organizations have mushroomed, and contact with Anglo-Saxon countries, particularly the UK (i.e., the Sino-British Symposium on Social Enterprise and NPO in 2004), has sparked a new interest in the role of SE in the Chinese context. In Hong Kong, the 1997 Asian financial crisis changed the way welfare expenditures were managed, from a "passive giving" to "empowering" or welfare-to-work, which is more in line with the types of social investment known in the West (Ho & Chan, 2010). The more capitalistic and market-oriented Hong Kong has become a major force in the development of SE in China. As of May 2015, there were 457 social enterprises in Hong Kong, making it a region with one of the highest densities of SEs per each million population compared with Taiwan, Singapore or South Korea. What happens in the SE practices and development in Hong Kong is likely to naturally spill over to China as a form of transfer of best practices due to their similarities in culture, language and shared history.

Currently, little is known about *how and why certain social enterprises are successful in the Chinese context*. Most research on SE in the Chinese and Hong Kong contexts are either conceptual, descriptive or review papers (Ho & Chan, 2010; Man & Terence, 2013; Poon, Zhou, & Chan, 2009). We know very little about high-performing social enterprises that make a difference to their field of work and the SE sector in general. Moreover, while the teaching side of SE has mushroomed in Hong Kong and China, where the major universities in Hong Kong all offered one or more courses in SE in 2015, there remains a dearth of serious scholarly research on SE in this context that would be equally useful for scholars, practitioners, policymakers and students of SE. In-depth studies of social enterprises in the Chinese context are likely to be a good starting point, as they will add to our understanding of what works, what does not work, why it works and how it works, and they will delve beyond the macro (and descriptive) perspective that has dominated SE research in the Chinese context (Ho & Chan, 2010; Man & Terence, 2013; Yu, 2011; Zhao, 2012). Obviously, there is still a great deal of work to be conducted to further advance SE research using micro-level perspectives involving the in-depth case study method and focusing on the organizational side in the Chinese context.

This study seeks to close this gap by exploring one of the most successful social enterprises in Hong Kong, Diamond Cab, which has successfully created a specialty taxi market from the ground up and turned it into a legitimate market in less than five years, in order to understand the key lessons from its success for theory, practice and policy. In this study, I ask: *what factors explain the successful development of Diamond Cab?* In the next section, I will first offer an overview of SE. I will then explain the methodology and discuss the findings. I conclude with the implications of the study and suggest avenues for future research.

An overview of social entrepreneurship

SE as a field of research and practice has existed for at least two decades. SE has been regarded as a central tenet of regional development strategies in the UK, especially in areas of deprivation (Parkinson & Howorth, 2008). As a new field, SE still lacks a clear definition. Some call it a 'contested concept' (Choi & Majumdar, 2014). Other scholars define it as using practices and processes that are unique to entrepreneurship to achieve aims that are distinctly social, regardless of the presence or absence of a profit motive (Short et al., 2009). Another definition states that social value creation is a process in which resources are combined in new ways to meet social needs, stimulate social change, or create new organizations (Mair & Marti, 2009). The hybrid nature of SE, as the pursuit of social and business goals, which has been called *hybrid organizing* (Battilana & Dorado, 2010; Doherty, Haugh, & Lyon, 2014), has become one of scholars' most-used theoretical lenses to study SE. Others define SE using an organizational identity perspective and define it as organizations that combine both *utilitarian/commercial* and normative/altruistic identities (Moss, Short, Payne, & Lumpkin, 2011; Stevens, Moray, & Bruneel, 2014).

A more recent view of SE has seen 'empowerment' as its dominant goal, by means of *optimizing* value creation and *satisficing* on value capture (Santos, 2012). Santos' definition emphasizes the importance of maintaining a *predominant focus* in organizing, either on *value creation* or *value capture* but not both. The former refers to the externalities of organizational activities after accounting for the opportunity costs required in mobilizing resources to achieve organizational goals. The latter refers to the generation of business value through organizations' commercial activities after deducting the expenses needed to mobilize resources to achieve organizational goals. The inability to maintain a predominant focus can lead to 'mission drift' by social enterprises (e.g., the case of the Mexican bank Compartamos; Kent & Dacin, 2013; Santos, 2012). *Empowerment*, rather than control, is a useful concept to describe SE. Empowerment refers to capacity and self-efficacy building (Chetkovich & Kunreuther, 2006; Ozer & Bandura, 1990; Santos, 2012) where individuals are given the ability, knowledge, skills and resiliency skills (e.g., positive self-beliefs) to exercise greater control over their lives, alter their environments (Ozer & Bandura, 1990; Spreitzer, 1995) and make strategic life choices (Kabeer, 1999). Empowerment in SE tends to refer to an important but not sole aspect of SE; the dominant goal of empowerment must be working together and being supported by social enterprises' business and operations models (Sodhi & Tang, 2011; Yunus, Moingeon, & Lehmann-Ortega, 2010).

One example is Germany's Andreas Heinecke, who, after his encounter with a blind colleague, started a lifelong quest to seek solutions that improve the well-being of disabled people. He developed a social enterprise called Dialogue in the Dark (DiD) that *empowers* visually impaired people by *training* and *employing* them as blind guides in the DiD's seventy-five-minute dark tour. The social enterprise charges an entrance ticket for individual visitors and corporate clients and manages the *revenue* to cover its costs. The excess funds are used to support its *global expansion*. This social enterprise engages in various social innovation activities, from its legendary dark-room tour, to dinner in the dark, concerts in the dark and many others. Today, DiD is a multinational social enterprise and has operations in over thirty countries (http://www.dialogue-in-the-dark.com/about-us/history-founder). Unlike for-profit and non-profit organizations, social enterprises *generate income* by selling products and services, but their purpose is to *create social value* and *empower society*, not to simply create wealth. Their focus is predominantly value creation, not value capture. They combine *social business* and *operations models* with *empowerment* goals.

Methodology

To answer the research question, I conducted an in-depth interview with the founder of Diamond Cab, Doris Leung, and invited her to give a series of guest lectures to an SE course where I am a course leader. To gain a holistic understanding of the case, I also interviewed Francis Ngai, the CEO of Social Ventures Hong Kong (SvHK), which is a venture philanthropy organization that provides funding and technical expertise to Diamond Cab, and invited him to give guest lectures in my SE course. I also attended the two informants' talks during the Hong Kong SE Summit in 2014 to enrich my understanding of the case. I further conducted a media article search on Diamond Cab to gain a more holistic understanding of the case and fill in the gaps not covered by the interviews and guest lectures. This *iterative process* of data collection and immersion helps develop a *rich and thick* understanding of the social enterprise and is crucial in the analysis stage to identify the factors that explain the success of the SE. Prior to the analysis stage, all interviews were transcribed by a native-English-speaking transcriber. In the next section, I illustrate the historical development of the social enterprise in question and use subheadings to organize key thoughts about the case.

The history of Diamond Cab

Personal values and prior knowledge

Diamond Cab CEO Doris Leung graduated from Hong Kong Polytechnic University, where she studied language and communication. She later finished a masters in journalism at Hong Kong University in 2003. She grew up in a middle-class family. Her father is a butcher and her mother helps her father in the meat stall. After graduating in 1993, she worked for many years as a *journalist*, mostly covering social and grassroots issues, including poverty, the elderly, disabled, social workers, etc. This *sensitized* her to various social problems in Hong Kong, particularly ageing, disability and poverty. She claimed that her passion for social issues and activism started at a young age, when her parents and family, particularly her aunt, often taught her about *social (in)justice*. She illustrated this using an example where she picked a fight with a foreign visitor who did not queue in the crowded Disneyland in Hong Kong. Based on my observation of her Facebook activity between July 2014 and July 2015, Leung is a highly active user of Facebook and often writes about social issues, from supporting gay rights and democracy to elderly rights.

Personal distress and opportunity recognition

Ms. Leung had the idea to start the Diamond Cab social enterprise in 2008–2009 following her difficulties trying to transport her middle-aged mother, who was suffering from brain tumors (interview with Doris Leung, 2013), to medical appointments. The experience made Leung realize how difficult it was for elderly wheelchair users and their relatives to get to medical appointments using standard public transport. "As the main caregiver, I experienced the frustration of trying to take her wheelchair to frequent doctor visits," said Leung. She learned of popular but *illegal and often unsanitary vans* that frequently transport elderly wheelchair patients. She was surprised that the illegal van operators charged hefty amounts to transport the elderly using vehicles that also transported live chickens and pigs and vegetables, among other cargo. The illegal van operators' advertisements listed "the elderly" alongside "live animals" and "vegetables" (an interesting insight that Ms. Leung often used in the class discussion about her SE). She had an initial interest in the idea but did not become serious about it until many months later.

Not long after, circa 2008–2009, she sought ideas from her friends, "The 30s Group", a group of successful professionals in their 30s living and working in Hong Kong, to discuss her initial ideas. The group comprises bankers, accountants, management consultants, marketers, IT specialists and lawyers, among others, and has performed various volunteer activities. The 30s Group is an informal, civil society organization that emerged in response to the 2003 SARS (severe acute respiratory syndrome) crisis that hit Hong Kong. This acquaintance led Leung to Francis Ngai, the CEO of SvHK, a pioneer venture philanthropy organization that provides financial and non-financial support to social ventures and social purpose organizations; he is also a key member of the 30s Group. SvHK had been scouting for social innovations and there was a mutual interest in Diamond Cab.

Opportunity co-exploitation and resource bricolage

Diamond Cab was formed in early 2010, SvHK provided the initial financing [an undisclosed amount] and business expertise, networks and technical support. Diamond Cab's business model is no different from that of any other taxi operator. They buy taxi licenses – usually costing around HK$7 million per license (equivalent to a tiny two bedroom apartment in Hong Kong) – and hire kindhearted taxi drivers to serve the elderly, wheelchair users and people (elders and non-elders) who have difficulty traveling using regular public transport. Diamond Cab's taxi is not a standard taxi; instead, it is a modified version of a Toyota Noah with added features, including a specially designed back door as a point of entry to the taxi.

The taxi is designed in such a way that it can accommodate two wheelchair users (sitting in wheelchairs) and two caretakers in separate seats. Comfort, safety and dignity for the elderly are critical issues for Leung, which she frequently repeated in her interviews and lectures.

Diamond Cab relies on a partner's taxi call center (an existing taxi operator) to take taxi reservations. This strategy allowed the SE to quickly launch on a shoestring budget and avoid making a large investment in call centers. Diamond Cab became the first ever SE in China, perhaps even in Asia, to offer this type of service and model. It keeps a lean operation and has only one full-time staff member, whose duty is primarily to match taxi reservations with drivers, plus Leung herself, who does most of the marketing and fund raising. In its initial stages, Diamond Cab co-created the market for its taxi services by signing an agreement with two large elderly homes. The latter proved to be crucial for its early survival because it created a captive market. Overall, the founder raised HK$2,000,000 (US$258,000) as an initial investment from all shareholders, including SvHK, two elderly homes, a taxi operator and seven individual impact investors (Chan, 2013). They used the funds to purchase five Toyota Noah vans from Japan.

Social business and operations model

Diamond Cab generates revenue from several sources. The first source of revenue is the *taxi fees* that it charges customers, who usually need to book a taxi at least twenty-four hours in advance. The flat taxi charge (as of July 2015) is HK$115 (US$14.8), which is higher than normal taxi fare (HK$22 or US$2.8), and flag fall charges apply. This is logical because its target market base is much smaller than the mainstream taxi market. The taxi applies extra charges for passengers picked up in different zones to cover the extra costs incurred to its drivers. The taxi drivers pay a *fixed per-trip or per-day rent* to the SE and keep the remainder as their income. Thus, the SE shares business risks with its drivers.

As time passed, Leung developed innovative ideas to generate extra revenue. She created a mini Diamond Cab model car that she sells to corporate sponsors and corporate social responsibility programs at HK$500 per piece. She regularly organizes mini-sedan chair races, where groups of young men and women carrying passengers using China's traditional 'human bicycle' compete for prizes (see Figure 7.1). In such events, as Leung claimed, they easily sell 500 to 600 model cars to corporate sponsors. The SE also collaboratively works to promote disabled artists and displays the paintings of several disabled artists on the doors of its taxis.

Figure 7.1 The Diamond Sedan competition.

The Diamond Sedan competition is modeled after the means of transportation popular in the 1950s to 1970s in Hong Kong and China, where a vehicle is carried by manual power.

The photos are courtesy of Diamond Cab Ltd.

In 2013, Diamond Cab began selling advertising space to a regular advertiser, a company selling products for the elderly. In late 2013, a sixth Diamond Cab joined the fleet, funded by a social impact investor who bought a taxi license and signed a five-year deal to rent the cab to Diamond.

As the venture has grown, Diamond Cab has expanded its range of services to include aspects of *entertainment* in the lives of the elderly, disabled and wheelchair users. The social enterprise organizes events to encourage their clients to go out for leisure activities, such as the Charity Tour in collaboration with Disneyland Hong Kong and Diamond Luxury in collaboration with Hyatt Regency Hong Kong, and offers a means of transportation. The Charity Tour is an innovative product by Diamond Cab that seeks corporate sponsors to pay for a taxi trip plus entry into, for instance, one of Hong Kong's theme parks. It has received varying degrees of media attention in other countries, including India and Singapore. More recently years, Diamond Cab has partnered with Singapore's MRT Corporation, which has wheelchair taxi service for its train stations, to "raise awareness of wheelchair-friendly taxi services in both Singapore and Hong Kong, to facilitate planning for such local transport services when passengers travel between the two countries" (SMRT, 2014).

I also visited Diamond Cab's website (http://www.diamondcab.com.hk/en/story.php) and noted its mission statement:

> Diamond Cab Ltd.'s . . . mission is to provide "legal, safe and convenient point-to-point transportation for the wheelchair-bound passengers in Hong Kong," to help meet the large and growing needs of its aging population. Diamond Cab was launched in Feb 2010 and with six Diamond Cabs has provided over 76,500 single trips for elder wheelchair users. Diamond Cab has 17 [paid] cab drivers who provide wheelchair-accessible transportation. However, Diamond Cab is not just a non-emergency ambulance that takes elders to medical appointments, but it organizes weekly evening social events to "help the elderly enjoy barrier-free activities like karaoke parties or night sightseeing tours."[1] . . . Diamond Cab's mission is "to promote active ageing through providing easier access to public transport for our senior citizens, thereby helping them stay mobile and independent." It also serves the disabled, including children, and their caregivers.

Social and financial performance

As of May 2015, Diamond Cab operates six taxis and has run over 70,000 wheelchair trips. The enterprise broke even in its second year of operation. The impact investment by SvHK "has expectation of return but funds are recycled" (interview with Francis Ngai, 2015), although there are other co-impact investors who expect some returns. The overall shareholders consist of SvHK (65 percent), individual investors (15 percent), elderly homes (10 percent) and a taxi operator (10 percent). Diamond Cab was one of the finalists of the UK Social Enterprise Awards 2012, and the founder was listed as a top three finalist (Asia Pacific) in the Cartier

Women's Initiative Awards 2013. In mid-2015, the social enterprise joined crowd-funding via indiegogo.com to finance its further expansion.

Discussion

Porterian focus strategy: from opportunity space and operations to identity

Diamond Cab's success may be attributed to several strategies. One important strategy used by Diamond Cab has been the "focus" strategy (Porter, 1996). That is, the social enterprise *focuses on creating a specialty taxi market* and *develops its organizational capabilities in this market* and nothing else. It does this by refining its initial ideas to provide point-to-point transportation for the elderly, disabled and wheelchair users consistently. This facilitates a "hockey stick" organizational learning, allowing the social enterprise to kill bad ideas faster and find its opportunity space earlier (Chandra, Styles, & Wilkinson, 2015). It has not attempted to enter any other new lines of businesses in its critical years (this holds true as of July 2015). This is in contrast to some of the slow-growing local social enterprises that try to engage in more than a dozen businesses, from handling the disabled to opening retail shops, cleaning services, tourism, and cafes, which retards the learning curve.

Another favorable aspect of the focused strategy is that it allows Diamond Cab to *systematize its operations*, which is crucial for its scaling up/replication stage. The founder had no prior experience in the taxi market, let alone the specialty taxi market, and thus experienced a steep learning curve. For instance, the enterprise relies on an existing taxi operator's call center to help operate the business and uses a manual booking system to match taxi drivers with passengers, and its taxis require special repair and maintenance services because the company relies on a non-standard taxi (Toyota Noah). Taxis are a retail business with a high level of interactions with passengers, and systematic daily operations are therefore central to the functioning of the enterprise. By being focused on the one thing it does best, the social enterprise is able to manage its *operations* in delivering the best possible services to the target beneficiaries. Scholars call social enterprises enablers of financial, informational and demand-and-supply flows (Sodhi & Tang, 2011), but this study enriches the literature by highlighting the role of social enterprises as enablers of people flows.

Another key advantage of the focused strategy has been the development of a clear *organizational identity*, both normative and utilitarian (Moss et al., 2011). The social enterprise carries a strong *normative identity* as a service provider to Hong Kong's neglected communities, particularly the elderly and disabled, and empowers them to live to the fullest with the freedom to travel and be looked after by kind-hearted taxi drivers. The enterprise also has a strong *utilitarian identity*, as a new solution to Hong Kong's ageing problem that is financially sustainable and does not depend on government grants or subsidies. This clarity of organizational identity helps build Diamond Cab's reputation and *legitimacy* as a player that has created a specialty taxi market. Importantly, the focus strategy helps the media to generate publicity about what Diamond Cab is all about and leaves people with a clear idea about what it stands for and why, and what it is good at.

Social design orientation: compassion and designing a new compensation model

Another important driver of Diamond Cab's success could be its *social design orientation* (Brown & Wyatt, 2010; Hillgren, Seravalli, & Emilson, 2011) in regard to its founding and business management. The social design orientation is deeply rooted in the founder's desire to create an enterprise that would provide better services than the illegal van operators, who were deficient in providing safety, hygiene and respect to elderly and disabled passengers. The illegal van operators in Hong Kong typically use the same space where they store livestock, vegetables and other goods with their elderly and disabled human passengers. Driven by a strong sense of *compassion* (Arend, 2013; Miller, Grimes, Mcmullen, & Vogus, 2012), the founder and her business partner, Social Ventures Hong Kong, were able to seek solutions that precisely fill in the gaps in the market by providing a *unique taxi design* that creates strong *social value* and high value for the target beneficiaries. In other words, the social enterprise humanizes the elderly and disabled passengers through the unique interior design of its taxi fleet.

Another key issue in social design is how the social enterprise designed its *compensation model for its taxi drivers*. In the traditional compensation model, a taxi driver leases a taxi from an operator and then races against the clock to cover his costs and make an income. To achieve its social mission to make elderly and disabled people more mobile, Diamond Cab challenges and redesigns this model by creating a *per-trip* or *per-day compensation model* scheduled around the driver's available work hours. The social enterprise focuses on hiring drivers who share its mission, such as assisting the elderly and disabled passengers to board and disembark from the taxi and providing special attention as required, not profit-hungry drivers. The unique taxi design and the per-trip/per-day compensation model are novel and have never been tried in the Hong Kong market. While this new compensation model has not turned mainstream, it demonstrates that it has a value in the society and fills a void in the market. This demonstrates the *institutional constraints* faced by the social enterprise and how it *innovates* to break the constraint and *recreates a new market and institutions* around it (Cajaiba-Santana, 2014; Weerawardena & Mort, 2012).

Social bricolage

Diamond Cab faced high uncertainty in its initial years as it attempted to create a new market that did not exist: a specialty taxi market. This represents the Knightian uncertainty (Knight, 1921; Langlois & Cosgel, 1993) with no model, no proof of concept or past data for extrapolation to make a go or no-go decision. For-profit investors will likely be averse to this type of investment. In the face of such uncertainty, particularly in dealing with the institutional constraints (i.e., the specialty taxi market did not exist in Hong Kong at that time) and resource constraints (i.e., the social enterprise had a minuscule startup budget), the social enterprise engages in *social bricolage* (Baker & Nelson, 2005; Di Domenico, Haugh, & Tracey, 2010; Vanevenhoven et al., 2011) by drawing on the *resources of other actors* (i.e., the partner venture philanthropy and an existing taxi operator who shares a similar vision) and *key stakeholders* (i.e., two elderly homes) to co-create the specialty taxi market.

The outcome of social bricolage speaks for itself. Bricolage not only reduces the uncertainty and the high potential loss in case the social enterprise fails but also brings in cross-sector partners as stakeholders and co-owners of the social enterprise.

Formal and informal advice and resource networks

Among the least frequently mentioned success drivers of Diamond Cab are the people behind the scenes who *formally and informally* contribute ideas, expertise and resources to the social enterprise. In the initial stages, the informal 30s Group, a volunteer group of successful professionals in their mid-30s (bankers, accountants, marketers, IT specialist, lawyers, etc.) was responsible for the initial recognition and validation of the founder's vision to create the social enterprise. Interestingly, a key member of the group, Francis Ngai (the CEO of Social Ventures Hong Kong, one of the pioneer venture philanthropies in Hong Kong) had recently made a successful turnaround of an almost-bankrupt NGO. This led him and the Group to believe that business skills can be fruitfully used to solve social problems.

They were also influenced by Mohammed Yunus' talk on social business (interview with Francis Ngai, 2015), which prompted their interest in offering assistance to the founder's idea for Diamond Cab. This led the social enterprise to SvHK, an official partner that brought managerial expertise, funding, and contacts that helped the founder tame uncertainty. As stated by the founder, each new service or product concept is tested in the market anonymously before it is launched, at which point the press are called for a press conference. This strategy appears to be trivial, but it provides important feedback that helps the social enterprise succeed.

The sheer number of experts that are connected to the founder and social enterprise facilitates the cross-pollination of ideas that creates superior ideas. This reminds us of the application of the 'innovation tournament' process (Terwiesch & Ulrich, 2009) that drives the founder's sound operational, financial and strategic decision making.

Conclusion

Despite the burgeoning interest in social enterprises, entrepreneurship and innovation in the Chinese context, current research in SE in the Chinese context has largely been descriptive, conceptual or focused on the macro-level perspectives of the field. There is a dearth of in-depth studies that examine factors and contexts that explain the successful development of social enterprises in the Chinese context. To fill in this gap in the literature, I engaged in a three-year study of one of Hong Kong's (and China's) first and perhaps most successful social enterprises and sought to understand what accounts for its success. Within less than five years, the Diamond Cab social enterprise has created a new market: a specialty taxi market that serves a neglected segment of the elderly, disabled and wheelchair users.

The study reveals a number of important themes and variables that explain the successful development of the social enterprise in question. First is the importance of the role of *personal values, personal distress, prior knowledge of social problems* and their interactions that trigger *entrepreneurial alertness*, leading to the decision and activities to start a social enterprise. The founder has a strong sense of *social justice* and has been involved in *social activism* from a young age, which reflects the *personal values* (Hemingway, 2005; Miller et al., 2012; Tan, Williams, & Tan, 2005) that drive the person's interest in SE. The founder's *personal distress* (Yiu, Wan, Ng, Chen, & Su, 2014) after her mother was diagnosed with a serious illness and the inconvenience of having to personally take her mother to medical appointments was an important direct trigger that strengthened her alertness to the opportunity to create a social enterprise. The founder's *prior experience* as a journalist covering social issues, including ageing, poverty and disability, help *sensitize* her to problems around her and what human beings can do to alleviate the sufferings of others. This highlights the role of *prior knowledge* (Chandra, Styles, & Wilkinson, 2012; Shane, 2000) as a trigger of social entrepreneurial action. These variables are critical not only in starting but also sustaining the social enterprise. It is easy to see people starting a social enterprise and later "throwing in the towel" to do something else, such as engage in a for-profit enterprise, or being subject to "mission drift." It takes a certain type of person under certain circumstances to create a social entrepreneur. This may reveal the importance of the *traits-based perspective* of social entrepreneurship and the *situational thesis* of human behavior.

Second, this study reveals a *social constructionism view* (Downing, 2005) of social entrepreneurship and innovation whereby opportunities for social value creation are not a lone person or linear act, but rather a *collective act* (Montgomery, Dacin, & Dacin, 2012; Parkinson & Howorth, 2008) involving a *dynamic and complex process* of sense making and sense giving (Downing, 2005). Much behind this process lies in the use of *social bricolage* (Desa, 2012; Di Domenico et al., 2010) for managing institutional constraints (where the specialty taxi market is illegitimate and did not exist legally) and resource constraints (where the infant social enterprise has few resources with which to pursue opportunities). The socially constructed market space is also a reflection of the role of *informal and formal networks* (Birley, 1985) that are connected to the social enterprise. At least, as this study shows, informal networks play a crucial role in providing and validating a new idea that has long been embedded in the informal entrepreneurship sector (i.e., the illegal van operators). The formal networks seem to be more crucial in bringing social investment resources together and facilitating the co-exploitation of social business opportunities.

The last point concerns entrepreneurial strategies as they are employed by the social enterprise. The *focused strategy* (Porter, 1996) seems to be effectively working in this context where the specialty taxi market did not exist. The focused strategy allows the social enterprise to craft its *opportunity space* (Chandra et al., 2015) over time until it appears to be a legitimate industry. This means that there was plenty of trial and error and eliminating "false opportunities" (consisting of partners, investors, resources, and ideas) in the early stages of the opportunity space development. Unlike any social enterprise that enters an already established social market, Diamond Cab had no *templates* or *prototype opportunity* (Chandra et al., 2015; Elsbach & Kramer, 2003) to refer to at the outset as if there were an *institutional distance* between the founder/SvHK and the non-existing specialty taxi market. The efforts of Diamond Cab to learn and develop opportunities, systematize its daily operations and management, and sharpen its normative and utilitarian identity are largely influenced by the focused strategy. A final important factor is the social enterprise's *innovation* at the product, process and system levels. Research demonstrates that innovativeness in SE is critical to a social enterprise's sustainability and ability to create social value (Weerawardena & Mort, 2012). This study demonstrates that *social design orientation* (Brown & Wyatt, 2010; Hillgren et al., 2011), which involves prototyping, designing with social value and not profit, as the main focus and empathy for target beneficiaries, is critical to successful market creation. Through this orientation, the social enterprise created a new compensation model (i.e., per-trip or per-day compensation) that had never been attempted in Hong Kong (China) and that balanced the needs of social value and business value creation.

Implications

The Diamond Cab experience offers several implications for theory, practice and policy. At a theoretical level, this study highlights the *individual, network and strategy* level factors that are associated with a high-performing social enterprise. While this study is just a single case, it does offer evidence that the *traits and values* of individuals (e.g., passion for social justice), *personal distress* (i.e., having a sick parent) and *prior knowledge of social problems* play critical roles in motivating a person to become a social entrepreneur. These are important contributions made by this study. While research in SE has focused on *organizational* level variables (Battilana & Dorado, 2010; Ebrahim, Battilana, & Mair, 2014), there is still a lack of research on the *micro-foundations* of SE, particularly the role of *the persons behind social enterprises, their emotions, cognition and behavior*. For example, how social enterprises address the ups and downs of managing the difficulties in running a social enterprise is unknown. We also do not know how social entrepreneurs motivate themselves and their teams to pursue their hybrid goals and how the tensions that arise in balancing conflicting goals may affect what they do and their performance. What does it take to be an effective SE leader?

At the network level, this study reveals the prominence of *social bricolage* as a principle in dealing with institutional and resource constraints when creating a non-existent market. Although this finding is consistent with prior research on the importance of social bricolage (Baker & Nelson, 2005; Di Domenico et al., 2010), we still know little about the boundary conditions of social bricolage and to what extent it may hamper the success of a new social enterprise. Future research can examine different institutional contexts and how social bricolage is practiced and its eventual outcomes, as well as how it links up with different types of network measures (i.e., strong vs. weak ties; network centrality, density, etc.). Importantly, this study contributes to SE research by highlighting the role of *informal institutions as an early supporter of a social innovation.* As is true in the Chinese context as well as elsewhere, *informal institutions* (Webb, Bruton, Tihanyi, & Ireland, 2013; Webb, Tihanyi, Ireland, & Sirmon, 2009) play a specific role in creating and impeding the rise of a new social order. This means future research should study how and why informal organizations can function to enhance (or not) social innovation and what it means to formal institutions. Will informal institutions be more receptive or restrictive to new, change-making ideas, and how can social entrepreneurs address this?

At the strategy level, this study contributes to the SE literature by revealing the role of *focused strategy, creating social opportunity space* and *social design orientation* as possible antecedents of a high-performing social enterprise. The next questions will be the boundary conditions of the focused strategy and whether it is the only way to pursue high social impact and financial sustainability in SE. Does any other strategy exist? Some social enterprises are very successful because they pursue a "low-cost" strategy (Porter, 1996). However, are those that pursue a diversified strategy (at early or later stages of a life cycle) likely to be as successful? Does a social design orientation produce less than optimal outcomes compared with for-profit design orientation in the creation of social good? How can social enterprises strategize in the context of a non-existent market? What is the role of effectuation strategy as a means to address uncertainty (Sarasvathy, 2001)?

For practitioners and policymakers, this study highlights that there are ways for social investors and government as funders to spot the right candidates for social investment. This study shows that an understanding of the *biographical profiles* of a would-be social entrepreneur can help these stakeholders make better decisions by investing their funds in the "right" social entrepreneurs. SE is a long-term game, not a short, one-shot game; therefore, there must be identifying signals that are crucial for impactful investment. Second, would-be and current social entrepreneurs can benefit from the *principles and strategies* adopted by Diamond Cab (e.g., social bricolage, focused strategy, social design orientation, etc.) in how they start and manage a social enterprise. While there may be tacit knowledge involved and processes, procedures and mechanisms that cannot be easily transported to other organizations, the government can take note of the Diamond Cab recipe as points for debate in designing its future economic and welfare policies. For instance, will the Hong Kong government's *direct funding* for social enterprises be beneficial for the SE sector in the long run? How the government balances the need to *support, govern and regulate* the SE sector without *interfering* too much in the sector may be crucial. The Diamond Cab case shows that a laissez-faire government in regard to SE policy appears to help, not hamper, development. Finally, this study points to the role of *ideological compatibility* between SE and formal institutions. *Capitalism* is alive and well in Hong Kong and China and therefore the *social business* concept will be welcome in Hong Kong and today's China. Future models of hybrid organizing for social good may face less resistance because they are more ideologically compatible with existing institutions.

Note

1 www.indiegogo.com/projects/diamond-cab-taxi-accessible-for-aging-hong-kong#/story

References

Arend, R. J. (2013). "A Heart-Mind-Opportunity Nexus: Distinguishing Social Entrepreneurship for Entrepreneurs", *Academy of Management Review*, 38: 313–315. doi:10.5465/amr.2012.0251

Baker, T., & Nelson, R. (2005). "Creating Something from Nothing: Resource Construction through Entrepreneurial Bricolage", *Administrative Science Quarterly*, 50: 329–366.

Battilana, J., & Dorado, S. (2010). "Building Sustainable Hybrid Organizations: The Case of Commercial Microfinance Organization", *Academy of Management Journal*, 53(6): 1419–1440.

Birley, S. (1985). "The Role of Networks in the Entrepreneurial Process", *Journal of Business Venturing*, 1: 107–117.

Brown, T., & Wyatt, J. (2010). "Design Thinking for Social Innovation", *Stanford Social Innovation Review*, 8: 30–35.

Cajaiba-Santana, G. (2014). "Social Innovation: Moving the Field Forward. A Conceptual Framework", *Technological Forecasting and Social Change*, 82: 42–51. doi:10.1016/j.techfore.2013.05.008

Chan, O. (2013). Diamond Cab (Hong Kong) Ltd. http://epaper.chinadailyasia.com/focus-hk/article-1477.html

Chandra, Y., Styles, C., & Wilkinson, I. F. (2012). "An Opportunity-Based View of Rapid Internationalization", *Journal of International Marketing*, 20(1): 74–102.

Chandra, Y., Styles, C., & Wilkinson, I. F. (2015). "Opportunity Portfolio: Moving Beyond Single Opportunity Explanations in International Entrepreneurship Research", *Asia Pacific Journal of Management*, 32(1): 199–228.

Chetkovich, C. A., & Kunreuther, F. (2006). *From the Ground Up: Grassroots Organizations Making Social Change*. Ithaca, NY: Cornell University Press.

Choi, N., & Majumdar, S. (2014). "Social Entrepreneurship as an Essentially Contested Concept: Opening a New Avenue for Systematic Future Research", *Journal of Business Venturing*, 29(3): 363–376.

Dacin, M. T., Dacin, P. A., & Tracey, P. (2011). "Social Entrepreneurship: A Critique and Future Directions", *Organization Science*, 22(5): 1203–1213.

Defourny, J., & Kim, S.-Y. (2011). "Emerging Models of Social Enterprise in Eastern Asia: A Cross-country Analysis", *Social Enterprise Journal*, 7: 86–111.

Defourny, J., & Nyssens, M. (2010). "Social Enterprise in Europe: At the Crossroads of Market, Public Policies and Third Sector", *Policy and Society*, 29(3): 231–242. doi:10.1016/j.polsoc.2010.07.002

Desa, G. (2012). "Resource Mobilization in International Social Entrepreneurship: Bricolage as a Mechanism of Institutional Transformation", *Entrepreneurship: Theory and Practice*, 36: 727–751. doi:10.1111/j.1540–6520.2010.00430.x

Di Domenico, M., Haugh, H., & Tracey, P. (2010). "Social Bricolage: Theorizing Social Value Creation in Social Enterprises", *Entrepreneurship: Theory and Practice*, 34(4): 681–703.

Doherty, B., Haugh, H., & Lyon, F. (2014). "Social Enterprises as Hybrid Organizations: A Review and Research Agenda", *International Journal of Management Reviews*, 16: 417–436. doi:10.1111/ijmr.12028

Downing, S. (2005). "The Social Construction of Entrepreneurship: Narrative and Dramatic Processes in the Coproduction of Organizations and Identities", *Entrepreneurship: Theory and Practice*, 29: 185–204. doi:10.1111/j.1540–6520.2005.00076.x

Ebrahim, A., Battilana, J., & Mair, J. (2014). "Research in Organizational Behavior. The Governance of Social Enterprises: Mission Drift and Accountability Challenges in Hybrid Organizations", *Research in Organizational Behavior*, 34: 81–100.

Elsbach, K. D., & Kramer, R. M. (2003). "Assessing Creativity in Hollywood Pitch Meetings: Evidence for a Dual-process Model of Creativity Judgments", *Academy of Management Journal*, 46(3): 283–301.

Hemingway, C. (2005). "Personal Values as a Catalyst for Corporate Social Entrepreneurship", *Journal of Business Ethics*, 60: 233–249. doi:10.1007/sl0551–005–0132–5

Hillgren, P.-A., Seravalli, A., & Emilson, A. (2011). "Prototyping and Infrastructuring in Design for Social Innovation", *CoDesign*, 7(3–4): 169–183. doi:10.1080/15710882.2011.630474

Ho, A. P.-Y., & Chan, K.-T. (2010). "The Social Impact of Work-integration Social Enterprise in Hong Kong", *International Social Work*, 53(1): 33–45.

Kent, D., & Dacin, M. T. (2013). "Bankers at the Gate: Microfinance and the High Cost of Borrowed Logics", *Journal of Business Venturing*, 28(6): 759–773. doi:10.1016/j.jbusvent.2013.03.002

Kerlin, J. A. (2006). "Social Enterprise in the United States and Europe: Understanding and Learning from the Differences", *Voluntas: International Journal of Voluntary and Nonprofit Organizations*, 17(3): 246–262.

Kerlin, J. A. (2010). "A Comparative Analysis of the Global Emergence of Social Enterprise", *Voluntas: International Journal of Voluntary and Nonprofit Organizations*, 21, 162–179.

Knight, F. (1921). *Risk, Uncertainty and Profit*. New York: Hart, Schaffner and Marx.

Langlois, R. N., & Cosgel, M. M. (1993). "Frank Knight on Risk, Uncertainty, and the Firm: A New Interpretation", *Economic Inquiry*, 31(July): 456–465. doi:10.1111/j.1465–7295.1993.tb01305.x

London, T., & Hart, S. L. (2004). "Reinventing Strategies for Emerging Markets: Beyondthe Transnational Model", *Journal of International Business Studies*, 35(5): 350–370.]

Mair, J., & Marti, I. (2009). "Entrepreneurship in and around Institutional Voids: A Case Study from Bangladesh", *Journal of Business Venturing*, 24(5): 419–435. doi:10.1016/j.jbusvent.2008.04.006

Man, C. K., & Terence, Y.Y.K. (2013). "An overview of social enterprise development in China and Hong Kong", *Journal of Ritsumeikan Social Sciences and Humanities*, 5: 165–178.

Miller, T. L., Grimes, M. G., Mcmullen, J. S., & Vogus, T. J. (2012). "Venturing for Others with Heart and Head: How Compassion Encourages Social Entrepreneurship", *Academy of Management Review*, 37(4): 616–640.

Montgomery, A. W., Dacin, P. A., & Dacin, M. T. (2012). "Collective Social Entrepreneurship: Collaboratively Shaping Social Good", *Journal of Business Ethics*, 111: 375–388. doi:10.1007/s10551–012–1501–5

Moss, T. W., Short, J. C., Payne, G. T., & Lumpkin, G. T. (2011). "Dual Identities in Social Ventures: An Exploratory Study", *Entrepreneurship Theory and Practice*, 35(4): 805–830.

Ozer, E. M., & Bandura, A. (1990). "Mechanisms Governing Empowerment Effects: A Self-efficacy Analysis", *Journal of Personality and Social Psychology*, 58(3): 472–486. doi:10.1037/0022–3514.58.3.472

Parkinson, C., & Howorth, C. (2008). "The Language of Social Entrepreneurs", *Entrepreneurship & Regional Development*, 20(3): 285–309.

Poon, P. S., Zhou, L., & Chan, T. S. (2009). "Social entrepreneurship in a transitional economy: A critical assessment of rural Chinese entrepreneurial firms", *Journal of Management Development*, 28(2), 94–109.

Porter, M. (1996). What Is Strategy? *Harvard Business Review* (December). doi:10.1098/rspb.2008.0355

Rivera-Santos, M., Holt, D., Littlewood, D., & Kolk, A. (2015). "Social Entrepreneurship in Sub-Saharan Africa", *Academy of Management Perspectives*, 29(1): 72–91.

Salamon, L. M., & Anheier, H. K. (1998). "Social Origins of Civil Society: Explaining the Nonprofit Sector Cross-Nationally", *Voluntas: International Journal of Voluntary and Nonprofit Organizations*, 9(3): 213–248.

Santos, F. M. (2012). "A Positive Theory of Social Entrepreneurship", *Journal of Business Ethics*, 111(3): 335–351.

Sarasvathy, S. D. (2001). "Causation and Effectuation: Toward a Theoretical Shift from Economic Inevitability to Entrepreneurial Contingency", *Academy of Management Review*, 26(2): 243–263.

Shane, S. (2000). "Prior Knowledge and the Discovery of Entrepreneurial Opportunities", *Organization Science*, 11(4): 448–469. doi:10.1287/orsc.11.4.448.14602

Short, J., Moss, T., & Lumpkin, G. (2009). "Research in social entrepreneurship: Past contributions and future opportunities", *Strategic Entrepreneurship Journal*, 3: 161–194.

Sodhi, M. S., & Tang, C. S. (2011). "Social Enterprises as Supply-chain Enablers for the Poor", *Socio-Economic Planning Sciences*, 45(4): 146–153. doi:10.1016/j.seps.2011.04.001

SMRT. (2014). Press release. http://www.smrt.com.sg/Journey-with-Us/Taxis/Wheelchair-Accessible-Taxis

Stevens, R., Moray, N., & Bruneel, J. (2014). "The Social and Economic Mission of Social Enterprises: Dimensions, Measurement, Validation, and Relation", *Entrepreneurship: Theory and Practice*, 39(5): 1–32.

Tan, W.-L., Williams, J., & Tan, T.-M. (2005). "Defining the 'Social' in 'Social Entrepreneurship': Altruism and Entrepreneurship", *The International Entrepreneurship and Management Journal*, 1(65): 353–365. doi:10.1007/s11365–005–2600-x

Teasdale, S. (2011). "What's in a Name ? Making Sense of Social Enterprise Discourses", *Public Policy and Administration*, 27(2): 99–119.

Terwiesch, C., & Ulrich, K. T. (2009). *Innovation Tournaments: Creating and Selecting Exceptional Opportunities*. Boston: Harvard Business School Publishing.

Vanevenhoven, J., Winkel, D., Malewicki, D., Dougan, W. L., & Bronson, J. (2011). Varieties of bricolage and the process of entrepreneurship. *New England Journal of Entrepreneurship*, 14(2): 7.

Webb, J. W., Bruton, G. D., Tihanyi, L., & Ireland, R. D. (2013). "Research on Entrepreneurship in the Informal Economy: Framing a Research Agenda", *Journal of Business Venturing*, 28: 598–614. doi:10.1016/j.jbusvent.2012.05.003

Webb, J. W., Tihanyi, L., Ireland, R. D., & Sirmon, D. G. (2009). "You Say Illegal, I Say Legitimate: Entrepreneurship in the Informal Economy", *Academy of Management Review*, 34(3): 492–510. doi:10.5465/AMR.2009.40632826

Weerawardena, J., & Mort, G. S. (2012). "Competitive Strategy in Socially Entrepreneurial Nonprofit Organizations: Innovation and Differentiation", *Journal of Public Policy & Marketing*, 31(1): 91–101. doi:10.1509/jppm.11.034

Yiu, D. W., Wan, W. P., Ng, F. W., Chen, X., & Su, J. (2014). "Sentimental Drivers of Social Entrepreneurship: A Study of China's Guangcai (Glorious) Program", *Management and Organization Review*, 10(1): 55–80.

Yu, X. (2011). "Social Enterprise in China: Driving Forces, Development Patterns and Legal Framework", *Social Enterprise Journal*, 7(1): 9–32.

Yunus, M., Moingeon, B., & Lehmann-Ortega, L. (2010). "Building Social Business Models: Lessons from the Grameen Experience", *Long Range Planning*, 43(2–3): 308–325.

Zhao, M. (2012). "The Social Enterprise Emerges in China", *Stanford Social Innovation Review*, Spring, 31–35.

8 Public-private partnership in the development of social entrepreneurship in mainland China

The case of NPI

Ding Li

This chapter provides a case study of Mr. Zhao Lu, a social entrepreneur who established Non-Profit Incubator – an intermediary agency with multiple platforms to support the development of social entrepreneurship in China through mobilizing all kinds of social resources, especially funding and policy advocacy from government agencies. This case study is one of the first analyses to examine the perplexing relationship between government and social entrepreneurship development in China. According to a 2011 study of family philanthropy in Asia by UBS (a Swiss-origin bank) and INSEAD business school, "mainland China has the strongest level of government control over philanthropy of the Asian countries surveyed. Also 40% of the China-based respondents rated the emergence of social entrepreneurship as the most highly-anticipated trend" ("Social Entrepreneurship Takes Off in China" by Juliana Liu Hong Kong, correspondent, BBC News, 23 September 2012). This situation is embedded in the peculiar development stage of socialism with Chinese characteristics in mainland China. Since 1979, China has managed to carry out economic reform successfully without major political reform.[1] In 2013, The GDP of China reached US$9.4 trillion, with a world ranking of no. 2.[2] However, underlying changes accompany the dramatic economic growth, which create severe societal problems in a broad range. The most pressing challenges include ever-increasing income inequality, a widening gap between urban and rural areas, environmental issues caused by rapid industrialization and urbanization and migrant workers and children who live in poor conditions and have difficulty accessing health care and education, among others.

Unlike many Western countries, since 1949 the provision of social services in China has been dominated by various government agencies and quasi-government agencies – such as Public Service Institutions,[3] People's Organizations[4] and government organized non-governmental organizations (GONGOs).[5] As a matter of fact, the government had been the sole provider of health care, schooling, senior care and disaster relief, amongst other social services, till the end of 1970s. Starting from the beginning of the 1980s, to cope with the open door policy on economic reform and eager to keep up with the trend in developed countries, the Chinese government founded many GONGOs. Up to now, most GONGOs still rely solely on government appropriation, have limited autonomy and incentive in providing social services and innovative solutions beyond executive orders given by their supervising government organs. As for the registration of NPOs, a dual administrative system has been running in China for more than three decades, which makes it almost impossible for any grassroots NPOs to get registered, but things are getting better since 2005 in several pilot cities.

The above-mentioned situation has been gradually changing. In February 2008 during the Second Plenary Session of the Seventeenth Central Committee of the Chinese Communist Party (CCP), former president and party leader Hu Jintao announced the "views of deepening the reform of administrative management system", indicating the political winds started to shift toward a more progressive approach in the social management system. And further in November 2013, the "Decision of the Central Committee of CCP on Some Major Issues Concerning Comprehensively Deepening the Reform" was approved and announced by the new leadership lineup of the CCP during the Third Plenary Session of the Eighteenth Central Committee. In this report, "to form a social governance system" was first mentioned and strongly advocated "limited government" and a "bottom-up approach to promote community resilience", initiating chain reactions in the following months in the field of philanthropy. Several favoring policies have been issued by central and local government, including "speed up the legislation of Charity Law", "Revoke the dual management system for domestic charities plus detail rules on implementing the regulation", etcetera, attempting to encourage more Chinese citizens to set up NPOs providing much needed social services. From early 2014, China has officially revoked the dual administrative system nationwide and started to simplify the registration process for a limited number of domestic charities.

Social entrepreneurship and social entrepreneur development in China

There is no consensus on the definition of social entrepreneurship globally, since it is still a relatively new term in the field of philanthropy, especially in China. NPI believes that social entrepreneurship is the process of pursuing innovative solutions to social problems and that "social entrepreneurs play the role of change agents in the social sector by (1) adopting a mission to create and sustain social value and (2) recognizing and relentlessly pursuing new opportunities to serve that mission" (J. Gregory Dees, "The Meaning of Social Entrepreneurship," 1998, revised May 2001. CASE at Duke) and agrees that "social entrepreneurship focuses on the social impact that an endeavor carries" (Wee-Liang, John Williams and Teck-Meng Tan, "Defining the 'Social' in 'Social Entrepreneurship'", *International Entrepreneurship and Management Journal*, no. 3, 2005: 353–365) and that "social entrepreneurs operate within the boundaries of two business strategies: Non-profit with earned income strategies . . . and for-profit with mission-driven strategies" (Social Entrepreneurship: Definitions and Boundaries by Samer Abu-Saifan, February 2012).

The first batch of Chinese social entrepreneurs emerged in the mid-1990s. The fourth World Conference on Women was held in September 1995 in Beijing – this event inspired some elite public intellectuals and scholars to establish domestic NGOs in the field of poverty alleviation, environment protection, gender issues and so on. Later on, with support from the Global Fund (www.theglobalfund.org) and several other institutions, many LGBT groups also formed grassroots organizations on HIV/AIDS prevention. Since the majority of funding for these grassroots NGOs was coming from international NGOs, charity foundations, embassy and multilateral organizations, and many organizations are rights-based and conduct advocacy campaigns, the Chinese government has been quite skeptical about their purpose and not willing to cooperate with them, thus most grassroots NGOs are not registered as legal entities and only a few are registered as companies. After the 2008 world economic crisis, international funding for Chinese grassroots NGOs slowly dried up, and for those that could not rebuild the business model and find alternative funding supports, many first-generation NGOs ceased their activities.

With the publication of the Chinese version of "How to Change the World: Social Entrepreneurs and the Power of New Ideas" by David Bornstein in 2006, "social entrepreneur" became the new buzz word in the Third Sector gradually. Around the same time, urged by the intensified social challenges and inspired by the story of Ashoka and Professor Muhammad Yunus, a small group of social entrepreneurs emerged in China. Unlike the first batch of grassroots NPOs, leaders in the 1990s and early 2000s were largely public intellectuals, scholars and LGBT activists, with highly diversified backgrounds: business entrepreneurs, school teachers, managers from the private sector, former public servants, overseas returnees, even fresh graduates. Their business model is quite different, often using hybrid income streams; they provide services and products for the people they serve while getting donations and revenues earned from public tendering programs. They are acting like service providers, quietly gain momentum through increase of awareness and profile of targeted societal challenges and advocate for support from government agencies and the general public by clear demonstration of excellent social services they provide.

Nowadays, it seems that for the very few prominent NPOs and social enterprises such as the Beijing Global Village Environmental Education Center and the Shenzhen Canyou Group, it is relatively easier to scale their organizations with high awareness, sufficient capital and intermediary resources; however, even the startups are actually quite promising ones, but are struggling on a day-to-day basis to find much needed financial and non-financial resources in their business models and basic infrastructure development. These issues, along with the other cultural and regulatory obstacles, simply make existing social entrepreneurs have a difficult time surviving and hinder many passionate people from becoming social entrepreneurs. Meanwhile, the general public is still unfamiliar with the notion of social entrepreneurship and knows very little about civil society and social entrepreneurs, thus does not provide funding to support their causes.

How Non-Profit Incubator got started to build public-private partnerships for social entrepreneur development in China

The predecessor of Non-Profit Incubator was the China NPO Information Network (CNPON). The first NPO supporting organization was founded by Yusheng Shang – a public intellectual and son-in-law of Wu Zuoren – a prestigious Chinese painter in 1998. With support from several international charity foundations, CNPON trained more than 500 GONGO and grassroots NGO leaders and systematically introduced the concept of civil society and NGO management by translating and publishing dozens of books on the above-mentioned topics.

From mid-2005, Zhao Lu became the deputy director of CNPON; he got to know Yusheng Shang when he was the chief editor for the *Philanthropy Times*, the official newspaper of the Ministry of Civil Affairs. Mr. Lu has a singular life experience compared with his fellow classmate. After graduating in 1992 from progressive Peking University, where he majored in Chinese literature, he became a journalist at the prestigious Xin Hua News Agency led directly by the Party Central Committee for two years, then in 1994 Lu plunged into the business arena and became a serial entrepreneur for the next decade. An idealist at heart and always craving for social justice and innovation, he gradually developed an interest in the emerging philanthropy sector. From late 2003 till mid-2005, Lu took up the role as chief editor of the *Philanthropy Times*, which enabled him to connect with senior officials at the Ministry of Civil Affairs, and he started to make the acquaintance of dozens of the most prominent Chinese public intellectuals and NPO leaders, including Yusheng Shang; Yongguang Xu, secretary general of China Youth Development Foundation; and Tuan Yang, deputy director of the Center for Social Policy Studies of the Chinese Academy of Social Sciences. Later on, these people become the board members of the nascent Non-Profit Incubator.

On 10 June 2005, the Pudong New District of Shanghai was chosen by the State Council to have a pilot project on Comprehensive and Co-ordinated Reform, which enabled the Pudong New District Civil Affair bureau to partially remove the dual administrative management system for some NPOs, especially for NPO supporting organizations, in order to cultivate more capable grassroots NPOs as much needed service providers to meet the huge unmet needs of the local community and vulnerable groups. In August 2005, Shang Yusheng and Lu Zhao were invited to Shanghai by Yili Ma, director of the Pudong New District Civil Affairs Bureau, a highly visionary yet pragmatic leader who has a rich knowledge and deep understanding of NPO development and social innovation, as well as their intertwined relationship. As a matter of fact, around the late 1990s, she actually had a ten-month secondment at Xu Chuan Zhuang Elderly Care Institution at Okayama City, one of the largest NPOs in Japan taking care of disabled people and senior citizens. In 1995, when she was the director of the Social Development Bureau of Shanghai Pudong New District, Ma contracted YMCA Hongkong (http://wfh.ymca.org.hk) to manage Luo Shan Community Center, pioneering government purchasing of social services from international NPOs in China. The meeting with Madam Ma went really well, the three of them hit it off right from the start and they talked for more than two hours like old friends.

A major decision was made shortly after the Shanghai meeting: the board of CNPON accepted the proposal from Ma that Zhao Lu would establish a new facility in Shanghai with full support from the NPO Information Center. On 18 January 2006, the Shanghai Pudong NPO Development Center (literally translated from the Chinese name; the formal English name, Non-Profit Incubator, did not exist until late 2006) got formally registered with the "Fast Pass" sanctioned by Ma herself. And in the spring of 2006, Lu Zhao left his wife and newborn baby in Beijing and moved to Shanghai alone, starting his endeavor as a social entrepreneur.

However, the first three months were really tough, even for a veteran entrepreneur; from day one the board confirmed that the mission of this nascent organization was "to advance social innovation and cultivate social entrepreneurs. Lu was told that he just needed to replicate the business model of the NPO Information Center to provide capacity-building courses for NPO leaders in Shanghai. However, after two months of thorough investigation, he found out that unlike in Beijing, even in the second-tier cities of Xian, Chengdu and Kunming, there were only a handful of grassroots in Shanghai and neighboring cities already being served by the Shanghai NPO Development Center – another NPO supporting organization registered in Pudong New District a few months earlier with generous support from Madam Ma, hence there was no ready market left for his new organization.

This is largely caused by the unique position of Shanghai being the most affluent city in China, yet it has little political and cultural influence with the power center. International NGOs and multilateral organizations do not have an interest to support the local social entrepreneurs; moreover, government control over international NGOs and grassroots NGOs were really tight in the past. Lu also tried to target a few thousand GONGOs in Shanghai; unfortunately at that time, none of them had an interest in receiving training programs because of lack of incentives to change the status quo to improve their capacities. However, Lu did find a silver lining in a near desperate situation – there were some compassionate citizens who wanted to set up grassroots NPOs to alleviate some pressing problems that had come to their attention, but still hesitated due to a lack of sufficient supports, such as office space, registration, funding opportunity and capacity building.

Being inspired by the business model of Silicon Valley to support startup high tech companies and NPO Incubating Centers in Japan and Taiwan, in May 2006, while lying on the beautiful beach in the Philippines on a family vacation, Lu finished the concept paper of the Non-Profit Incubator. After he came back to Shanghai, he started to widely spread the word and talk to all the key stakeholders to get their support and potential funding. Things did not go well at the very beginning, especially with the government agencies; even Madam Ma herself was quite supportive, although the majority of her fellow officers in the Civil Affairs Bureau still thought that more grassroots NPOs meant more trouble, and the National Security Bureau and the Police Department were even worried that the motivation of Lu and these grassroots NGOs he was going to incubate might bring potential hazards to society. Nothing could stop Lu from pursuing his dreams once he had made up his mind. After five months' arduous persuasion, he finally got the green light from all related government agencies and initial RMB1.2 million funding from the Ford Foundation and the Narada Foundation at the end of 2006.

And at the same time, Lu chose to use "Non-Profit Incubator" as the formal English name for the newborn organization. Few month later in early April 2007, Lu and his three team members launched the program in Shanghai and started to provide crucial supports for five startup NPOs and social enterprises, including free office space and shared facilities, micro-grants, training and guidance to these early-stage social entrepreneurs on institutional capacity building. Furthermore, NPI provides assistance on registration, fund-raising, policy influence and advocacy for the better development of NPOs and social enterprises. In July 2007, Liguo Li, the vice minister of the Ministry of Civil Affairs, visited the NPI office in Shanghai. He spoke highly of the Incubator model and its slogan "Enlightening and empowering your loving hearts", expressed his willingness to support it and promised to reduce redundant registration procedures to create a more favorable environment for grassroots NPOs. This visit was the symbolic event for NPI to establish a public-private partnership for early-stage social entrepreneurs in mainland China. NPI soon extended its presence and operated Incubator programs in Beijing, Chengdu and Shenzhen from 2008 till the end 2009. The NPI program was regarded as a major innovation in the Third Sector and gained lots of attention.

To fulfill the mission of cultivating social entrepreneurs, for Lu to build trust among government agencies was only the first step. He decided to go further to leverage more tangible resources from government. At the same time, Lu was also thinking about the sustainable funding mechanisms for the NPOs. He noticed that in many developed countries, government agencies purchased the social services from NPOs and social enterprises for local community members and people in need, and he was keenly aware that this would be inevitably the trend in mainland China too. In November 2007, entrusted by the Civil Affairs Bureau in Pudong New District, NPI carried out two research projects, on "government purchase of NGO service" and "effectiveness of government subsidies on Community Day Care Centers for elder people". The former project proposed an overall framework of purchasing services from NPOs and detailed suggestions on its management and operation, while the latter project helped the government to better support the Community Day Care system based on evaluations on its current status and the efficiency of financial investment by introducing a public bidding system.

Luckily enough, all the suggestions were accepted by the supervising government agency and soon after, the public bidding system for government to purchase social services from NPOs (including many grassroots) and social enterprises was released in Pudong. NPI was among the first batch of beneficiaries from this policy. At the beginning of 2008, the Sanlin World Expo Garden Public Center, the largest and most comprehensive community center in Shanghai, entered the bidding procedure to select the daily operator, since the government agency decided to step down from the day-to-day management of this huge and often empty 8,000-square-meter community center. After a fierce competition with the YMCA and another NPO, NPI won the bid for the contract from the government of Sanlin town and started to manage the daily operation for San Lin World Expo Garden

Public Center. Also around the same time, Lu initiated the Enrichment Community Service Platform. Unlike the usual methodology to run community centers, NPI does not want to be the all-around service provider; instead NPI conducts a thorough investigation within the community and then develops screening criteria to invite and select capable NPOs and social enterprises to provide the professional services to the local community members.

One of the major purposes for Lu to set up the Enrichment Community Service Platform is to help NPOs enter communities and gain access to people in need. The platform focuses on the following main areas: undertaking entrusted management of public facilities, including the Community Center and other platforms; training social workers to better serve community members; and enhancing community resilience via capacity-building programs for local volunteers and opinion leaders; among other activities. By 2010, other than the Sanlin World Expo Garden Public Center, the center had won several entrusted projects, including the Neighborhood Center of Yanji subdistrict office in Yangpu District, the Service Center for Disabled People of Shanggang subdistrict in Pudong New Area and the Yanji Community Social Service Center in Yangpu District. In 2010, the Enrichment Community Service platform also expanded to Sichuan Province, where NPI launched two major programs, including the management of the Nokia Sunshine Community Service Center and sixteen urban and rural community centers established in the disaster areas within Sichuan province, along with the Youth Apartment Center in Chengdu Hi-Tech Zone (three youth community centers, each covering more than 1,500 square meters).

As for the Incubator program, the opportunity for massive expansion appeared in early 2010. The Ministry of Civil Affairs formally recognized the Incubator model and started to promote it nationwide; within just three years' time, local government agencies set up hundreds of NPO Incubators across China. From then on, NPI started to receive lots of inquiries and invitations from all over the place to set up offices, run Incubator programs and provide consulting services. Up to now, NPI had already incubated over 300 excellent NPOs and social enterprises with an 85 percent success rate, operating the Incubator program in its Shanghai, Beijing, Shenzhen, Dongguan, Zhuhai, Nanjing and Chongqing offices directly and providing consulting services to other NPO Incubators in Jiaxing, Suzhou, Qingdao and Erdos. Also from the start of 2010, all the office space for Incubator programs was provided by the local government agencies free of charge, and the government became the major funder for this program. It is estimated that over 70 percent of incubated NPOs can get registered as NPOs within one year and then sanctioned for the government procurement system to get funding for their projects.

Other than the Incubator program and Enrichment Community Service platform, Lu is actively exploring diversified resources and models to cultivate social entrepreneurs from very early stages of NPI. At the end of 2007, NPI successfully convinced the Lenovo corporate social responsibility (CSR) department to carry out the Lenovo Venture Philanthropy Program. Initiated and implemented by NPI, funded by Lenovo, this program aims to support innovative grassroots

NPOs with high potential in China on institutional capacity building. NPI was responsible for designing the framework of the whole program, drafting relevant documents for Lenovo, providing counseling to the Lenovo CSR department, corporate volunteers and social entrepreneurs and being in charge of the application process and project evaluation. By 3 March 2008, NPI had received ninety-six applications. The Program offers a total of RMB2,360,000 to 16 NPOs in the first phase. Furthermore, NPI organizes capability-building teams made up of volunteers from Lenovo and external experts to help these grassroots NPOs, which include strategic planning, marketing, human resource management, accounting and IT. The program continued to support another 26 NPOs in the following year, with a roughly RMB2.5 million budget. Unfortunately this program only lasted two years, since in 2009 the head of the Lenovo CSR department left the position and his successor put more efforts into PR and media exposure. The collaboration with NPI was continuous, but the content shifted toward supporting college students to design and implement charity projects. However, the model inspired Madam Ma. She reached out to Lu and asked NPI to come out with a proposal to set up a similar program to support innovative and effective community service projects. From mid-2009, the Shanghai Community Services Venture Philanthropy Competition, hosted by the Shanghai Civil Affairs Bureau, was officially launched, run by NPI. The competition helps more than one hundred community projects by 60 NPOs (over 60 percent are grassroots) get RMB10 million funding support in year one. And because the Community Service Venture Philanthropy Competition in Shanghai offers a pioneering approach in China, as a result it has been well received as a role model. Starting from 2010, this model has been replicated in many cities by the local civil affairs bureaus across China. Currently NPI is still directly managing four municipal and district level competitions in Suzhou, Dongguan, Zhuhai and Pudong New District of Shanghai. All these years, NPI managed to leverage more than RMB200 million to support over 600 NPOs and social enterprises through this platform.

NPI also initiated the NPO Projects Exhibition program in 2009, aiming to raise the profile of social entrepreneurs and create more media exposure and funding opportunity for them. The first NPO Fair was held in Beijing from 12 to 14 August 2009, attracting 128 prominent grassroots NGOs and 14 major public charity foundations in China. The event, with projects covering the areas of post-disaster reconstruction, environmental protection, culture and education, poverty alleviation, assistance to disabled people, community service and fair trade, is recognized as the largest event in the country to comprehensively showcase domestic NGOs. Being inspired by this successful event, Lu began to seek government support to make the NPO Fair become an annual event in the Third Sector. After one and a half years of searching and negotiations, NPI finally reached an agreement with the Shenzhen Civil Affairs Bureau. The second NPO Fair was organized in spring 2011 in Shenzhen, with more than 150 grassroots NPOs and 80 charity foundations and CSR programs attending the event. It immediately got attention from the Ministry of Civil Affairs. Starting from August 2012, the Ministry of Civil Affairs became the host of the China NPO Fair (http://www.cncf.org.cn/).

Since then, NPI has kept playing an important role to organize the grassroots NPO section. Each year over 300 grassroots organizations come to Shenzhen to showcase best practices. Although the booth decorated by grassroots NPOs are normally quite shabby, it still attracts the most visitors because of the innovative and vigorous projects.

Up to now, NPI had been an aggregation of several NPO supporting organizations, with 165 full-time employees working with fourteen independent legal entities (based on the regulation, an NPO is not allowed to set up subsidiaries, so NPI's field office in every city and sometimes even in different districts of major cities has to be registered as an independent legal entity) located in eight cities: Shanghai, Beijing, Chengdu, Shenzhen, Dongguan, Zhuhai, Nanjing, Suzhou, plus six program sites, in Hangzhou, Tianjin, Jiaxing, Chongqing, Qingdao and Erdos. With an annual budget around RMB61 million in 2013 (including RMB24 million from the Shanghai United Foundation, which was initiated by NPI in 2009), NPI is supporting over 1,000 social entrepreneurs and their organizations each year through various programs such as the Incubator, Enrichment Community Service Platform, Venture Philanthropy Competition, Capacity Building Program delivered by Social Entrepreneur Institute, Social Entrepreneur Magazine, China NPO fair, The Nest Program, a public funding mechanism by the Shanghai United Foundation, etcetera. In the past eight years, NPI incubated over 300 NPOs and social enterprises, many of them regarded as the most outstanding rising stars in their fields. NPI is also managing over 60,000 square meters of space and facilities for social entrepreneurs to run charity programs and community services programs, and providing capacity-building programs to several hundreds of social entrepreneurs.

However, for NPI, there is still a long way to go to build effective public-private partnerships to support early-stage social entrepreneurs' development. On the one hand, it is never easy for a grassroots NPO to collaborate with government agencies as an equal partner, especially when the funding for some platforms, such as some project sites of the Enrichment Community Service program and some new field offices, is almost entirely coming from a single government agency. It highly depends on the team leader's individual ability and wisdom in dealing with government officials and innovation, if the local team has failed to expand the sources of funding or renovate the projects to boost the performance of local government agencies, within one or two years the team will find themselves in a dilemma, if they bend to accommodate the dominant culture and bureaucratic process from the government. Getting too close with government, they will soon lose the touch and capacity to provide good services to those social entrepreneurs and community members; however, if they do not have the street smarts to be sophisticated enough to mingle with government officials, they will find it quite hard to implement the programs. And once the more reform-minded officials in charge transfer to other posts, it means starting all over again to gradually build the mutual trust with the new leadership team. In some extreme cases, NPI had to withdraw from partnership agreements on certain programs. In 2012 NPI conducted a stakeholder survey, and results showed that NPI was perceived as a very close ally to the government agencies internally and externally by its employees, partners from the government agencies, private sectors, other NPOs and social entrepreneurs NPI is serving. NPOs which receive government funding through Venture Philanthropy Community Service Competitions managed by NPI need to be supervised by the NPI staff to maintain high-quality standards and the rigorous budget control requested by the government agencies. Occasionally social entrepreneurs felt that they were being pressured by NPI staff and complained about NPI "wearing the hat of the government", focusing more on protecting the interests of the government, less on the development of grassroots NPOs.

On the other hand, like most NPOs in mainland China, NPI itself constantly faces the challenge of human resources – it is hard to find good talents and easy to lose them due to low salary and a high pressure working environment. In 2013, the turnover rate reached a staggering 43 percent, making effective knowledge management a mission impossible. Last but not least, to gain the recognition and support from government agencies is relatively easy, compared with mobilizing corporations and the general public's engagement in terms of supporting early-stage social entrepreneurs. We found that most big companies, both multinational and domestic, still chose to donate to quasi-government agencies and GONGOs continuously for establishing good government relations despite the Guo Meimei scandal tie up with the China Red Cross in June 2011. Due to long-lasting mistrust in Chinese society, many citizens simply do not donate to any charity institutions, including grassroots; they tend to search for the people in need by themselves and then hand out the money in person. Considering this, NPI initiated the Shanghai United Foundation at the end of 2009, the first public charity foundation ever founded by a grassroots NPO, in order to support the effective and innovative charity projects being carried out by professional organizations set up by social entrepreneurs, helping them organize public fund raising campaigns like the "50 KM Walkathon for Eggs Project" and tailor-made funding mechanisms engaging corporate volunteers to donate for grassroots NPOs. Also started in 2010, NPI strove to actively involve corporations in every major platform and convince them to provide funding, volunteers and channels for social entrepreneurs. It is quite clear that NPI will further explore the cross-sector collaboration with government agencies, corporations and charity foundations to build effective public-private partnership and to mobilize more resources to better serve the needs of emerging NPOs and social enterprises.

Among all the institutions supporting the development of social entrepreneurs in China, NPI is quite unique in its endeavor to build public-private partnerships nationwide but at the same time be deeply grounded at the local level using bottom-up approach. This case study is an exploratory analysis to examine how Zhao Lu tried to build up the new paradigm to satisfy the heterogeneous requirements for establishing the enabling environment for social entrepreneurs in China. The key for successful political reform is to ensure that the role of government will change from omnipotence to limited functions, as was addressed in reforms outlined by the country's new leadership for the next decade at the Third Plenary Session of the Eighteenth Central Committee of the CCP held in March 2103. On the one hand, the rise of social entrepreneurship will rely on the new policy and substantial support from the related government agencies; however, more social entrepreneurs will bring more innovative solutions. In turn it will also help to speed up the transformation of government functions. With the deepening of economic and political reform in China, more and more supporting organizations for social entrepreneurship will emerge. We hope this case study can provide useful information for philanthropists, social entrepreneurs and scholars to better understand the current situation and future direction in China regarding the development of the Third Sector and social entrepreneurship.

Appendix 1

The composition of NPI full-time employees (as of 2013)

NPI has a young, highly educated and diversified workforce; the average age of full-time employees is twenty-nine; over 90 percent have college degrees, and more than 35 percent have masters (or above) degrees. About 30 percent come from a business background; 30–40 percent have served in the Third Sector for years, 25–30 percent are fresh graduates, others are coming from freelance, media backgrounds and so on. There are three female trustees among eight board members. Female employees constitute 70 percent of NPI staff, a strong majority (see Table 8.1).

Table 8.1 Diversity information, 2013 (including only full-time employees)

	Female	Male	Total
Board	3	5	8
Professional staff	130	35	165
Classification	Number		
Minority	3		
Disabled	0		
Female	130		
Female manager	22		
Total staff promoted in 2013	21		

List of some excellent NPOs and social enterprises incubated by NPI

  Xintu Center for Community Health Promotion (www.xintu.org) is a registered grassroots NGO committed to health and development for people and their communities.
  1 KG More (www.1kg.org) is a social enterprise dedicated to promoting responsible tourism by encouraging travelers to help children in poor areas through simple caring actions.

Xingeng Workshop (www.xingeng.org) is a social enterprise providing job opportunities for underprivileged people in urban and rural areas by means of fair trade.

Sowosky (http://job.sowosky.org) is a professional NGO helping social workers to serve their target groups better and pushing the specialization and professionalization of social work in China.

Raleigh China (www.Raleigh.org.cn) is a local NGO committed to the improvement of personal qualifications and environmental protection consciousness of Chinese youth. It serves as a platform for the youth to know, to challenge and to improve themselves.

Hand in Hand Care in Hospice (www.handinhandchina.com) is an NGO providing comprehensive services to solve the psychological problems of terminal patients, their families and the doctors and nurses. It cultivates a professional team of teachers and volunteers to promote hospice serves.

Club for Grow Up Happily (www.growinghome.org.cn) is an NPO dedicated to helping children grow up in a more balanced way through networking among children, parents, teachers and experts.

China Doll Care for Rare Disorders (www.chinadolls.org.cn) is an NPO dedicated to provide services to people who are suffering from osteogenesis imperfecta (commonly known as brittle bone disease) and other patients who have rare diseases. They also conduct policy advocacy for these patients to be included in the social welfare system and get substantial support from the government and general public.

Current board members of NPI in 2013

Wei He, male, chairman of the board, NPI

Graduated from Zhejiang Normal University in 1982, Chairman of the board of Narada charity Foundation, COO and board member of Shanghai Zhong Qiao Construction Co., Ltd. Member of Supervisor Committee of Shanghai Nandu Group Co., Ltd.

Kathy Cheng, female, board member, NPI

Former Deputy Secretary General of Narada Foundation. Ph.D. from University of Chicago, master's in Psychology of Iowa State University. Market Research and Consulting expert. In 2001, Kathy Cheng joined McKinsey and was responsible for restructuring of large state-owned telecommunication and insurance companies. After 2006, Kathy initiated the Philanthropy project of McKinsey. Kathy was the director of AC Nielsen Beijing branch in 1996, and then served as director in two well-known international market research companies.

Qingzhi Zhou, male, board member, NPI

Honorary President of Narada Charity Foundation, CEO and Chairman of the Board of Shanghai Zhong Qiao Construction Co., Ltd. Founder of Shanghai Nandu Group.

Yusheng Shang, male, board member, NPI

Chairman and co-founder of China NPO Information Network (CNPON); graduate from Department of Physics, Peking University. Before taking the position of Secretary-General of National Natural Science Foundation of China in 1986, Mr. Shang was doing academic research at the Physics Institute of China Academy of Sciences. As one of the founders of CNPON and China Foundation Center, Mr. Shang also serves as Secretary-General of the Wu Zuoren International Foundation of Fine Arts. For the past twenty years, Mr. Shang has committed himself to Scientific Foundation Management, the study and the practice on Third Sector leadership, NGO capacity building and networking system.

Zhiyun Wang, female, board member of NPI

From early 2013, Secretary-General of Shanghai United Foundation. MBA from Zhejiang University. She has eight years of experience as Procurement Manager working for large state-owned company: Oriental Communication Co., Ltd., and Multi-National company: Phillips Electronic Co., Ltd. From 2010 to 2013, Vice President of NPI.

Yuesheng Xin, male, board member of NPI

B.A. in International Economics from Peking University; MBA from Harvard University; Director of CITIC Capital Co. Ltd.

Before joining CITIC, Mr. Xin worked for McKinsey in both Washington and Shanghai offices as a senior consultant.

Tuan Yang, female, board member of NPI

Founder and Chairman of the board of Beijing Home of Nong He Consulting Center, Deputy Director, Center for Social Policy Studiers, Chinese Academy of Social Sciences. Director, Professional Committee of Social Policy, Chinese Sociological Association.

Graduated from Capital University of Economics and Business; further studied at McMaster University (Canada) and New York University. Ms. Yang has undertaken many research projects, and her academic research covers the social security system, civil society development, social policies and rural medical care reform, etc.

Lu Zhao, male, founder and CEO of NPI, board member of NPI

EMBA, and B.L. from Peking University. Lu Zhao used to be a journalist of Xinhua News Agency, and the founder of the first professional financial publications *China Securities*. Besides, he has many years of experience in business management as an entrepreneur. Lu Zhao worked as the chief editor of *China Philanthropy Times*, Director-General of Corporate Citizenship Community. He was also one of the main organizers of the first "China Charity Conference".

Notes

1 Regarding the origin of China's economic reform, the open door policy was confirmed and issued at the Third Plenary Session of the Eleventh Central Committee of the CCP (China Communist Party) in Dec 1978; the policy implementation started from 1979.
2 Source of data: The National Bureau of Statistics of China, March 2014.
3 Public Services Institutions (a.k.a: Institutional Organizations) in China are the subsidiaries of certain government agencies including public schools, hospitals, research institutes, museums, orchestras and various social welfare organizations. There are no official statistics of how many people are working for Public Services Institutions; however, according to some experts, an estimated 40 million full-time employees exist.
4 People's Organizations in China are quasi-government agencies, under the direct leadership of the State Council or CCP. The origin of People's Organizations can be traced back to the civil war in the 1930s. The majority of People's Organizations were established in the early 1950s and 1980s. It is estimated that more than 7 million People's Organizations, including their subsidiaries, exist in China. Some of the most prominent People's Organizations are:

> Red Cross Society of China
> Communist Youth League of China
> China Welfare Fund for the Handicapped
> Children's Foundation of China
> All-China Women's Federation
> Song Ching Ling Foundation
> All-China Federation of Trade Unions
> China Welfare Institute
> China Enterprise Management Association
> China Young Pioneers
> All-China Federation of Industry and Commerce
> All-China Youth Federation
> Chinese Medical Association
> Source of the information: Baidu encyclopedia online

5 GONGOs in China have three major types of registration – the first comprises Public Charity foundations such as the China Youth Development foundation and provincial and municipal charity foundations across China; the second comprises Guild/Associations, including various professional and trade associations; the third comprises NPOs (official name: civilian-run non-enterprise working units). It is estimated that half a million GONGOs exist in mainland China.

9   Project Flame
The CityU story

Linda Wong

The origin of Project Flame

The appearance of Project Flame in the City University of Hong Kong in 2012 has created quite a buzz in the local community. That this new kid on the block, in the modest architecture of Hong Kong's social entrepreneurship landscape, has been greeted with such interest and good will is amazing. To those of us who are part of its story, the birth of Project Flame has been fortuitous. At the same time, it is also a product of the particular social and academic ecosystems in Hong Kong.

In 2011, Linda Wong was appointed acting head of the Department of Public and Social Administration (renamed the Department of Public Policy). The start of the new term highlighted the planning of activities, including staff development. To encourage colleagues to enroll in the popular Hong Kong Social Enterprise Summit, then in its fourth year, a departmental subsidy was offered, to take advantage of the early-bird offer just announced. This aroused a good deal of interest. A number of colleagues had done research on social enterprises and planned to continue. Some felt that social entrepreneurship could enable us to break out of the narrow confines of public administration teaching and build a space to integrate learning from various professions and perspectives. A quick search also identified people with similar interests in other academic departments. In September/October 2011, faculty members in the College of Liberal Arts and Social Sciences and College of Business started to come forward to discuss how they could take their interest in social entrepreneurship further. A first meeting took place on 2 October 2011, attended by a dozen faculty members, with the provost in attendance. The consensus of the meeting was that social entrepreneurship could become a powerful platform to kick-start interdisciplinary teaching and research among faculty and students. In the following months, this ad-hoc group reached out to more faculty members from across campus. Our bottom-up initiative also took advice from a few pioneers in the social enterprise space.

For Hong Kong higher education, 2011–2012 was an exciting, even feverish, year. The following year saw the introduction of the four-year curriculum (from three years). Adding an extra year to undergraduate studies created room for reform and innovation. CityU chooses to introduce a Discovery Enriched Curriculum (DEC) to enable all students to discover new knowledge and innovate on learning during their course of study. One way of doing this is to expand Gateway Education (GE; previously called General Education) courses open to all students to broaden their horizons and enrich interdisciplinary learning. New funding for GE course creation, teaching support and idea incubation gave faculty incentive and resources to experiment and innovate. Another salient development was the adoption of a performance-based pay review system, which replaced annual increments in staff salaries. This carrot and stick approach, variously seen as admirable, bold, or unacceptable, produces results. From 2011 to 2013, the number of GE courses rose sharply, from 127 to 225; student enrolment more than doubled, from 10,390 to 29,726 (City University of Hong Kong, 2013). The fortune of the Social Entrepreneurship Group, as we called ourselves then, found a germane institutional context.

A succession of fortuitous happenings appeared shortly after the group's formation. In late 2011, a private foundation invited City University and all local universities to apply for funding to promote service leadership education in Hong Kong. This initiative was a response to the need to groom service leaders in Hong Kong, a quintessential service economy providing 93 percent of GDP and over 80 percent of employment in 2011 (Hong Kong Government, 2013a). Recognizing the potential of our informal group, the university asked us to submit a project proposal. We responded immediately. To us, social entrepreneurship provides a good conceptual framework to integrate the practices of service innovation, leadership and entrepreneurship not only in business but across all professional spectrums. All our students, in whatever discipline, could benefit. Staff also stands to gain; being involved in teaching, research and innovation is self-enhancing and allows us to contribute to society. We thus put in a proposal built on a holistic model of service leadership and social entrepreneurship. Our bid was a success. Getting a three-year grant is a morale booster. It gives us the resources to start work as well as good leverage to get additional support. Another stroke of good fortune followed soon after. The Hong Kong government announced a matching grant scheme for donations raised by local universities. This will bring in matched funding for two years. Securing public money strengthened our case to ask for university support. We borrowed office space from the College of Liberal Arts and Social Sciences. In addition, we obtained seed money from the vice president (Research and Knowledge Transfer), College of Liberal Arts and Social Sciences, and my own department, to carry out our work before the arrival of external funding. This allowed us to assemble a small staff, headed by an executive director. As luck would have it, we learned that our ideal candidate, one of Hong Kong's most experienced social entrepreneurs, was available at the time. After painstaking persuasion and negotiation, we finally secured our executive director. Two junior staffers were also recruited. Thus, ten months after holding its first meeting, the SE Group was in business.

Nothing is more important than the recruitment of members. At the start, the core members came from Public and Social Administration and Applied Social Studies, also Asian and International Studies, Management, the Provost's Office, Chinese Translation and Linguistics, School of Creative Media, Office of

Education Development and Gateway Education, Asian and International Studies, Economics and Finance, Marketing, the Advanced Institute of Cross-Disciplinary Studies, Student Development Services and the Dean of Students. Later on, we reached out to more colleagues in science and technology, from the Departments of Mechanical and Biomedical Engineering, Computer Science, Systems Engineering and Engineering Management, and Electronic Engineering. Now, our thirty members are truly interdisciplinary, belonging to eighteen departments and units. Growing the membership was hard work. It normally took person-to-person canvassing to recruit a member. A small number were introduced by others. In contrast, sustaining involvement and building solidarity is even more challenging. Academics these days are extremely busy. Junior faculty is even more pressured to secure research grants and publish. I shall analyze the academic environment in the university system later on.

The search for identity occupied much of our thoughts in mid-2012. We were known as the SE Group for almost a year. Yet we were not entirely happy with the name. The name we choose reflects our self-identity and how we want others to view us. On campus and in Hong Kong generally, social entrepreneurship is not a common term. Nor is the English pronunciation easy. We toyed with a number of variations but finally settled on Project Flame with a subtitle, Social Innovation and Entrepreneurship at CityU. We want the title to baffle and challenge the reader or listener to find out what it means and the subtitle to define our mission. In sum, the two parts convey our passion – there is a flame in our hearts which we want to ignite, to keep our concern for people and society alive, and we do this by being innovative and entrepreneurial.

To appreciate the importance of the idea of flame, we must look at the character of our age. We live in an age of uncertainty. In particular it is a time of discontent. Young people, our students included, struggle to find their place in society, yet feel frustrated by the foreclosure of mobility channels. Most cannot see their future clearly. Many feel powerless and lose their self-confidence. To energize our students, nothing is more important than keeping their passion and self-belief burning. Acquiring skills in innovation and solution seeking through an entrepreneurial approach builds up their capacity and sense of personal efficacy. As teachers with many years of experience in higher education, we also detect a change in our students' values and outlook in recent years. Getting a good professional education and a well-paid job after college is still important. It is not enough. Nowadays students care for society and the environment. They want to express their creativity. They want to make a difference. Embracing social entrepreneurship will show them how to become change makers.

We adopted our new name in July 2012. What followed was a frantic preparation to announce ourselves to colleagues and incoming students. The arrival of the double-cohort, the last batch of the A-level graduates and the first cohort of the six-year high school leavers, was a monumental event for the university. We have no time to lose to let students know about Project Flame. This we did through designing our website, handing out flyers and small souvenirs, making class visits, asking course leaders to recommend our courses to their students, attending student briefings and so on. We also made a big splash through holding the Social Entrepreneur in Residence Program at the start of the semester. This was a two whole-day program designed by two prominent social entrepreneurs, Andreas Heinecke of Dialogue in the Dark and K. K. Tse of Hong Kong Social Enterprise Forum and Education for Good. This intensive program catered to students, fellow academics and senior leaders of the university (provost, vice presidents, college deans and heads of departments) in joint and separate sessions. Different types of activities were included – for example, mass lecture, session for business educators, local social entrepreneurs, power lunch for deans, heads of departments and key administrators, student elevator pitches, case and personal narratives and sharing with alumni.

The Social Entrepreneur in Residence Program was the first of its kind in Hong Kong. Participation was good – about 400 participants attended various segments. At the same time, we realized that the program was too ambitious. Some target audiences were hard to reach, like parents, alumni and senior administrators. The program was followed by a Community Forum on Social Innovation, conducted by Andreas Heinecke and Ada Wong, local founder of MaD (Make a Difference), which specializes in promoting creativity and solution seeking among young people. In this forum, Project Flame was formally introduced to academia and the local community. About 120 people took part. We announced ourselves with a bang, not a whimper.

At the start of 2013–2014, we choreographed another colorful event, a fashion show. Student models pranced down the catwalk wearing secondhand donated clothing to show their passion for conservation and responsible consumption under the expert guidance of a fashion coordinator and makeup artists. The glitz and glamor turned many heads on the campus and brought in good business to our secondhand shop. A week later, we organized an innovation and solution seeking workshop for students (called Mini-MaD) on the theme of zero food wastes. Both programs were useful in spreading the message of social innovation and entrepreneurship.

What followed was a solid program of academic and co-curricular activities. We adopted a four-pronged approach which comprises professional and academic development, research and knowledge transfer, social innovation incubation and student service leadership. The following section will elaborate these endeavors. Meanwhile, we continued to apply for competitive university funding for new initiatives, including the Interdisciplinary Professional Development Award, which supports the development and delivery of new GE courses and the Campus Sustainability Fund. A key accomplishment was a bid for a new faculty position in social entrepreneurship. The post is shared between the Department of Public Policy (under the College of Liberal Arts and Social Science) and the Department of Management (under the College of Business), a first for the university and in Hong Kong academia.

At the same time, we sought out faculty training opportunities. Capacity building was vital if we were to spread our message and groom our students. So we gave support to colleagues to attend training workshops, seminars, study tours and overseas visits. Investing in ourselves as well as novel programs allowed us to demonstrate results. So far, we have been lucky in marshaling resources. The fact that a large part of our income came from extramural sources gave us a bit more financial autonomy. This does not mean we are exempt from following existing campus guidelines. On the contrary, negotiating the myriad rules and regulations in our administrative landscape has been a big challenge. As Elkington and Hartigan (2008) point out, social entrepreneurs are "unreasonable people" who are not content with the status quo and resort to stirring up change. Project Flame people may be seen in the same light.

The academic milieu and its dilemma

Why do we want to start a social entrepreneurship movement in our university? The answer comes from how we see the place of a university today and the values we embrace. As academics, we see universities imbued with several missions – to transmit knowledge, nurture talent, serve society and promote innovation. At least that is as far as theory or rhetoric goes. If we take a real look at how universities perform, a different picture emerges. Most universities focus more of their energies on the first two functions (transmission of knowledge and training of talents) than the other two (contributing to society and promoting innovation). On the transmission of knowledge, many universities lean towards specialist and professional education. General education that broadens student learning and studies across disciplinary boundaries are often neglected. As far as the student grooming function goes, the stress is on enhancing intellectual abilities and professionalism, not whole-person development. Most universities want their students to become socially responsible citizens. However, more is said than done. It is equally hard to prove how effective universities have been in spearheading social innovation.

Why is the gap between theory and practice so prominent? We can look to the milieu of higher education, in particular how universities strategize to remain competitive. It is no secret that competition among universities is fierce – for research grants, for prizes, for star professors, for global ranking. This has been increasingly so in Hong Kong. Herculean efforts are spent in attaining these objectives. It is equally well known that promotion for academic faculty is primarily based on research output. Professors who excel in teaching but are weak in research may not even keep their posts. The pressure is relentless for young untenured faculty. What is the result? Many universities become mills for journal papers. Research undertaken by staff has become more specialized and cutting-edge. Whether or not research findings have any practical or social value becomes a secondary consideration. When more and more professors bury their heads in research and publication, fewer have time to guide and interact with their students. What does this mean for universities? For institutions which are adept at the game, they gain more prominence and respectability. For university education as a whole, the result may be a distortion of its nature and function.

A university is a treasure trove of knowledge. It houses a vast pool of talents. It is a base to nurture social elites. Universities enjoy generous support from their communities. They should use their intellectual resources to help society find effective solutions to social problems and take the lead in social innovation. In the past two decades, many universities in the UK, USA and Europe have taken the gauntlet to foster social innovation and entrepreneurship through education, research and social engagement. On some campuses, students have demanded that their universities offer more socially relevant, applied and interdisciplinary studies and provide chances for service. Brown University is one example. Many top universities have set up innovative education programs, social businesses, and social innovation research centers. Good examples are the Said Business School Skoll Center for Social Entrepreneurship at Oxford University, the Stanford Graduate School of Business Center for Social Innovation, the Social Entrepreneurship Initiative at the University of Michigan Center for Entrepreneurship, the INSEAD Social Innovation Centre, and the Center for the Advancement of Social Entrepreneurship at the Fuqua School of Business at Duke University. In particular, Ashoka University specializes in promoting and supporting different universities in social entrepreneurship education. In the past year, Ashoka has conducted faculty seminars and training workshops in Hong Kong. More than a dozen universities in America have become change-maker campuses. We believe CityU can and should follow similar roadmaps.

City University is one of eight publicly funded universities in Hong Kong. It was established in 1984 as the City Polytechnic of Hong Kong. It acquired university status in 1994 and now enrolls some 20,000 students for associate degrees and undergraduate and postgraduate studies. Over the last twenty years, the university has made remarkable strides. One indicator is its global ranking. According to the 2012 QS World University Rankings 2012, CityU was ranked number 95 in the world, 12th in Asia and 9th among young universities (under fifty years old). The pressure to excel in education and research, especially the latter, is keenly felt by the university faculty.

CityU embraces two parallel missions: the nurturing of well-rounded graduates to serve as competent professionals and future leaders of society, as well as the creation of applicable knowledge to support social and economic advancement. Consistent with its commitment to professional education and innovative research, the university seeks to support students and faculty to prepare for and respond to the changing needs of society. The introduction of the "Discovery-Enriched Curriculum" at City University, led by the Provost's Office through the blueprint for CityU's Academic Development Proposal 2012–15, creates the space to combine academic discovery and innovation with the rising awareness of social enterprise and social entrepreneurship among faculty and students. It also accords well with the university's commitment to act positively on the environment and society and develop students' social responsibility. As said before, the conversion to a four-year structure is a boon to curriculum reform and innovation. Likewise, rewarding staff through performance-linked pay steers faculty efforts to areas that give the best rewards, especially research, publication and grant capture. Under this context, involvement in Project Flame may not offer enough incentive to pressurized faculty. The fact that we managed to develop a critical mass in our endeavor is encouraging, even extraordinary.

In the past year, our experience in teaching an introductory course on social entrepreneurship has been very positive. Open to all students on campus, the course allowed students to break out of their chosen disciplines and apply knowledge and creativity to solve social and environmental problems. In actually working on group projects, disciplinary boundaries become less relevant than staying focused on selected issues and seeking whatever solutions that works. As teachers, we are energized by this spirit. We become more aware of the need to extend our own knowledge, pedagogy and skill sets and venture out of our comfort zones when we teach and do research. A practical step is to reach out to colleagues from other disciplines, their students, the government and community agencies to launch research, incubate new ideas, explore workable strategies and initiate attempts to solve problems. University leaders must recognize and support such efforts if they are serious about their social missions.

The social ecosystem and its challenge

The other driver underpinning our push for social entrepreneurship is the state of our social ecosystem. We live in any age of uncertainty and discontent. Social problems become more and more complex. What used to work in the past seems to have lost its efficacy. In Hong Kong, mainland China and many places, public discontent on unresolved social issues has escalated into angry protests. Many problems remain indomitable. Examples include widening social inequalities, narrowing of social mobility channels, employment difficulties of young people, galloping rents and house prices, acceleration in aging, shortfall in health services, environmental pollution and so on. To solve these problems, markets, governments and civil society organizations have thrown in immense resources and greatly expanded services. Each year, more than 40 percent of Hong Kong's government spending goes to the social services (HK Government, 2013b: 392). However, service shortfalls remain as acute as ever. New needs keep arising. The tolerance of our citizens is near the breaking point. Confidence in government and trust in political institutions in meeting public demands plummet to dangerous levels.

Young people in our midst face many pressures. Many become confused and angry. University students and graduates face daunting challenges: to get a job with reasonable prospects, pay off their government loans, find affordable housing, develop a career, save up for marriage or enroll in further studies. Even with a degree, many become disheartened knowing how difficult it is to realize their goals. Some lose their confidence and sense of efficacy. In our university, most of our students come from modest backgrounds, with household incomes at median level and half living in public housing. It is even more important for them to develop trust in themselves and see beyond their own life pressures to contribute to society. From our observation, our students do care about society and the environment. Many do not know what they can do and how. Social entrepreneurship education and practice offers a useful platform to empower them and add value to their education experience. In many places, very few graduates will start a social business after they leave university. The vast majority will take up mainstream jobs. During their course of study, we can make a difference in their education by nurturing their social passion, developing positive mindsets and acquiring entrepreneurial skills to solve problems they care about.

In the last two decades, Hong Kong's economy has undergone a paradigm shift with the shedding of its manufacturing base. Now Hong Kong has become a quintessential service society. In 2011, the service sector contributed 93 percent to our GDP (from 75 percent in 1990) and employed 84 percent of local manpower (Hong Kong Government, 2013a). Under such circumstances, the enhancement of student service and leadership takes on critical importance for higher education institutions. Employers have been calling for the strengthening of students' service skills, attitudes and leadership. According to the 2010 Survey on Opinions of Employers on Major Aspects of Performance of Publicly Funded First Degree Graduates in 2006, commissioned by the Education Bureau, employees' sense of responsibility and commitment were highly valued. In terms of performance, the 2006 graduates were generally able to meet their employers' required standard in most skill areas. Graduate performance was strongest in Cantonese (the lingua franca in Hong Kong), sense of responsibility and commitment and ability to make use of the Internet to benefit business. By comparison, graduates were weaker in management skills and use of Putonghua (the spoken language of China). Some employers suggested graduates enhance their willingness to take on responsibilities and make commitments. They were also urged to be more enthusiastic about their work and take more initiative at work. We believe that exposure to social innovation and entrepreneurship strengthens students' social awareness, utilizes their passion in creative ways and cultivates their mind set and skills for solution seeking. These will stand them in good stead in facing work and life when they graduate.

We are increasingly struck by the realization that many of our environmental and social problems cannot be solved by the efforts of one sector or discipline alone. Business, government, nonprofits and private individuals must work together. In the last two decades, a global movement in social innovation, enterprise and entrepreneurship has emerged as a driving force to reshape public, private and nonprofit activity, promote socially responsible business, locate new sources of funding and encourage social and technological innovation (Bornstein, 2007; Hayllar and Wettenhall, 2010, 2012). In 2013, the UK had 70,000 social enterprises employing a million people and contributing £24 billion to the economy (Social Enterprise UK, 2013: 6). Across Asia, particularly in Bangladesh, also in India, the Philippines, Taiwan, Korea, Singapore and Hong Kong, the movement has arrived and thrived. In Hong Kong, social enterprises took the early form of sheltered workshops and service projects for marginalized groups after the Second World War. It was not until the last decade or so that social enterprises, as we know them today, mushroomed. In the beginning, most social enterprises were started by NGOs to respond to challenging problems at the time: work integration for the disadvantaged, poverty, ethnic discrimination, and community problems. A key instigator has been the government, which became increasingly concerned about worsening poverty, unemployment, and community malaise. Another push factor was the change of the welfare subvention system, which motivated NGOs to generate incomes through new initiatives and adopt business practices to improve efficiency (Fisher, 2010). Later on, the social enterprise landscape became more mixed (Lee, 2012). Across the spectrum are mission-linked projects pioneered by business entrepreneurs, social franchising, impact investing, education and training, incubation and support programs. In 2013, there were 400 social enterprises in Hong Kong (Social Enterprise Directory, 2013).

Social entrepreneurship lies at the heart of social enterprise activity. Bornstein and Davis consider social entrepreneurship to be a "process by which citizens build or transform institutions to advance solutions to social problems, such as poverty, illness, illiteracy, environmental destruction, human rights abuses and corruption, in order to make life better for many" (Bornstein & Davis, 2010: 1). The roles played by social entrepreneurs are crucial: it is they who relentlessly pursue new opportunities to create public or social value by "engaging in a process of continuous innovation, adaptation and learning" (Dees, 2001: 4). As the field of social innovation and entrepreneurship expands, more critical research is required. This involves research into a wide range of issues, such as the rationales and motivations underlying social innovation and entrepreneurship, policy support and constraints, performance evaluation, social enterprise certification and social franchising. Hong Kong has a lot to catch up on concerning social entrepreneurship education and research. As far as education is concerned, there have been pioneering efforts in practitioner training, short courses, publication of newsletters and case studies, as well as faculty workshops making use of overseas experts and local pioneers. Very few universities have offered courses in social entrepreneurship. The landscape is about to change. A number of universities have introduced related courses as part of the common core curriculum and general education. Social entrepreneurship content is being infused into business, management, and entrepreneurship courses at undergraduate and master levels. Project Flame commits itself to this vital process.

Achievements and challenges

Project Flame embraces two missions. Our first mission is to become a leading tertiary center in Hong Kong, China and Asia to advance knowledge transfer and practice in social innovation and entrepreneurship. The second mission is to foster social innovation and transformation through education, innovation incubation, research and knowledge transfer and engage in proactive collaboration with partners in civil society, business, industry, academia and government.

Our missions are buttressed in our values. We are committed to a holistic model of social innovation and change underpinned by our belief that enduring and impactful change is a complex phenomenon. To produce sustainable change in an academic setting, the change model has to be embedded in the multiple missions of a university. These missions include knowledge transmission, knowledge creation and evaluation, innovating new ideas and service application. Each of these strands is interrelated and mutually reinforcing.

In knowledge transmission, the core task is the offer of meaningful curricular and co-curricular programs. In knowledge creation and evaluation, we pursue research to develop and assess knowledge and ideas. The integration of teaching and research will enrich education and our understanding of the world. In innovating new ideas, we seek to extend our grasp of change strategies and fine tune them to produce the desired outcome. In service application, we look for practice opportunities and learning through service. The fruits of such learning will allow us to incubate creative approaches, invigorate our teaching and construct more useful tools in research. We believe that all four missions must be embraced simultaneously. To leave out any one goal will produce incomplete results.

As far as social entrepreneurship is concerned, we believe that our university should offer an energetic program of SE education and praxis. On the one hand, we are committed to excellence in professional education and research. On the other, we are devoted to the pursuit of equitable and sustainable solutions to local and global problems through social innovation and student leadership development. These goals are pursued through four sets of analytically distinct but programmatically complementary activity areas. They are Academic and Professional Education, Research and Knowledge Transfer, Social Innovation Incubation and Student Service Leadership.

In the Academic and Professional Education area, two new Gateway Education Courses were launched in Semester B 2012–13. They are GE1218 Make a Difference: the Challenge to Social Entrepreneurship in a Globalized World and GE1220 Enhancing Your Service Leadership for the 21st Century. These courses have enrolled 250 students to date and have received excellent feedback. Two new GE courses – GE2246 Changing Our Society: Turning Social Problems into Business Opportunities, and GE2245 Professions in Hong Kong: Critical Insights and Issues – are ready for implementation. A fifth GE – Social Innovation and Entrepreneurial Venture Exploration – is in the pipeline. All these are open to students from all disciplines and departments.

To cater to students who want to deepen and broaden their training as change makers, a minor in Social Entrepreneurship is in preparation. If approved, the fifteen credit unit program offers in-depth study of the fundamentals of social entrepreneurship. The aim is to provide students with both the theoretical knowledge and practical skills to diagnose social problems and to generate intervention ideas for systemic change from multidisciplinary perspectives. The minor consists of one mandatory core course and four elective courses offered by cognate departments (Public Policy, Applied Social Science, Management, Marketing and College of Business). This will be the first such program in Hong Kong.

The Student Service Leadership Initiative received extramural funding from a private foundation in Hong Kong and intellectual support from the Hong Kong Service Leadership and Management Institute. The various GE courses fulfilled the objectives for service leadership and social entrepreneurship. In June 2013, we organized a four-week student internship for eight students in Zhongshan city, China. The students worked in the city's innovation park to promote youth innovation projects. In July 2013, a study tour to social enterprises in Singapore was conducted for fourteen students. In December 2013, another group of students (fourteen) took part in a study tour in Shanghai with students from Shanghai and Taipei. This tri-city cultural learning and exchange experience adds dimension to the students' learning and extends their personal networks. Funding for overseas service learning experiences came from a medley of internal and external sources. It was far from enough. Continuous fund raising is critically important given the high costs involved and the students' financial limitations.

To foster social innovation, our goal for the past year was not incubation as such. Rather the aims were to introduce the notion and promise of social innovation to faculty and students, arouse interest through relevant activities, and expose participants to simulated experiences. Our endeavors include: submitting a funding proposal to set up a Learning Commons for Social Innovation and Incubation to the government (which was not successful), taking part in the Diamond Cab Sedan Competition to raise money for wheelchair bound users in 2012 and 2013, co-sponsoring the Fifth (2012) and Sixth (2013) Social Enterprise Summits, holding a "Photo with a Message" Competition and launching a secondhand shop. The Hand 2 Spot is now our flagship program to promote innovation, entrepreneurship, and conservation. Students are trained to operate the outlets on campus and student residence. The latest extravaganza was the fashion show of secondhand clothing described earlier. The event attracted maximum publicity – many watchers and press coverage. In October 2013, we commissioned a Mini-MaD event to be held, to let students brainstorm and develop proposals to eliminate the food waste problem on campus.

In the area of Research and Knowledge Transfer, we rolled out a number of initiatives. The objectives are to broaden understanding of social entrepreneurship within and without the university and to share best practices. The past year's highlights include the following:

- The Social Entrepreneur in Residence Program (SEiR) took place in September 2012, the first of its kind in Hong Kong featuring Andreas Heinecke, founder of Dialogue in the Dark, and K. K. Tse, founder of Hong Kong Social Enterprise Forum and Education for Good; 400 students, faculty and alumni took part in the two-day event.
- The Community Forum on Social Innovation was held immediately following the SEiR. This drew 120 people from the university and the community. Andreas Heinecke and Ada Wong, founder of Make a Difference in Hong Kong, spoke at the Forum. The birth of Project Flame was officially announced by our president.
- Discussions have been carried on with a government unit to conduct a public service flow review project. This will involve students from different universities to form teams to study the public service delivery system with a view to improve service efficiency and customer satisfaction.

- At the request of a local association of old age care homes, Project Flame co-organized a workshop to introduce new Medicine Management Systems in institutional settings in December 2012. Eighty participants included home managers, government officers, doctors and pharmacists.
- Nine Project Flame members paid a visit to social innovation parks in Shunde and Zhongshan, China, in January 2013 to explore the social innovation landscape in these cities and to offer advice to the new social entrepreneurs. This visit and a return visit by Zhongshan officials resulted in the 2013 student internship in that city.
- Project Flame maintains a vigorous program of agenda visits and sharing by prominent practitioners. Agencies visited include government departments, NGOs, utility companies and social enterprises. Prominent social entrepreneurs were invited to conduct guest lectures and tell their personal stories.
- We collaborated with the Hong Kong General Chamber of Social Enterprises on the development of a Social Enterprise Certification System. Project Flame was commissioned to develop a certification tool, and pilot and refine it for implementation. The research was funded by a leading Hong Kong bank (the local branch of a global financial institution). The research began in November 2013 and is expected to take fifteen months.
- In November 2013, we organized the International Symposium: Discovery and Idea Incubation for Realizable and Scalable Social Impact. The five-day program was conducted by an international and regional panel of experts to share and incubate new ideas of starting, coaching and scaling up social enterprises. Highlights will include pitching for prizes and a master class with Michael Norton, co-founder of UnLtd and the International Centre for Social Franchising.

How far has Project Flame fulfilled its missions through the four-pronged approach so far? When we count up the plethora of activities which address the goals of education, research, innovation and service leadership, the volume and range of work is quite extensive. Our GE courses have been popular. Many activities are well attended. The higher education and social enterprise sectors commented warmly on our holistic vision and programs. To our supporters, Project Flame has been an extraordinary story. Since its ten month gestation period (October 2011) and infancy (from July 2012), we have built up a thriving platform for interdisciplinary collaboration. Our brand name is becoming widely known on campus. Outside the university, we have collaborated actively with community partners to grow the social entrepreneurship space in Hong Kong. Our external liaisons extend to China, Taiwan and Singapore. Yet we have a lean staff consisting of one half-time executive director and four research associates. The project's faculty leadership, namely the director and the four associate directors who oversee the core areas, put in their own time on top of their normal work load. Indeed all members work for Project Flame on a voluntary basis. Looking back, we have to admit that our progress has far exceeded our expectation.

What accounted for our modest success so far? First, being a bottom-up initiative – Project Flame members bring with them passion and dedication on a personal and voluntary level. There is a lot of fire among loyal members of the team who, as long-serving teachers, are devoted to developing the full potentials of our students. The fact that many of us are tenured faculty also helps. Good knowledge of the organization is definitely useful considering how complex a university system is. More importantly, loyalty and performance generates trust from our seniors, whose endorsement is absolutely vital to the continuation of the project.

Second, the ability to reach out to colleagues in other disciplines gives us credibility as a truly interdisciplinary platform. In other universities, the social innovation initiative is located either in the faculty of business or in the faculty of social sciences. At CityU, our members come from eighteen academic and support units. We are glad to have made a good start. The need to broaden membership is more challenging still.

Third, the success in attracting extramural funding is critical in enhancing our credentials as a worthy initiative. Nowadays universities put a premium on external research income, corporate sponsorship in research and commercialization of knowledge. More and more, these measures will be taken as performance indicators of a successful university. They will as well influence the size of government funding. The soft money we raised from outside sources strengthens our case for intramural support. It also gives us more autonomy to fund student activities and staff development programs.

Fourth, student support is crucial. The offering of GE courses anchors our initiative in the core business of a university. Ongoing enrolments generate resources for departments. In our case, responding to the university's initiatives to implement a discovery-enriched curriculum and campus sustainability bring in resource support and one new faculty post. Our co-curriculum activities enrich teaching and learning. They also widen contacts with the student population. We are glad that over the past year, we had inspired a small but dedicated group of student fans and helpers. Without their support, we would not be able to roll out our ambitious programs.

In the past year, we encountered many trials and challenges. A key obstacle is space, a scarce and costly resource in Hong Kong. We resorted to borrowing. We are very grateful to the College of Liberal Arts and Social Sciences, which came to our rescue. Yet the location is far from ideal. Tucked away in a side corner of the campus, the building in which we are housed is not easy to find. Poor access creates difficulties even for participants. A good example is our secondhand shop. We ameliorate this handicap by posting items on our website for potential customers to book online. This helps, but our location does deter the pickup rate. One interim solution is "hawking" outside the student canteen. Again, the space we are assigned is too restricting. The worry is that as long as we do not have a suitable site for the secondhand shop, its full potential cannot be realized.

Negotiating through the university's maze of administrative and financial rules and procedures has been a key challenge. Project Flame is a new initiative in the university. It serves as a campus-wide platform. Yet it does not fit under the existing organizational structure. It is not an academic unit or department. Neither is it a research center. Nor is it part of student development services. Its portfolio is wide and multidimensional. However, the lack of a regular administrative status creates ambiguities in reporting and accountability. A case that belies our identity confusion is our unsuccessful attempt in acquiring research center status. We did not secure this status because we are not focused enough on research. At the same time, our work spills into too many areas. We are still searching for an appropriate organizational status to attract the resources, space and staffing we need. Likewise, we find it difficult to make our needs understood by the administration. Oftentimes, the existing rules are not made for a new project like ours. Hence, how to accommodate our special requirements and at the same time uphold the consistency of the existing system calls for a great deal of patience and mutual accommodation.

To make our initiative more sustainable, wide faculty involvement is crucial. In our experience, this is not easy at all. We still need to reach out to faculty in some disciplines, such as science, engineering, law, communication and business. In these areas, the pressure to do cutting edge research and get published is immense. In particular, it is even more difficult to recruit young non-tenured faculty. Yet we need their dynamism and creativity to enrich and propel our movement. At the same time, we have to replenish the leadership in the project to ensure succession and renewal. Up to now, the culture and incentive structure in a university is still not conducive to widening faculty engagement in practice and innovation.

Project Flame – summarizing our experience

The emergence of Project Flame owed much to luck and the needs of our eco-systems. When we review the endogenous and exogenous factors in the last two years, the institutional, academic and social systems were ripe for change. I believe Kingdon's (2011) theoretical perspective in analyzing public policy is useful in explaining the emergence of Project Flame. Kingdon attributes public policy to two factors. The first is the participants inside and outside the government. The second is the process, which includes the problem stream, the policy stream and the political stream. Each of these streams has its distinct life, but when they come together, a specific problem becomes important on the agenda, policies that match the problem get attention and then policy change becomes possible. The coupling of streams opens up a policy window for entrepreneurs to advocate their proposals and even succeeds in pushing through change.

Applying Kingdon's theory to Project Flame, we find a good fit with the confluence of factors and agents in seizing a precious moment for change. To begin with, we have a group of interested faculty who strongly believe in seeking a new approach to the way we teach, conduct research and contribute to society. At the same time, there is the convergence of three streams. Specifically, the failure of the traditional sectors to solve social problems and the role confusion of universities (the problem stream), the usefulness of social innovation and entrepreneurship framework in addressing the social and educational deficiencies (the policy stream) and the emergence of facilitating factors within our institutional context (the politics stream) have come together. The chance arrival of donation income and government matching grants turn our wish into reality. We all welcome luck in whatever we do. When luck descends, the fact that all conditions are ripe gives us the moment to start.

Project Flame has had two amazing years. We all learned a lot, which is enriching and satisfying. At the same time, the test has been daunting. To account for the difficulties in grafting a new initiative to a well-structured organization, the notion of intrapreneurship has been useful. Intrapreneurship is understood as the act of behaving like an entrepreneur while working within a large organization. In 1992, The American Heritage Dictionary acknowledged the popular use of a new word, "intrapreneur", to refer to "a person within a large corporation who takes direct responsibility for turning an idea into a profitable finished product through assertive risk-taking and innovation" (American Heritage Dictionary, 2013). Project Flame leaders are intrapreneurs in an academic setting. To find our way through the complex university landscape, we are constantly required to explain our needs and plead for greater flexibility. This is inevitable; what we are doing may look risky and even subversive to the system. As a learning organization, we hope the university will reinvent its systems to cope with new situations. At the same time, we know we must work within its confines and work out appropriate solutions. The lesson we learned in the past year is this: patience, resourcefulness and good will are essential in building trust and cooperation. The role of an intrapreneur is inherently challenging. Only when we do this well can we create real change within and beyond our familiar context.

References

American Heritage Dictionary (2013). 3rd edition. Boston: Houghton, http://www.intrapreneur.com/MainPages/History/Dictionary.html, accessed 23 August 2013.
Bornstein, David (2007). *How to Change the World – Social Entrepreneurs and the Power of New Ideas*. Oxford and New York: OUP, Updated Edition.
Bornstein, David, & Davis, Susan (2010). *Social Entrepreneurship: What Everyone Needs to Know*. New York: OUP.
City University of Hong Kong Education and Gateway Education Office. (2013). http://www.cityu.edu.hk/edge/ge/ (accessed on 8 January 2016)
Dees, J. Gregory "The Meaning of 'Social Entrepreneurship'", Duke University Fuqua School of Business, original paper in 1998 and revised in 2001. https://entrepreneurship.duke.edu/news-item/the-meaning-of-social-entrepreneurship/
Elkington, John, & Hartigan, Pamela (2008). *The Power of Unreasonable People – How Social Entrepreneurs Create Markets That Change the World*. Boston: Harvard Business Press.
Fisher, Stephen (2010). "Development of Social Enterprises in Hong Kong", paper delivered at the *Symposium on Social Enterprises for a New Age: Six Cases in China*, 10 May 2010, Hong Kong Baptist University, Hong Kong.
Hayllar, Mark Richard, & Wettenhall, Roger (2010). "Public-Private Partnerships: Promises, Politics and Pitfalls", *Australian Journal of Public Administration*, 69: S1-S7, 3/2010 London: Wiley-Blackwell Publishing.

Hayllar, Mark Richard, & Wettenhall, Roger (2012). "Social Enterprise: What Is It, and How Can It Be Strengthened", *The Asia Pacific Journal of Public Administration*, 3(1): 21–40.

Hong Kong Government. (2013a). *Hong Kong: The Facts – Hong Kong as a Service Economy*, http://www.gov.hk/en/about/abouthk/factsheets/, accessed 9 September 2013.

Hong Kong Government. (2013b). *Hong Kong Government Yearbook 2013*. http://www.yearbook.gov.hk/

Kingdon, John W. (2011). *Agendas, Alternatives, and Public Policies*. London: Longman Publishing Group.

Lee, Jane. (2012). "The Broad Spectrum and Ecology of Social Enterprises", in Michael Luk, Jane Lee & K. K. Tse (Eds.), *We Can Change the World – Collection of Essays from Hong Kong Social Enterprise Leaders and Social Entrepreneurs*. Hong Kong: Cloud Publication, pp. 16–19 [in Chinese].

QS World University Rankings. (2012). http://topuniversities.com/university-rankings, accessed 9 October 2013.

Villenueve-Smith, F., & Chung, C. (2013). *The People's Business: The State of Social Enterprise Survey 2013*. Social Enterprise. London, UK.

10 Empowerment in social entrepreneurship

The case of DID Hong Kong

Antony Pang, Hang Chow, Cora Chu,
Fiona Wat and Julian Zhu Min

Introduction

Empowerment of the disadvantaged has been the focal point of both academia and practitioners in fields of rehabilitation, psychology and social work. The notion of empowerment is commonly associated with a process of change and the power and ability to make choices (Kabeer, 1999). Wallerstein (1992), for example, defined empowerment as "a multilevel construct that involves people assuming control and mastery over their lives in the context of their social and political environment" (Purdue & Howe, 2012). Peterson (2014) emphasized the dynamic nature of the notion as "an active, participatory process through which individuals and groups gain greater control over their lives, acquire rights and reduce marginalization".

Whilst empowering the socially excluded or disadvantaged is one of the popular missions of social enterprises, there are very few cases that successfully transcend social innovation into fulfilling the social mission while keeping the social business financially sustainable at the same time. Dialogue in the Dark Hong Kong Limited (DID HK)[1] is a social enterprise originated from Germany holding the mission to empower people of differences (PODs) by creating an authentic experience led by visually impaired (VIs) or, later, hearing-impaired (HIs) in a complete darkness or silence for the participants. The venture is a perfect example of empowering with social innovation. The unique experience aims to challenge the perceptions of the participants towards VIs/HIs through the original experiential learning process.

With the aims to 'turn sympathy into empathy', to empower the physically challenged to lead a fruitful life by utilizing their strengths and talents and to inspire positive actions to transform the world, DID HK has successfully facilitated empowerment from individual to organizational and community levels. Operating in the form of social enterprise, DID HK was praised for its adoption of the creative model and the high level of sustainability. DID HK is undoubtedly a social innovation operating in the form of social enterprise, in which the original and innovative inputs have effectively enabled empowerment of PODs and the participants at individual, organizational and community levels.

Drawing upon the practitioners' experience of the authors, the scoping research conducted by Chui (2014) and other secondary resources, this chapter summarizes and analyzes the elements enabling the innovative process of empowerment of DID HK based on the concepts of social innovation and empowerment. This chapter is structured as follows. Firstly, the conceptual understanding of empowerment and social innovation is discussed. The second section is a brief description of the development of DID HK since its establishment in 2009. In the third section, the empowering processes of DID HK are analyzed at psychological, organizational and community levels. We argue that DID HK provides a unique model of empowerment to both the PODs and its customers.

Social innovation

Whilst the idea of social innovation can be traced back to Max Weber's study of the relationship between social order and innovation (Hubert, 2010), social innovation in recent years has spread to other disciplines such as business studies, social work, development studies, sociology and politics, etc. Despite the wide-ranging definitions of social innovation, Mulgan (2007) extracted some important elements of the concept. First, social innovation is 'new ideas that work'. The element of 'new ideas' emphasizes the importance of originality and creativity. The effectiveness in addressing the issue is also highlighted. Second, the innovative activities shall be motivated by the goal of meeting social needs and predominantly developed and delivered via social organizations (ibid). This differentiates social innovation from business innovation.

It is argued that by adopting the model of social enterprise and a novel idea to reverse the roles of PODs and the participants to achieve empowerment, DID HK is a good example of social innovation for empowering PODs.

The transformation journey of DID Hong Kong

Disappointed by the strong prejudice against the visually impaired, the DID was founded by Dr. Andreas Heinecke in Germany to address the issue of the lack of understanding of the general public towards the visually impaired and therefore to "engage people of differences to create social impact". Dialogue in the Dark was brought to Hong Kong by Patrick Cheung and Tse Ka-kui through social franchising. By allowing participants to go through an authentic dialogue experience in complete darkness or silence, the Dialogue Experience is a unique model that makes participants aware of their own value system towards oneself and others. Since its startup in 2009, DID HK Ltd has become one of the most successful self-sustaining social enterprises in Hong Kong. Chui (2014) summarized the key developmental milestones for DID HK Ltd. From experiential stage to continuous innovations in the last five years, the development of DID HK Ltd is an ever-evolving journey. The four phases of development are 'before financial breakeven', 'financial breakthrough', 'scaling up through consolidating resources' and 'rebranding to sustain and expand the social impact'.

From 2009 to 2011, DID HK struggled through a stage of business model trial. It started with mobile experiential workshops in 2009, which had successfully attracted public attention and witnessed an increase in sales revenue. DID HK moved to a fixed location in 2010 and started to receive regular walk-in visitors. Whilst still recording a deficit on its balance sheet, it was the strong will of the then general manager to create an environment to facilitate bottom-up dynamics that help increase the income to exceed the expenditure in seven months (Chui, 2014). The proactive strategies of the leader include setting sales targets and facilitating referrals of potential corporate clients to the sales team. These practices were successful in reversing the financial imbalance in a short period of time.

Phase two witnessed a breakthrough not only in financial terms, but also in terms of innovation via various experimentations, as well as partnership with corporates. New brands such as 'Birthday in the Dark' and 'Dating in the Dark' were created. Amongst the new ideas, 'Concert in the Dark' soon became one of the flagship events of DID HK. 'Concert in the Dark' is another groundbreaking and innovative venture. It is the first ever live concert set in a completely dark environment. Audiences are guided to their seats by the VIs and they are able to experience a unique entertainment brought by voices and sounds. The event secured sponsorship from a local mobile network carrier as a part of its corporate social responsibility programme, which lowered the cost of operation and opened the opportunities to attract corporate and community partnerships. Apart from the innovative nature and the support from the corporate partners, the success of 'Concert in the Dark' is also a result of the bottom-up efforts. The idea of the event was created by a team of staff, who were satisfied with their 'ownership of the innovative idea and its successful implementation'. The open working culture also helped incubate a new business venture: 'Dialogue in Silence' workshops in 2011, involving hearing-impaired as the programme runners. According to Chui (2014), DID HK achieved HK$654,408 profitability by the end of 2011 and received several awards recognizing its outstanding performance as a social enterprise in social innovation.

Since 2012, DID HK has been striving to scale up. By integrating the elements of Dialogue in the Dark and Dialogue in Silence, the corporate training programs were rearranged to be more versatile to maximize the learning of the trainees. As a newly developed venture, the Silence Experience continued to develop 'impactainment' programmes. In 2012, DID HK opened the second space as the 'Dialogue Experience Square'.

In 2012, DID HK conducted internal soul searching and re-branding exercises with its staff and a social impact project to assess the performance of the ventures. More emphases were put on 'empowering the physically challenged' and inspiring the public to take actions in transforming the world, as the social mission of DID HK (Chui, 2014).

'Dialogue Experience' is the present HK trademarked Social Franchising Brand developed under DID HK. It is renowned for its financial stability, social impact, innovation, alternate leadership and company culture to incubate social entrepreneurship of their staff.

Empowerment theory

According to Zimmerman and Warschausky (1998), empowerment theory combines the perceptions of control, positive approach to life and the ability to understand and participate in the sociopolitical environment. Empowerment may be analyzed at three levels: individual, organizational (structural empowerment) and community empowerment.

Psychological empowerment is defined as the process and a multi-level construct by which people gain control over their lives, participate in political and community decision making and grow the awareness of the sociopolitical environments (Christens, 2012; Zimmerman, 2000). Zimmerman (1995) proposed a three-factor nomological network for psychological empowerment, including (1) an intrapersonal component referring to how people think about themselves; (2) an interactional component indicating a person's understanding about their community and sociopolitical issues; and (3) a behavioral component emphasizing the actions and behavior of people. Zimmerman (1995) also argued that the nomological network of psychological empowerment is related to self-efficacy, self-esteem, competence, mental health and power.

Extending the intrapersonal empowerment to the interactional level and organizational context, Kanter defines power as the capacity of accessing information and opportunities, mobilizing resources, and obtaining support to achieve goals (Meng et al., 2015). Empowerment in the context of an organization is a set of imperative managerial techniques that lead to higher effectiveness and encourage innovation from the inside. According to Conger and Kanungo (1988), organizational or structure empowerment can be viewed as a relational construct and motivational construct. In the relational construct, it is assumed that the organizational actors possessing more power are more likely to achieve their outcomes and are more likely to influence actors with less power. Therefore, empowerment in this context is the process by which the managers share their power with the subordinates. In the motivational construct, however, power is portrayed as an internal need that fulfills the personal self-efficacy and motivates individuals in an organization. Therefore, empowerment in this sense means enabling rather than simply power delegation (Conger & Kanungo, 1988).

At the community level, empowerment is a collective action that connects the people in need with the community to enhance their quality of life (Zimmerman & Warschausky, 1998). The empowerment process includes providing equal access to resources, enhancing the understanding of social and community issues and allowing participation in community activities.

Zimmerman and Warschausky (1998) also delineate three dimensions of empowerment theory: values, processes and outcomes. Values include "attention toward health, adaptation, competence, and natural helping systems" (ibid). Processes are the mechanism through which people, organization and community gain control over their lives, by collective learning and providing opportunities to influence the sociopolitical environment (ibid). Outcomes of empowerment may differ at different levels. At the individual level, the empowerment outcomes may refer to the increase in control and participation in individuals' lives. For an organization, the empowerment outcomes may be indicated by enriched linkages with other organizations, enhanced policy and productivity as a result of the empowerment practices. An empowered community may have enhanced responsiveness to the protection of people's quality of life, effective civil society to respond to social needs and more opportunities and channels for civic participation in community decision making, etc.

In the next section, DID HK will be used as a case to illustrate the process and outcomes of empowerment to PODs at individual, organizational and community levels.

Innovation in empowerment processes of DID Hong Kong

Psychological empowerment

As a social business operated with a strong social mission, human-oriented organizational culture and unique business model, DID HK is successful at empowering VI/HI employees as well as the participants/customers on a psychological level. For VIs and HIs, the model creates an effect of a narrative therapy by reversing the power relationship between PODs and the participants. VIs and HIs are empowered by demonstrating their competence in mastering an environment of constraints over the other participants. They gain self-esteem and self-efficacy through their work. For the participants, the experience is a combination of entertainment and generates positive changes in their perceptions towards PODs. By departing from their comfort zone, the participants are able to 'adventure' in complete darkness and experience the excitement of navigating in the world that they have never reached, while being able to taste and understand the challenges of VIs and HIs.

Transformational learning process for participants

The core value of Dialogue Experience (Dark and Silence experience) is to run a social enterprise with the mission to create social impact by engaging the PODs to construct a transformational experience for all participants, including the PODs. Experiential learning is the process whereby people engage in direct encounter, then purposely reflect upon, validate, transform, give personal meaning to and seek to integrate their different ways of knowing (McGill & Warner Weis, 1989). Dialogue Experience has designed its programs to align with that experiential learning approach together with a carefully designed program rundown in which participants are directly put into unfamiliar or disoriented scenarios.

By going through an authentic dialogue experience in complete darkness or silence, participants are able to be more aware of their own value system to themselves and the others. They are put under a constructed environment which creates disorientation and a disenabling effect that creates the reversal of roles and power relations. Participants are taken away from their comfort zone to be placed in a comparatively disadvantaged position. After the tours, participants are debriefed by experienced VI/HI trainers to help digest and connect the experience with their personal perceptions. The tours are designed to inspire participants to conceive a positive notion towards the disabled. As Chui suggested, the VI and HI trainers are the core of the value chain creation of the Dialogue Experience (Chui, 2014). Apart from being guides through the experience in the dark or silence that facilitates self-reflection, the VI and HI trainers are also sources of inspiration in the whole package of the Dialogue Experience. Participants are able to see how these trainers overcome their disabilities, leading a dignified and rewarding life with strong competence. According to the interviews conducted by Chui (2014), participants started to pay more attention to the PODs and increased their awareness of facilities for the disabled. They tended to have different attitudes towards future adversity after the transformational learning process.

According to Mezirow (1991), there are ten steps in the transformation process: disoriented dilemma situation, self- assessment process, building empathy and recognition towards others under similar situations, trying to explore options for change and then plan a course of action to address the disorientation. After the first five steps, one will need to acquire new skill and knowledge to adapt to the change, practice the new role and build up competence and collaborative excellence jointly with the team or the group. The last step is reintegrating back the new role and actions into one's life or workplace with a transformed perspective. Indeed, disorientation still exists as it is, but the mentality and the perspective has changed. DID HK has started to conduct social impact measurement research projects, a critical step with the objective to validate the impact level among various stakeholders of the organization and its partners. Obvious transformational learning outcomes were found among corporate clients, staff and partners, including exploration self-awareness, enhancement of leadership, more patience in listening and communicating with others (Chui, 2014).

Participants of the Dialogue Experience are inspired and transformed from the tours at both intrapersonal and interpersonal levels, in which the participants experience a deep, structural shift in the basic premises of thoughts, feelings and actions. At an intrapersonal level, participants will embrace the possibilities of changes by appreciation of people of differences with empathy, followed by the changing perspectives to bring in new behaviors and new habits. At an interpersonal level, participants shall develop trustful relationships and strong bonding among teammates by going through the collective Dialogue Experience, which nurtures teamwork and effective communication among participants with team excellence.

Narrative therapy for visually and hearing impaired individuals

From the perspective of VI and HI trainers, the intervention that positions them as the trainers in the Dialogue Experience facilitates narrative therapy for the trainers themselves. The concept of narrative therapy describes how people can be redefined through the creation of a double story based on the people as their own agency. There are three basic ideas in narrative therapy (White, 2007):

1 Problems are socially constructed. The problem is the problem and not the person is the problem.
2 Life experiences and encounters create a story plot for our identities over time.
3 Identities can be re-authored.

It was a common perception that the disabled are a disadvantaged group where most are unable to be self-reliant, let alone have a fruitful life and career. With this assumption in mind, PODs are sometimes stigmatized as being incapable to work and contribute to the community. Dialogue Experience is a life experience that changes not only the POD employees but also the entire community. By playing a core role in the social business model, these PODs demonstrate their capability to not only work and produce something, but also change the mentality of the public towards disability.

The case of Julian Zhu is a good example to demonstrate how the life of a visually impaired trainer was changed by the venture. Back in 2008, Zhu was the first Chinese-speaking freelance trainer with the Germany-based Dialogue Social Enterprise. He flew there from time to time to receive training and take part in delivering Dialogue in the Dark workshops mostly in international business events. While Zhu very much enjoyed creating dark experience for clients in every workshop, he never dreamed of doing the same thing in Greater China. Having heard that DID HK Ltd made a dramatic impact in Hong Kong and adjacent regions, as well as being fascinated by the passion and leadership of Dr. Andreas Heinecke, the founder of Dialogue Social Enterprise in Germany, Dr. K. K. Tse and Patrick Cheung, the co-founders of DID HK, Zhu decided to join them in the mission of promoting social inclusion and encouraging local social entrepreneurship, which was at that time an uphill climb. Zhu eventually took up the challenging tasks of recruiting VI staffs, as well as working with master trainers from Germany in localizing black box content and pre-job internal training of new recruits. With the work opportunities provided by DID HK, Zhu has been empowered to make his own living and, more importantly, find the meaning in his work to promote a better future with his peers.

In the survey conducted by Chui (2014), most VI and HI staff express that their power of expression has been enhanced and many find meaning in their work in helping the general public to understand their world.

Organizational empowerment

In the scoping report of DID HK, Chui (2014) summarized seven organizational factors that facilitate the transformation and empowerment process.[2] When the DID HK's recipe of success is understood in the context of organizational empowerment, there are three key elements that allow the organization to operate effectively in accomplishing its goals. DID HK has been strongly empowered by its values and social mission, organizational culture and management philosophy that facilitate bottom-up innovation and staff diversity.

Values and social mission

As a social enterprise, the mission of DID HK is simple and direct: to engage people of differences to create social impact. The four core values are:

1   Demonstrate enthusiasm in every encounter.
2   Bring up problems and have the courage to take initiatives to change.
3   Value differences in people.
4   Enjoy work and togetherness.

DID HK embraces the ambition to empower not only the VI staffs, but also the whole team as well as members of the general public who benefit from its expanding scope of services. Running a social enterprise with the mission to create social impact by engaging PODs to construct a transformational experience is the core value of Dialogue Experience.

With the mission to empower the staffs in mind, internal management, including personnel, promotion and black box content design, is delegated to VI colleagues. This enables outstanding employees to develop leadership. With this arrangement, an encouraging message is delivered to the local blind community: PODs can be more than just happy receivers of social service or decent subordinates in a sheltered workplace. They can be an important part of the organization, delivering valuable services to the community. Up until now, there were six blind employees taking managing positions, such as recruitment, internal training, quality control, human resources management and representing the Experience Management team in decision making at the company level. DID HK aims to unleash their potentials, and to encourage them to take the lead is the main challenge of the program. Dialogue Experience Silence places HIs at different positions based on their talents and empowers them to take the lead. They encourage work ownership, which in turn brings job satisfaction and sense of achievement. During their daily operations, HI team members are trained to be what DID calls 'Experience Architects', who are responsible for designing, tailor-making, hosting and managing unique silent experiences to hearing participants. The responses from participants are positive, which encourage and motivate the HI team members to realize and accept their abilities.

In terms of the business model, DID HK is a privately owned business without any subsidies from any external funding bodies, which is a common practice in most of the socially owned enterprises. By not taking government subsidies or charity donations, trainers and staff of DID HK are motivated and incentivized to work hard, which is one of the reasons for them to have gained respect from the community. Social enterprises share their commercial needs to balance the financial sustainability and social impact. Derived from the idea of Heinecke and Vaidyanathan (2009), it is important how all these 'invisible' ideologies are put into company culture. DID HK has less than one-third of the net profit to be shared by shareholders and one-third goes to the charity.

Organizational culture and management philosophy facilitating bottom-up innovation

Embedding the social business model, the social mission to help PODs and the leadership incubation into its management philosophy and organizational culture, DID HK has a flat hierarchy, lean management and liberal environment that lead to mushrooming bottom-up initiatives. The successes of these initiatives have repeatedly brought DID HK under the spotlight and created more intensive connection and collaboration with other stakeholders in the community.

According to the interviews with the staff in DID HK (Chui, 2014), the flat hierarchy in the organization allows the growth of freedom of expression. An intimate environment where even the lowest in the power structure will have frequent opportunities to sit around with the founders and managers in meetings makes the VIs/HIs and junior members of the organization feel respected and equal. They are also likely to have a strong sense of ownership in the company. From the perspective of management, the managers of DID HK are able to strike a balance between staff empowerment and control with provision of discretion and trust to enable bottom-up innovation.

Another striking feature of the organizational empowerment in DID HK is its liberal and democratic culture. Chui (2014) summarized that DID HK provides the sense of freedom, support, cooperation and pro-communication environment for the employees. First, with a simple hierarchy, employees are able to interact with almost all members in the organization and external guests. They also feel the freedom to speak their minds.

Second, staffs are encouraged to be 'intrapreneurs' to create and pursue their own innovative ideas and even corporate-to-corporate collaboration. The company will provide financial support and advice to incubate their innovations. The championship of Dialogue Experience Silence by Fiona Wat[3] and the brand 'non-visual based design' and Dark Theatre created by the visually impaired colleagues Alex Chan and Comma Chan are examples that illustrate innovation, double identities and administration.

Third, as the ventures of Dialogue Experience are expanding, there are increasing opportunities of cooperation within the organization and with external stakeholders.

Fourth, the diversity of staff also facilitates communication. DID HK has VI, HI and abled staff. Despite the different needs in communication, the staff are very willing to engage in more direct communication such as phone or face-to-face. The diverse staff team also includes the key roles of young graduates from universities. These young staff have a strong sense of social mission and passion in helping the POD community. A bottom-up managerial atmosphere through freedom, a supportive tone and facilitating cooperation and communication are important factors facilitating innovation. As Brown and Duguid (1991: 54) argued, 'Within an organization perceived as a collective of communities, not simply of individuals, in which enacting experiments are legitimate, separate community perspectives can be amplified by interchanges among communities. Out of this friction of competing ideas can come interchanges among communities . . . can come the sort of improvisational sparks necessary for igniting organizational innovation. . . . Organizations reflectively structured are perhaps particularly well positioned as highly innovative to deal with discontinuities. If their internal communities have a reasonable degree of autonomy and independence from the dominant world view, large organizations might actually accelerate innovation.' The trust and respect built in the supportive and caring organization culture have contributed to the incubation of some popular innovation projects under the venture of Dialogue Experience.

DID HK is successful at boosting the morale and satisfaction of their staff with a bottom-up approach by encouraging their staff to bring up innovative ideas, which in turn bring the continuing success of the company.

Successful cases of bottom-up innovation

It is the combination of the aforementioned organizational culture and management practices that allows successful incubation of innovations within the organization. After some phases from introducing Dialogue in the Dark via social franchising from Germany, there are numerous Dark experiences innovated in HK such as executive workshops, Experiential Exhibition, Dinner in the Dark, Birthday Party in the Dark, and other thematic Experiential Exhibition tours like Dating in the Dark, Dark Christmas and Summer in the Dark, etc. Concert in the Dark is the largest scale of its kind in the world. All these innovations are the results of teamwork. DID HK is dedicated to nurture a creative culture in the company. All these innovations started with small innovation circles, which are composed of VIs/HIs, sales teams and operation colleagues. This practice shows their emphasis on capacity building, innovation and empowerment in the organization.

The creation of the Silence Experience[4] is a successful case demonstrating the outcome of the pro-empowerment organizational culture of DID HK. In 2010, DID HK Ltd started to consider engaging more PODs like HIs in their core business. Silence Experience was created. It was originally in the form of executive workshops and 'impactainment', interestingly defined as entertainment with social impact, to showcase the ability of HIs. Silence le Cabaret[5], as a flagship venture of Silence Experience, uses interesting and animated gestures during a performance in silence to touch the hearts of the hearing audience. During the development of Silence le Cabaret, HI members are in charge of script writing, acting and stage management. The program is now a platform to showcase a spectrum of talents that surprises the audience.

The company subsequently came up with its Hong Kong brand 'Dialogue Experience' to cover 'Dark' and 'Silence' experiential platforms. With this Dialogue Experience brand, DID HK is able to franchise out the original experience globally. These experiences share the fundamental elements such as a pre-set environment to show the ability of PODs, role exchange of PODs and participants and promotion of positive image of PODs.

Community empowerment

With only several years of operation, DID HK has managed to empower the community by its clear, yet effective, social mission and its strong engagement with different stakeholders of society.

A mission to promote the values of PODs

PODs are commonly perceived as disabled in society, who require supports and sympathy. Having set a clear target of beneficiary to VIs and HIs, DID HK plays an important role to develop and promote their unique skills in a dark or silent environment to promote their strength and competence to the public. With this kind of experiential creation, they are empowered to unleash full potential in the spotlight of the public.

By setting itself as an example and endeavoring to spread the ideas of hiring PODs, DID HK creates social impact in the commercial sector using diverse hiring practices in organizations that help create job opportunities for the differently abled. The purpose of engaging HIs in the Silence experimental products is to create awareness and understanding between differently abled groups and the rest of society. The company encourages empathetic, positive and appreciative attitudes towards PODs in society. As an encouraging outcome, the head of human resources of a well-known international chain coffee was inspired to place deaf/hard of hearing staff in the front line. Not only did he offer additional work opportunities in the deaf/hard of hearing community, the abilities of HIs were recognized, which helps to avoid stereotyping and misunderstanding by the public.

The Dialogue Experience cleverly taps the ability of PODs being fully mobile and competent in the dark and silence to create an innovative model that is able to raise public awareness of PODs on one hand, and provide professional training of transferrable skills and education to the PODs on the other. At the founding stage, a team of founding members visited the local rehabilitation, advocate and social service organizations in Hong Kong to learn about the needs of the VIs. The team soon found out that among the many people with visual impairment, only about 1,000 of them were actively participating in various training and self-developing programs. VIs in Hong Kong in general need the resources and opportunities to get adequate education, training, social exposure and job experiences in order to be competent and competitive for jobs. In this regard, DID HK provides trainings in languages, communication skills and literacy for the POD trainers to equip them with adequate capacity to lead and guide the workshops and exhibition.

The employment opportunities and job satisfaction provided by DID HK to PODs are remarkable. In January 2009, DID HK recruited the first batch of blind trainers in the dark. In January 2010, the company started the recruitment and training of the guides. As business expanded throughout the years, the company continued recruiting and providing internal trainings. By summer of 2014, DID HK had sixteen staff with visual impairment employed on a full-time basis and another thirty VI part-time employees. Furthermore, DID HK strives to create work opportunities in different areas for those VI employees with potential. For example, some capable VI staff were sent to carry out the social responsibility duties outside the company and work together with various stakeholders. At this moment, one partially sighted employee has joined the cause-related marketing team, one is with the sales team and business development and one is in charge of organizational learning and talent development for the whole company.

Co-evolvers and local elements

DID HK is a learning organization which is constantly seeking opportunities to collaborate with various community stakeholders and being innovative in creating new ideas to meet new challenges. Engaging 'co-evolvers' in its development strategy is an important step to expand the impact of community empowerment. In this section, the cases of 1O1O, a local mobile brand under CSL Mobile Limited, and MTR, the mass transit railways of Hong Kong (MTR Corp, 2014), are elaborated to illustrate the roles of 'co-evolvers' in creating social impact and empower the community.

As an important co-evolver with DID HK, 1O1O, a local mobile network company in Hong Kong, has been the major sponsor for Concert in the Dark, the signature event of DID HK, since 2009. It was from the perspective of 1O1O that the company is in need to remain competitive in the local mobile market by evolving itself from the traditional model of corporate social responsibility to generating business values through business innovation collaboration with DID HK, a successful brand of social enterprise. By associating with DID HK in the flagship event like Concert in the Dark, 1O1O is able to brand the uniqueness of its service as delivering a unique "communication" experience for its premium customer to stand out from other competitors. However, Dialogue Experience is more than a social enterprise to 1O1O. They are partners and co-evolvers in the process of organizing events in the market. In 2014, this partnership moved further to deliver an exceptional experience to 1O1O prestigious customers in silence. Silence le Cabaret became the most expected event by the corporate customers of 1O1O.

The second example of co-evolver with DID HK is MTR (MTR Corp, 2014). With its own academy of training school for the staff, MTR adopted a dialogue experiential learning program as one of the key methodologies in sharpening various skills of the staff and amplifying the impact of its leadership program. DID HK designed the learning and development curriculum for their leadership program in addressing the current business challenges. With the business input from MTR, Dialogue Experience accelerated the product development process by launching workshop in the dark with a customized program rundown. Dialogue Experience has been learning from the partner in customizing program rundowns to achieve the desirable transformational learning outcomes. That process will keep on evolving with a dedicated joint effort from the experienced architects in Dialogue Experience as well as from the business partners.

Apart from the collaboration with the 'co-evolvers', DID HK also embeds local elements in their experiential products to increase the originality. To keep up with the fast pace and the changing needs of the Hong Kong community, Dialogue Experience Silence decided to extend its experimental programs from corporate training workshops to educational and entertainment programs, in one year after the launch of the business in Hong Kong. These new experimental products, Silence Yum Cha, Silence Dinner, Silence Motion, add cultural flavor to the original business concept and give room to expand the clientele. The new ideas with local elements attracted not only the Hong Kong participants, but also visitors and corporations from overseas.

To further expand the scope of business, Dialogue Experience Silence partnered with Ngong Ping 360, a cable car tourist attraction in Hong Kong, to create the Silence Motion 360. This new experimental product was designed and customized by taking advantage of the beautiful natural scenery surrounding Ngong Ping and a historical cinema. Led by the HI trainers, participants will be experiencing an advanced level of drama building programs in the one-of-a-kind sensory journey on a cable car ride and time travel through the beautiful scenery and historical areas. The new program targets not only local corporate customers but also MICE (Meeting, Incentive, Conference and Exhibition) tourists from overseas corporations.

Conclusion

In Hong Kong, there are around 2.4 percent visually impaired and 2.2 percent hearing impaired populations (CSD, 2014). While PODs have long been marginalized in society with widespread misconception and misunderstanding, there are courageous social ventures and innovative projects addressing this very issue. The popularity of DID HK has proven the success and effectiveness of this unique model in empowering the PODs and customers at psychological, organizational and community levels. While the participants go through the transformational experiential learning most notably as role reversal and change in power relations via the specially designed experience program, the VI and HI trainers also experience a process of narrative therapy in which PODs are empowered through guiding the participants in the dark or experience silence. At the organizational level, the social mission and values, organizational culture and management philosophy that facilitate bottom-up initiative have largely empowered the PODs and staff by providing them with freedom to create innovative projects. With the expanding success of these bottom-up projects, DID HK is also able to empower the POD community and general public. By spreading the empowering message through its services and advocacy activities, as well as strategically engaging corporates and other stakeholders in society as 'co-evolvers' and adopting local elements in their experiential products, DID HK provides a unique and all-rounded model in empowering various stakeholders in the community with innovative ideas.

Notes

1 Dialogue Experience (DE) was created by DID HK to design programs that align with an experiential learning approach together with a carefully designed program rundown in which participants are directly put into unfamiliar or disoriented scenarios.
2 The seven factors as concluded by Chui (2014) are: (1) VIs and HIs as the core of the value chain creation; (2) empowerment practices of the organization; (3) staff diversity; (4) shared values and identity brought by common social goals; (5) bottom-up enthusiasm; (6) a discovering and learning organization; and (7) proactively looking for collaboration opportunities.
3 Fiona Wat embarked on her journey as a social entrepreneur in 2011 with DID HK Ltd and founded both Dialogue Experience Silence and Silence le Cabaret. Dialogue Experience Silence received the respected 2013 Social Enterprise Champion Award– Innovation. Wat first joined the group as a volunteer. After twenty years of experience in the commercial world working mainly in marketing and brand management, she realized it was time to make a big change in her career life to bring positive messages to impact society. Being in a social enterprise, Wat's challenge is to foster collaboration among different sets of systems, values, beliefs and practices to run the business. Among all, the most important is to have the deaf community engaged in mainstream business activities and to provide a diversified work environment where everyone would appreciate the differences and the talents of every individual. Wat's professional background in the creative and marketing industry adds different perspectives in developing sustainable social enterprise projects, as a creative sense is important when solving problems.
4 Dialogue Experience Silence offers experiences that are conducted in silence that combine engagement, education and inspiration. Through the engagement and interaction between participants and HIs, varieties of silent experiential programs were developed through teambuilding workshops and impactainment programs facilitated by HIs to social sectors, including but not limited to commercial, academic, government and tourism. The programs break down barriers between people – participants and the deaf people alike. Positive impacts include team spirit, patience and empathy.
5 Silence le Cabaret is a combination of dinner and theatre, with a troupe of deaf performers leading the audience into the show, and in which the audience also plays an important part of the whole performance. By inviting every participant to dress up in themed costumes to align with the story, usually the play is based on a local well-known crime thriller written and directed by a hearing impaired person; in this silent theatrical performance featuring hearing impaired actors using only body language and facial expressions without any sound or sound effects, the audience was touched and admired this unique form of performing art.

References

Brown, J. S., & Duguid P. (1991). "Organizational Learning and Communities-of-Practice: Toward a Unified View of Working, Learning, and Innovation", *Organization Science*, 2(1): 40–57.
Census and Statistics Department Hong Kong Special Administrative Region (CSD). (2014). Social Data Collected via the General Household Survey Special Topics Report No. 62, Persons with Disabilities and Chronic Diseases, http://www.statistics.gov.hk/pub/B11301622014XXXXB0100.pdf, accessed August 2015.
Christens, Brian D. (2012). "Toward Relational Empowerment", *American Journal of Community Psychology*, 50: 114–128.
Chui, S. (2014). *A Scoping Study of Theory of Change of DiD HK Limited*. Centre for Human Resources Strategy and Development, Hong Kong Baptist University, Manuscript.

Conger, J. A. & Kanungo, R. N. (1988). "The Empowerment Process: Integrating Theory and Practice", *Academy of Management Review*, 13(3): 471–482.

Heinecke, A., & Vaidyanathan, M. (2009). Rethink-Redesigning-Rebuilding, Manuscript, www.dialogue-se.com

Hubert, A. (2010). Empowering People, Driving Change: Social Innovation in European Union. A Report. European Commission. Available online: http://ec.europa. eu/bepa/pdf/ publications_pdf/social_innovation.pdf.

Kabeer, N. (1999). "Resources, agency, achievements: Reflections on the measurement of women's empowerment", *Development and Change*, 30(3): 435–464.

McGill, I., & Weil, S. W. (1989). *A Framework for Making Sense of Experiential Learning.* Guildford: The Society for Research into Higher Education and Open University Press.

Meng, L., Liu, Y., Liu, H., Hu, Y., Yang, J., & Liu, J. (2015). "Relationships among Structural Empowerment, Psychological Empowerment, Intent to Stay and Burnout in Nursing Field in Mainland China – based on a Cross-Sectional Questionnaire Research", *International Journal of Nursing Practice*, 21: 303–312.

Mezirow, J. (1991). *Transformative Dimensions of Adult Learning.* San Francisco: Jossey-Bass.

Mulgan, G. with Tucker, S., Ali, R., & Sanders, B. (2007). Social Innovation: What It Is, Why It Matters and How It Can Be Accelerated (Working Paper). The Basingstoke Press.

MTR Corp. (2014). Annual Report, Manuscript, http://mtr.com.hk/chi/publications/ images/business_overview_c.pdf

Peterson, N. A. (2014). "Empowerment Theory: Clarifying the Nature of Higher-order Multidimensional Constructs", *American Journal of Community Psychology*, 53: 96–108.

Purdue, D.E.J., & Howe, P. D. (2012). "Empower, Inspire, Achieve: (Dis)empowerment and the Paralympic Games", *Disability & Society*, 27(7): 903–916.

Spreitzer, G. M. (1995). "Psychological empowerment in the workplace: Dimensions, measurement, and validation", *Academy of Management Journal*, 38(5), 1442–1465.

Wallerstein, N. (1992). "Powerlessness, Empowerment and Health: Implications for Health Promotion Programmes", *American Journal of Health Promotion*, 6(3): 197–205.

White, M. (2007). *Maps of Narrative Practice.* New York & London: Norton & Company.

Zimmerman, Marc A. (1995). "Psychological Empowerment: Issues and Illustrations", *American Journal of Community Psychology*, 23(5): 581–599.

Zimmerman, M. A. (2000). "Empowerment Theory: Psychological, Organizational and Community Levels of Analysis", in E. Seidman & J. Rapparport (Eds.), *Handbook of Community Psychology.* New York: Kluwer/Plenum, pp. 43–63.

Zimmerman, Marc A., & Warschausky, Seth (1998). "Empowerment Theory for Rehabilitation Research: Conceptual and Methodological Issues", *Rehabilitation Psychology*, 43(1): 3–16. American Psychological Association.

11 Multisided platforms strategy in social entrepreneurship

A case study of Taiwan's Duofu

Hsiang-Hsun Wu and Jennifer H. Chen

Introduction

Duofu Care & Service, established in May 2009, is Taiwan's first private "rehabus" service operator and is considered one of Taiwan's representative social enterprises. Duofu Care & Service (hereafter referred to as Duofu) is dedicated to providing a highly flexible, high-quality, barrier-free transport service for people with disabilities to resolve the transport inconvenience that typically forces them to remain at home. Since its establishment, Duofu has expanded into a multitude of extended services, such as accessible travel, commissioned operation of rehabus vehicles, and medication delivery, though travel transport remains the organization's primary source of income. The method by which Duofu achieved success is a good model for related service providers, particularly with regard to the following questions: How did Duofu develop itself? How did it overcome financial problems without accepting any government subsidies and still having to compete with other private rehabus service operators who did receive a considerable amount of government compensation? How did Duofu attract users? How did it later persuade vendors and tourism operators to participate in a travel service that had yet to be proven profitable? How should Duofu find a balance between its economic and social values to achieve multidirectional growth goals?

A multisided platform (hereafter MSP) describes the business logic that Duofu has embraced: Duofu creates value primarily by enabling direct interaction among people with disabilities and providers of accessible travel and related service. Platform refers to an "economic platform"[1] in which two or more distinct groups provide each other with network benefits (Eisenmann & Hagiu, 2008); a multisided platform is one in which the operator intends to facilitate direct interactions by offering infrastructure and rules between two or more distinct groups of affiliated users (Hagiu & Wright, 2011). In an MSP, users value the ability to interact, engage in transactions with, and cooperate with users from the network's other side(s). In the case of Duofu, the organization had no plans to develop an MSP to resolve its problems. Duofu initially focused solely on providing high-quality accessible transport services, actively cooperating with public service providers who offer accessible transport services, and vying for opportunities with disability groups, all in an effort to establish a positive word of mouth. When it had attracted a group of regular customers, it began developing new services, such as its traveling service, and gradually realized its unique role as a platform to attract other groups of users. Requests from third-party agencies led Duofu to add commissioned rehabus management, medication delivery, and food delivery services. Financially, the organization is still making a loss, but by using the MSP method it is expected to see benefits relating to economies of scale and economies of scope.

The example of Duofu provides social enterprises with a sustainable management reference for how to evolve from a single-service provider to embrace MSP. In this case as with others, social enterprises are inherently a two-sided platform, in which one side is a group formed for fulfilling social public needs, and the other side comprises participants who invest in such a group because of the group's business value (Baden-Fuller & Mangematin, 2013). One example in recent years is the development of e-commerce platforms, such as the business-to-business trading platform Alibaba in China and novel mobile applications like the Uber taxi service based out of the United States, which have proven beyond any doubt that an online business model can yield substantial economic value; and yet, studies on nonprofit organizations and social enterprises have largely overlooked this angle. If stakeholders in social enterprises can gain a new understanding of the intertwined nature of business value and social value from a platform perspective, social enterprises will be able to develop services and products that contribute even more to sustainability.

The major difference between the platform model of social enterprises and that of for-profit organizations is that social enterprises are required to mitigate conflicts that occur between social public ends and economic goals. The platform model of social enterprises also requires a large amount of capital to establish infrastructure, as with any enterprise model, but obtaining investments is more challenging for social enterprises because the goals they are pursuing (i.e., public benefits) can mean a possibility of no return on investment. Another problem that arises when the platform model is used is the chicken-or-egg question; a group of potential users would choose not to embrace a service or product at first and instead wait to see if others do so, but if nobody makes the first move to enable interaction, transaction, and cooperation, users may reject the platform model (Hagiu & Wright, 2011).

For-profit organizations can resolve that quandary by subsidizing the investment costs that early adopters expend on using a product or service; for example, family gaming consoles are typically sold lower than cost to increase the number of players willing to buy them. Cross-subsidization is not an unknown business model in social enterprises either, as seen with the Scojo Foundation (currently known as VisionSpring), which distributed reading glasses free of charge to rural residents in India and sold them to middle-class people in urban areas. However, social enterprises implementing cross-subsidization may encounter problems in (1) whether they should use capital acquired from nonprofit businesses to subsidize the development of new profit-making businesses (Kerlin, 2013); (2) whether profit-making businesses should extensively subsidize nonprofit businesses, and if so when they should cease subsidies; and (3) how social enterprises should respond when external investors of profit-making businesses move to reduce the focus placed by social enterprises on nonprofit businesses.

One approach that for-profit organizations typically employ to resolve their chicken-and-egg problem is providing exclusivity to attract user participation. In the gaming console example, this would be tying exclusive software to a specific console whenever a new generation is launched. Exclusivity entails requiring a large amount of investment in advance or seeking the full support of a third party (Casey & Töyli, 2012), and since such large-scale enterprise and capital is often unavailable to social enterprises, it is typically not viable for smaller social enterprises.

The infrastructure pertinent to an MSP is extremely expensive, and the process of building trust among various groups of users is time consuming. As such, failures in platform models are more common than success stories (Casey & Töyli, 2012). If social enterprises adopt a platform model at the beginning of their entrepreneurial ventures, their failure rate can be expected to be notably higher than at for-profit counterparts. For Duofu, there was at first that same lack of success in using a platform model, but it turned around its fortunes somewhat with a two-sided platform from which it then developed an MSP. The remaining sections of this chapter introduce Duofu's background and its initial method of cross-subsidization, then describe the developmental process that allowed it to move from a one-sided platform to a two-sided and then an MSP. Finally, based on this case study, three platform model concepts are proposed that are conducive to social enterprises seeking sustainable development.

Establishment: resolving the shortage of barrier-free transport services

In May 2009, Jeff Hsu resigned from his job as a documentary director and established Duofu Care & Service, prompted by his own grandmother, who was injured from a fall and found extreme inconvenience in travelling to and from the hospital because she lacked a document proving her handicap, making her ineligible to take public rehabuses. Public sector–managed personal transport services for the physically challenged also have a considerable number of restrictions, such as the need for advance reservations, intra-city transport limits, and the policy of only taking passengers to or from medical appointments. These limitations are time inefficient and physically and mentally hurt everyone involved while confining people with disabilities to a small living circle. Hsu's idea was that instead of complaining and hoping someone would make changes, he could develop a transport service himself that would fulfill the needs of the physically challenged. Thus, Duofu became Taiwan's first private service company offering accessible transportation and incorporating professional services into accessible transportation, a field hitherto dominated by traditional car rental service providers. With the introduction of his service, pregnant women, children, the elderly, and people with disabilities were finally able to travel whenever and wherever they desired.

Duofu's primary competitors remain the rehabus services subsidized by the government. Private sector operators have shied away from investing in rehabuses because (1) purchasing a six-seat shuttle and making the necessary modification requires a high investment cost of at least NT$3 million (US$93,800); (2) passengers are typically physically unwell, making each service trip prolonged and complex, meaning a rehabus makes considerably less than a taxi would in the same amount of time; and (3) modified buses cannot be sold on the secondhand market to recoup expenditures. The central government of the Republic of China (Taiwan) has therefore formulated subsidy policies that would encourage private organizations to invest in rehabus business, and local governments have developed rehabus services based on a public (government)-managed private business concept, encouraging business owners willing to provide rehabus service to participate in the tendering process, with successful bidders obtaining subsidies. In addition to their own vehicles, tenderers are also provided with rehabus vehicles owned by the local government. However, according to regulations, only individuals who hold a disability card are eligible to use the service. Taking a public-sponsored rehabus is usually inexpensive – a third of the standard taxi rate – and low-income households are even eligible for a certain number of free rides per week. Currently, operators who have cooperated with local governments to provide rehabus service include the Eden Social Welfare Foundation, e-Go, and e-Bus.

Despite the provision of government subsidies, public-managed private businesses remain incapable of resolving the severe social concern of rehabus shortages. As of the end of quarter one of 2014, some 1,125,000 people in Taiwan possess a disability card, accounting for 4.8 percent of the total population; the largest single category is people with limb disabilities, who account for 375,000 (33.3 percent) of card holders. Despite the high number of people in need of accessible transportation, there is an insufficient supply of ready vehicles. According to data presented by the Ministry of Health and Welfare, by the end of March 2014, just 1,382 vehicles were available around Taiwan for accessible transportation services. Based on the number of people in need across different cities and counties, 1.23 rehabus shuttles are needed on average per every 1,000 people with mental or physical disabilities. Taipei, the capital, has the highest number of shuttles at 2.3 per 1,000 people, and mostly rural Yunlin County in central Taiwan has the least at 0.32, demonstrating the uneven distribution of resources. Hsu estimates that the 60,000 people with disabilities who need to periodically visit medical institutions represent an approximate annual revenue potential of NT$4 billion (US$124.95 million) for the medical transport service sector.[2] For the entire nation, that would mean possible revenue of NT$25–30 billion (US$780.93–937.11 million).

The relatively low quality of service at public-managed private rehabuses is one aspect that has been criticized severely. Successful tenderers in various locales only provide services for the disabled whose household registration (permanent address) is set in that specific jurisdiction, and their focus has been maximizing the profits from the difference between subsidies and operating costs. To achieve this,[3] these service providers have tried to minimize costs for maintenance, safety equipment, and personnel training, engendering an unsafe environment and extremely poor service quality for passengers. To enhance vehicle use rate, many service providers have mandated that users must make bookings three to five days in advance and refuse to permit impromptu bookings. Moreover, users who miss bookings will receive penalty points as a form of punishment. For example, in Taipei, those who accumulate three penalty points are prohibited from using the service for a month. Vehicles are also typically prioritized for people with higher levels of disability, making it difficult to impossible for people with less severe impairments to use the service. If users opt for self-paid rehabus services, they could be charged at a rate as high as NT$900 (US$28.11) per trip. Not only have locals with disabilities expressed extreme dissatisfaction toward the existing rehabus services, foreign visitors have also gotten the impression of Taiwan as a disability-unfriendly nation.

In the first year (2009) of its establishment, Duofu, headquartered in Wenshan District of Taipei City, started serving people with disabilities in Taipei and neighboring New Taipei (then Taipei County) with two vans. Breaking from the practices of public-managed private rehabus services, Duofu allows users to book any time and cancel their bookings without penalty, and it provides transport to nearby cities and counties for any purpose. Its fees are also considerably lower than self-paid rehabus services, starting at a rate of NT$500 (US$15.61). The combination of unique services and a relatively low price at the early stage of this entrepreneurial venture rapidly attracted a wide range of customers who were left highly satisfied, including people with disabilities, pregnant women, children, and the elderly. Within a short period, Duofu was able to purchase another van at the end of 2009 and managed to break even in its first year. Duofu purchased three more vans in early 2010 to bring its fleet to six.

Making a platform: a bridge to customers

Initial service

In the first two years of its establishment, Duofu paid visits to various large and small disability associations with the hopes of becoming an accessible transportation partner, but it was foiled by a lack of trust from its potential partners. Nevertheless, Duofu's numerous advantages in cost, quality, and convenience spread through word of mouth and the Internet, helping the organization successfully establish its first group of highly loyal customers. Its transport service design is as follows.

Service standardization: Duofu has standardized service procedures from the first point of contact with customers to the satisfaction survey conducted afterward, and it also offers different services according to each rider's specific needs. During the standardization process, Hsu instructed drivers to first determine the specific inconveniences that passengers experience in order to effectively handle their difficulties. For example, when a passenger vomits in the car because of physical discomfort, the driver is supposed to check the passenger's condition and provide comfort accordingly while also contemplating how to clean up before receiving the next passenger. Duofu drivers are typically forty years old on average, ten years younger than those employed by other service providers, because Hsu believes that younger drivers are more likely to accept a customer-centered service model and abide by service regulations.

Home service: Hsu found that elderly people and patients who live in apartments equipped with no elevators are largely unable to leave their homes, severely curtailing their social lives and hurting their physical health. He approached this problem by introducing a stair-climbing machine for wheelchairs, enabling transport services to be extended into users' homes.

Safety as the top priority: To ensure a safe, comfortable ride and maintain passenger dignity, Duofu only uses vehicles that are a maximum of five years old and keeps only safety equipment manufactured by well-known, reputable brands. The modified vehicles must pass inspections before they are used on roads, wheelchairs are fastened with five seat belts, and all passengers are insured with the maximum insurance amount regulated by law.

Fixed pricing: Point-to-point pricing is used. For example, NT$600 (US$18.74) is charged per trip from Wenshan in Taipei City to Yonghe District in New Taipei, a ride of about fifteen to twenty minutes. The price shown is the price paid, putting customers at ease about hidden additional fees.

No advance bookings required: The twenty-four-hour service permits customers to make reservations any time of the day, including impromptu bookings and changes, as Hsu believes customers who are late for their reservations, who wish to use the service earlier than expected, or who have to cancel all have reasons for doing so. No fees are charged for any changes or scheduling, and when a sudden change does occur, Duofu tries to comfort customers by informing them that there is no penalty and that they should not worry about discontinuing use of Duofu services. To accommodate flexible scheduling, twelve or thirteen drivers work in shifts for every ten vehicles just in case of unexpected incidents. Hsu asserted that hiring extra drivers is an essential "waste" for enabling customers to enjoy the freedom of traveling.

No service restrictions: A fixed-point, periodic transport service is offered for people who need to visit medical institutions for medical consultations. In addition, customers are welcome to use the shuttles for visiting friends or for traveling.

To enable more people to benefit from its pick-up service, Duofu has vied to become the Taipei Metro's appointed wheelchair-accessible service partner. Following two years of promotion, Duofu has built a strong partnership with organizations such as the Taiwan Foundation for Rare Disorders, Sunable: Access for All in Taiwan, the Spinal Cord Injury Associations, and the Taiwan Motor Neuron Disease Association, all while participating in large-scale accessible transport projects, such as transport arrangements for the Association of Mouth and Foot

Painting Artists of the World in 2012, and the Accessible Transport Service for Taichia Matsu Procession in 2013. Duofu was extensively involved with the services in these projects, cooperating with organizers to improve barrier-free facilities such as adjusting entrance width to accommodate wheelchair entry and bed heights and preparing assistive devices for bathing.

Introducing a travel service

Duofu's accessible travel service was introduced six months after its establishment. Hsu recalled (interview with Hsu, the founder of Duofu [2013]):

> Duofu's customers with physical disabilities often said: "Because of limited transportation and other constraints, we cannot move about like others. Sometimes, when we have finally settled ourselves in a cab, we're not sure whether the place we're going is wheelchair friendly. Instead of getting there only to find that the place has no access for wheelchairs or has no bathrooms for disabled people, we'd rather stay at home and watch TV or play on the computer." (Translation)

Compared with services offered for hospital-to-home traveling, accessible travel is more complex. Duofu began by exploring tourist areas in an attempt to resolve problems concerning inadequate barrier-free facilities, leading Hsu to identify the following key needs[4]:

1   **Service group expansion**: Accessible travel offers caregivers and care receivers (family members) a solution to travel together. Previous efforts at accessible transport services have focused on care receivers, neglecting the prolonged stress imposed upon caregivers. Hsu asserted that "accessible travel is not only a service package provided to an individual, but is also a complete set of measures offered to an entire family or group." During holiday seasons or long weekends, families and companies have sought Duofu assistance because some members in the group used a wheelchair, telling Hsu: "As long as you can satisfy our accessibility needs, we'll entrust you with planning our entire trip!" Service group expansion signifies that Duofu can advocate the concept of accessible service to consumers without physical and mental challenges in addition to people with them.
2   **Increased revenue sources and profit margins**: The incorporation of caregivers in service groups indicates an increased inflow of income sources for the organization. The accessible travel is charged per head count with no relation to disability status, and it differs significantly from transport services in that travel service maximizes the passenger capacity of each vehicle. The transport service is based on a pick-on-call concept, in which additional vehicles and drivers are ready to provide services at any time. Additionally, Duofu's travel service involves a chartered service that is provided when the number of people in a group has reached the minimum threshold and charged

on a per-day basis. For these reasons, the operating costs of a travel service are relatively lower than those incurred for medical transport services.

Providing an accessible travel service begins with constructing a barrier-free environment. Taipei's accessible environment is lacking. Many tourist attractions offer relevant services or ramps for wheelchairs, but excessive obstacles remain throughout trips, such as stairs, posts, and objects or holes on walkways. Accessible services pertinent to bathrooms, meals, accommodation, and emergency medical treatment remain inadequate, disrupting accessible travel itineraries and activities. Even before Duofu, other social public groups (e.g., Eden Social Welfare Foundation and the Taiwan Access for All Association) have invested effort in offering accessible travel, but because of their status as a nonprofits, these groups cannot commercially promote their accessible travel service and have had to rely instead on lobbying. Duofu on the other hand has cooperated with Sunable on comprehensively linking aspects of accessible service. For instance, in Wulai, a popular hot springs district in New Taipei, Duofu and Sunable spent almost a year persuading owners of retail stores, bed and breakfasts, restaurants, and recreation areas that they can gain increased revenues and better reputations from tourists with disabilities by improving their accessibility. Duofu has through such efforts been able to rapidly develop a travel route in northern Taiwan spanning from Tamsui to the north of Taipei, down to Wulai to south of the capital, and out west to Daxi in Taoyuan City and along the North Coast Highway. In 2014, Duofu and major travel operator Lion Travel began working together to promote accessible travel that extends all the way down the coast to the tech capital of Hsinchu. Duofu's strategy is to start by offering services at a rate approximating its cost to establish its customer base, then offering added value travel service, and finally using its profits to subsidize the higher costs of its transport service.

Case in depth: from cross-subsidization to a platform

As mentioned earlier, Duofu didn't realize its platform role until the successful launch of an accessible travel service. More and more travel service providers became "affiliated" members offering qualified and certified services to people with disabilities. In this evolving process, we find that cross-subsidization plays a key role in keeping Duofu blooming on its way to becoming a platform. Contrary to past studies on MSPs taking cross-subsidization as an instrument for profit generating (Rochet & Tirole, 2003), the Duofu case shows that cross-subsidization is a probe to find the opportunities for growing into an MSP.

Cross-subsidization is a business practice commonly used by MSPs offering a cross-subsidization to other services in the same platform because the fees charged for that service are greater than the stand-alone cost of offering the service (Rochet & Tirole, 2003). For example, Adobe offers Acrobat Reader for free, enabling anybody to read PDF documents, while at the same time selling a pro version of Acrobat at a high price targeting users who need to edit and export PDF files. In other words, Adobe categorized users into subgroups according to price flexibility and user needs in order to make use of the influence that each subgroup exerts on each other; specifically, as the number of free users increases, the chance that these free users will convert into paid users increases.

It should be noted that cross-subsidization is not a sufficient condition for a platform. For example, Dropbox charges users who need a comprehensive file management function and a lot of storage space while providing free services to users who only require basic functionality for storing and accessing files online. Dropbox's freemium model is based on the concept of cross-subsidization, where monetary amount received from a few paid users is used to subsidize the free users who make up the majority. However, Dropbox is not a platform because free users and premium users have almost zero interaction through its service.

In an MSP model, cross-subsidization occurs between groups of users in **distinct networks**. Taking the credit card industry as an example, card holders often enjoy multiple special offers and lower card fees, whereas merchants are charged at a higher merchant discount rate (Rochet & Tirole, 2002). In the video game industry, Sony and Microsoft sell their consoles at a price lower than production costs, with subsidization capital derived from the high licensing fees charged to game developers. In the newspaper industry, news agencies charge more for ad agencies in order to subsidize lower prices for readers. And at shopping malls, shoppers benefit from free parking fees while vendors must pay a high premium for rent. The operator of a platform must decide which user group or groups benefit from a lower price aimed at ensuring participation during the initial stage of platform development (Eisenmann, Parker, & Van Alstyne, 2006; Rochet & Tirole, 2003). These examples indicate that if a wide variety of choices is offered to the subsidized side, operators who employ a platform model cannot increase prices to the subsidizing side (Eisenmann, 2007; Rochet & Tirole, 2003). For example, assuming players can simultaneously purchase multiple game consoles of various brands at a low cost, Sony and Microsoft cannot easily demand a high licensing fee from game developers. Therefore, platform operators must raise the incentives for the subsidized side to continue participating in the platform, or otherwise increase the costs for them to leave.

The transport and travel services that Duofu offers are a cross-subsidization in a same-side network, while its travel services and affiliate service providers form a cross-subsidization in a cross-side network. Because suppliers of accessible travel services in Taiwan are scant, customers are unable to find replacements for Duofu's services and are thus willing to pay higher prices. Customers of Duofu's accessible travel service are also typically users of its accessible transport service, and they are unlikely to use other accessible travel providers because of the trust in the brand they have developed. Tourism and travel-related service providers, meanwhile, are willing to accept almost immediately proposals from Duofu and its partners when they ask for improvement to accessible services and facilities. This is a strong contrast from Duofo's early stage, when it failed to construct an effective two-sided network for its accessible transport service because of a lack of trust on the part of health providers and the tendency to prioritize public-managed private rehabus services over private service providers. Figure 11.1

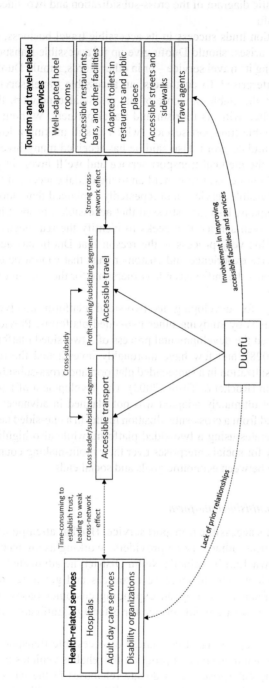

Figure 11.1 Duofu's cross-subsidization and two-sided platform.

illustrates a schematic diagram of the cross-subsidization and two-sided platform established by Duofu.

As the organization finds success in its accessible travel business, a predicament subsequently arises: should Duofu give up its accessible transport service to focus on managing its travel service – or in other words, should Duofu become a profit-making enterprise? To customers, an accessible travel service is irreplaceable, and it is the stable outcome of the cross-sided network that Duofu has jointly established with its tourism and travel partners. Without having to subsidize its accessible transport service (which is still making a loss), Duofu could rapidly accumulate profit. Hsu said he has received many investors' proposals to "remove the medical transport service and we'll invest in your business immediately," but he has firmly held on to the initial concept of "creating a comprehensive accessible service" and repeatedly explained that Duofu is not a profit-oriented company. Hsu also stressed that accessible transport has always been a customer-driven service that seeks to identify the real needs of people with disabilities. This very process is the reason that Duofu has accumulated irreproducible service experience and customer trust that cannot be established within a short period – the indispensable cornerstone for the growth of its accessible travel service.

Duofu's strategy for developing its two-sided platform involved providing novel perspectives by studying other two-sided platforms. Previous studies have rarely described the developmental process of a two-sided platform (Eisenmann & Hagiu, 2008), and few have thoroughly investigated the relationship between cross-subsidization in a same-sided platform and cross-subsidization in a cross-sided platform (Rochet & Tirole, 2003). The development of Duofu shows the platform model ultimately adopted was not planned in advance; instead, it gradually developed from a cross-subsidization model in a one-sided network into a business that operates using a two-sided platform, while also highlighting the increased difficulty for social enterprises over their profit-making counterparts to maintain a balance between economic goals and social ends.

Becoming a real multisided platform

To enhance Duofu's accessible transport service, Hsu has attempted to encourage participation from other service providers. Working as an accessible taxi instructor for Crown Taxi in Taipei's Neihu District, he advocated that accessible service providers should increase resources and generate social influence rather than focusing merely on expanding customer bases. Accessible transport is Duofu's most crucial service for offering significant social public benefits.

To strengthen the operating effectiveness of accessible transport, Hsu proposed a commissioned management program for rehabus vehicles in 2013 after realizing that many enterprises often donate rehabuses in the name of corporate social responsibility to private social welfare groups without considering whether these groups are capable of managing the donated vehicles. Typically, such groups are unable to afford the substantial costs required for keeping the vehicles up (e.g., fuel, parking fees, maintenance fees, labor fees) and are not professionally capable of managing vehicle dispatch. In addition, most enterprises have donated vehicles to groups based in metropolitan areas, neglecting the people who most need rehabuses in remote counties and cities (e.g., Hualien, Taitung). Therefore, Hsu and several other social welfare groups began formulating a commissioned management program to put Duofu in charge of managing the vehicles.

This program involves the donor (enterprises) providing rehabus vehicles to well-known social welfare groups (recipients) such as the Taiwan Foundation for Rare Disorders and the Taiwan Motor Neuron Disease Association, which then commission Duofu to manage these donated vehicles. These commissioners maintain priority use of the vehicles, but Duofu may use them when they are not otherwise occupied. According to the agreements, Duofu then gives the social welfare groups a proportion of profits earned from using the commissioned vehicles. This allows the recipients not only to gain monetary benefits, but also to save on the costs of managing vehicles and corresponding labor fees. To further incentivize the scheme, Duofu also gives the income earned from selling the vehicles later on to the social welfare groups. Duofu can thereby increase the scale of its operation without having to expend more on purchasing transfer vehicles. Donator enterprises can meanwhile study Duofu's detailed records to follow up on the number of people serviced and the mileage of each donated vehicle to assess the benefits of their investments in social public welfare. Figure 11.2 illustrates a schematic diagram of the commissioned management mechanism.

From the initial two-sided platform involving tourists with disabilities on the one side and tourism and travel-related service providers on the other, to establishing a multisided relationship comprising accessible transport customers, social welfare groups, and donators, Duofu intends to transform into a service company deploying an MSP. In this scenario, the subsidized side generally is not always supported by the subsidizing side; rather, the subsidized side endeavors to seek a platform that enables it to support itself while providing social public benefits.

As an MSP, Duofu is also a very attractive partner for many service providers who want to offer medication and meal delivery to the elderly. In its early stages, the organization introduced a stair-climbing machine for wheelchairs that allows customers who reside in apartments that are not equipped with elevators to travel outdoors, creating further opportunities for developing other multisided relationships. The stair-climbing service enabled Duofu to provide an integrated roadside and home-based service to elderly people, making it into an important strategic partner for homecare services. As a result, Duofu began collaborating in 2013 with iHealth, allowing female iHealth pharmacists to travel on its vehicles to deliver medication.

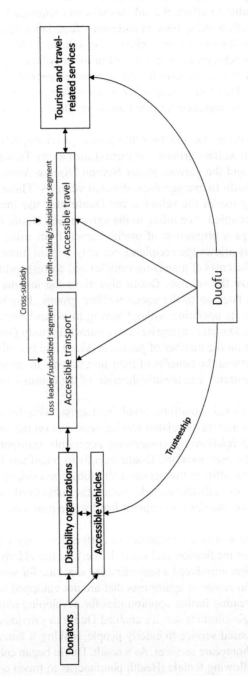

Figure 11.2 Duofu's commissioned management service mechanism.

Discussion and conclusion

Duofu's developmental process serves as a vital inspirational source to social enterprises developing a platform-mediated model. In this section, we conclude the case study of Duofu, presenting three platform-mediated business strategies worthy of subsequent investigations: (1) identifying two-sided platform business opportunities based on a one-sided cross-subsidization service, (2) realizing economic and social goals by expanding a two-sided platform into a multisided platform, and (3) expanding the overall profit pool by leveraging a platform-mediated business model.

Identifying two-sided platform-mediated business opportunities from a one-sided cross-subsidization service

Hsu first established Duofu Care & Service because he realized how inconvenient it was for people with disabilities to use rehabuses. As the number of customers increased and stabilized, Hsu introduced the accessible travel service at the recommendation of his physically challenged friends. Because Duofu cannot profit from providing transport services alone, Hsu used a cross-subsidy approach involving both services, using the earnings achieved from travel services to subsidize the financial deficiency of the transport service. Subsequently, Duofu attracted more users of travel services with the help of its transport service users. To expedite its tourism development, it then cooperated with tourism and travel-related service providers to improve the basic facilities required for an accessible travel service, thereby promoting a two-sided platform business model. In such a platform, physically challenged travelers and their families are motivated to use Duofu's travel service because of its exceptional service quality and variety of traveling routes; tourism and travel-related service providers are motivated to cooperate with Duofu because of the stable number of consumers. Tourism and travel-related service providers are the subsidizing side that offers free accessible services and facilities, whereas Duofu is the platform operator that selects participants and ensures a high service quality.

Social enterprises are by their nature a cross-subsidization in the same-sided platform. Based on this case study, if a cross-subsidization in the same-sided platform can be converted into a cross-subsidization in a two-sided platform, the social value and economic value that social enterprises demonstrate can be enhanced.

Realizing economic and social goals by expanding a two-sided platform into a multisided platform

Duofu started with only a single subsidized side in accessible transport, and the introduction of commissioned management and medication and meal delivery services engendered additional sides, forming a multisided platform and decreasing the extent to which its accessible transport service is subsidized. Because the services provided in the multisided platform established from its accessible transport service neared perfection as the number of cooperating operators increased, relevant customer switching costs also increased. Hence, operators who use a platform model can implement their long-term social-value goals because of the stable relationship they have with customers.

Expanding the overall profit pool by leveraging a platform-mediated business model

Because current self-pay accessible transport and tourism remain underdeveloped, Duofu's MSP has attracted multiple service participants, accelerating market growth. At the same time, by engaging in co-competition with a portion of its potential competitors, Duofu has enabled accessible service markets to expand further.

Social enterprises endeavor to identify entrepreneurial opportunities from among social concerns in an effort to provide social benefits while also attending to economic goals. What is key is figuring out how to inhibit organizational growth that can come from the conflict between social ends and economic goals. Dees (1998) indicated that for managers to maintain a harmonious relationship between two types of employees who hold distinct perspectives, they must ensure that while supporting commercialization, the business means is based on the organization's core values, enabling employees to trust one another. Managers must preempt conflicts that are likely to occur by determining their potential sources and educating employees to mitigate the negative effects of such conflict. That will allow employees on both sides of a divide to devise the most applicable method of action through communication and coordination. Salary issues, for example, may be one of these conflict sources, with some seasoned employees whose education and experience level are equivalent to those of newly hired employees, while new employees recruited from other industries may request a higher starting salary, making allocating employee pay a process that must be transparent. In this case study, the founder of Duofu, Hsu, served as the arbitrator whenever a conflict between social public benefits and economic goals occurred. But as Duofu's MSP becomes increasingly complex, it may require a more comprehensive managerial mechanism to avert conflict before it happens.

Notes

1 Other types of platforms such as product platforms – a set of product parts that are connected physically as a steady sub-assembly and are able to fit for different final models and also develop differentiated products – are not included in our discussion.
2 Calculated on the assumption that each person requires eight trips per month at NT$700 per trip.
3 City and county governments have specified that rehabus service providers must provide a certain number of services per month in order to receive the set subsidies; failure to do so results in a proportionate deduction. Reports have shown that operators have

attempted to maintain this standard by dispatching a bus to the residential area of users even after they cancel a service reservation, and operator personnel have been found to sometimes make their own arrangements via phone to satisfy the quota.

4 Summarized points based on the interview with Hsu in July 2013.

References

Baden-Fuller, C., & Mangematin, V. (2013). "Business Models: A Challenging Agenda", *Strategic Organization*, 11(4): 418–427.

Casey, T. R., & Töyli, J. (2012). "Dynamics of Two-sided Platform Success and Failure: An Analysis of Public Wireless Local Area Access", *Technovation*, 32(12): 703–716.

Dees, J. G. (1998). The Meaning of "Social Entrepreneurship", https://csistg.gsb.stanford.edu/sites/csi.gsb.stanford.edu/files/TheMeaningofsocialEntrepreneurship.pdf

Eisenmann, T. (2007). Platform Mediated Networks: Definitions and Core Concepts. *Harvard Business School Note*.

Eisenmann, T., & Hagiu, A. (2008). Staging Two-sided Platforms. *Harvard Business School Teaching Note*.

Eisenmann, T., Parker, G., & Van Alstyne, M. W. (2006). "Strategies for Two-sided Markets", *Harvard Business Review*, 84(10): 92–101.

Hagiu, A., & Wright, J. (2011). Multi-sided platforms. *International Journal of Industrial Organization*, 43: 162–174.

Kerlin, J. A. (2013). "Defining Social Enterprise Across Different Contexts: A Conceptual Framework Based on Institutional Factors", *Nonprofit and Voluntary Sector Quarterly*, 42(1): 84–108.

Rochet, J. C., & Tirole, J. (2002). "Cooperation among Competitors: Some Economics of Payment Card Associations", *Rand Journal of Economics*, 33(4): 549–570.

Rochet, J.-C., & Tirole, J. (2003). "Platform Competition in Two-sided Markets", *Journal of the European Economic Association*, 1(4): 990–1029.

Index

Enhancing Employment of People with Disabilities through Small Enterprise (3E) Project 20–1, 31–2, 41, 52, 55, 57–8; comparison with UnLtd on cost-effectiveness in funding SEs 67; funding 25; management by Social Welfare Department 34; median life span of SEs funded by 58–9; social return on investment 61, 66; workfare 61, 63, 66, 70n42; *see also* Stewards
Enhancing Self-Reliance Through District Partnership (ESR) Program 21, 25, 32, 33, 34, 35, 38, 40, 43, 52, 55, 57–8; launch 45n11, 45n14; percentage of profitable SEs funded by 59; social return on investment 41–2, 66; workfare generated by 61, 70n41
Environmental Protection Administration (EPA) 80, 81
EPA *see* Environmental Protection Administration
ESR *see* Enhancing Self-Reliance Through District Partnership (ESR) Program
European Union 75

Fairtrade International 98
Fair Trade USA 98
First Social Welfare Foundation 87n1
Fisher, S. 52, 53, 61
Flying V 103
for-profit enterprise 6, 7
Foundation for Women's Rights Promotion and Development 85
France: long-term unemployment 19
FSES *see* Fullness Social Enterprise Society
Fullness Social Enterprise Society (FSES) 22, 35, 38, 41–2, 43
Fuqua School of Business 146

Global Fund 128
Go Incubation Board for Startup and Acceleration Firms 97
GONGOs *see* government organized non-governmental organizations
Good Lab 22, 24, 40, 43
government organized non-governmental organizations (GONGOs): China 126, 129, 130, 135, 140n5; Taiwan 85, 86
grants 155; Hong Kong 35, 36, 37, 40, 41, 47n35, 116; research 143, 145; Taiwan 73, 74, 75–7, 79, 80–2, 83, 87, 87n7
Gre Tai Securities Market 97

Guangming Daily 6
Guangzhou Daily 6
"Guiding Principles for Social Gender Equality Policy" 85, 86
"Guiding Principles for Taiwanese Centenary Social Welfare Policy—Towards a New Society with Equity, Inclusion, and Justice" 84–5
"Guiding Principles for Taiwanese Social Welfare Policy" 84–5, 86

HAB *see* Home Affairs Bureau
Handerson Property 40
Hand in Hand Care in Hospice 138
Hartigan, P. 145
He, W. 138
Health Works 24
HEFCE *see* Higher Education Funding Council for England
Heinecke, A. 111, 144, 151, 158, 163, 164–5
Henderson Land Group 24
Higher Education Funding Council for England (HEFCE) 62, 63, 70n45
HKCSS *see* Hong Kong Council of Social Services
HKCSS-HSBC Social Enterprise Advancement Grant 24
Home Affairs Bureau (HAB) 21, 28n1, 34–5, 36, 37, 38, 46n18, 47n29
Home Affairs Department 21, 48n38, 59
Homemakers Union Consumers Co-op 95, 102
Hong Kong: blank spots and blind spots on social enterprise development 52–71; Central Policy Unit 53; civic society 21–3, 35–40; corporate social responsibility 23–4; definition of social enterprise 34–5; dependent and independent variables 56–7; economy 42–3; funding and incubation of SEs 38–40; Funding Periods 70n22; gross domestic product 148; Inland Revenue Ordinance 22; innovation 25–6; institutional logics for the future 27–8; legitimacy of social enterprise 24–8; legitimacy of social enterprise in the past 26–7; market orientation 24; misperception of social enterprise 34–5; social enterprise 19–29; social enterprise as a policy agenda 31–4; social enterprise development 52–3; social enterprise development over the

For Product Safety Concerns and Information please contact our EU representative GPSR@taylorandfrancis.com Taylor & Francis Verlag GmbH, Kaufingerstraße 24, 80331 München, Germany